DIRTY DEALING

DIRTY DEALING

The Untold Truth about Global Money Laundering, International Crime and Terrorism

Second edition

Peter Lilley

London and Sterling, VA

Also by Peter Lilley
Hacked, Attacked and Abused

First published by Kogan Page Limited in 2000
Reprinted 2001
Second edition 2003
Reprinted 2005

120 Pentonville Road
London N1 9JN
UK
www.kogan-page.co.uk

22883 Quicksilver Drive
Sterling VA 20166-2012
USA

ISBN 0 7494 4034 1

British Library Cataloguing-in-Publication Data

A CIP record for this book is available from the British Library.

Library of Congress Cataloging-in-Publication Data

Lilley, Peter, 1943-
Dirty dealing : the untold truth about global money laundering / Peter Lilley.-- 2nd ed.
p. cm.
Includes bibliographical references and index.
ISBN 0-7494-4034-1
1. Money laundering. 2. Organized crime I. Title.
HV6768.L55 2003
354.16'8--dc21

2003009200

Typeset by Saxon Graphics Ltd, Derby
Printed and bound in the United States by Thomson-Shore Inc.

Contents

There is no fortress so strong that money cannot take it.

(CICERO, 106–43 BC)

Gold is tested by fire, man by gold.

(ANCIENT CHINESE PROVERB)

Preface: My beautiful launderette

Behind every great fortune is a crime.

(HONORÉ DE BALZAC)

With few exceptions criminals are motivated by one thing – profit. Greed drives the criminal, and the end result is that illegally gained money must be introduced into a nation's legitimate financial systems... Money laundering involves disguising assets so they can be used without the detection of the illegal activity that produced them. This process has devastating social and economic consequences. Money laundering provides the fuel for drug dealers, terrorists, arms dealers to operate and expand their operations... Left unchecked, money laundering can erode the integrity of our nation's and the world's financial institutions.

(THE UNITED STATES DEPARTMENT OF THE TREASURY FINANCIAL CRIMES ENFORCEMENT NETWORK, *FINCEN ADVISORY*, MARCH 1996, **1**, ISSUE 1)

> *Money is laundered to conceal criminal activity associated with it, including the crimes that generate it, such as drug trafficking or illegal tax avoidance. Money laundering is driven by criminal activities. It conceals the true source of funds so that they can be used freely. It is the support service that allows criminals to enjoy the fruits of their crimes. It allows crime to pay and often, pay well.*
>
> (THE UNITED STATES OFFICE OF THE COMPTROLLER OF THE CURRENCY, *MONEY LAUNDERING: A BANKER'S GUIDE TO AVOIDING PROBLEMS*)

On 11 September 2001 the world changed. Very soon after the horrific events in the United States media attention was drawn to the underlying topic of the financing of terrorism. Since then the war on terrorism has, to a large degree, been focused on stifling the funding of such activities. Nearly every country has introduced, revised or strengthened its anti-money laundering regime; key nations have issued reports on just how well they are doing, quoting the amounts of terrorist funds that have been frozen or confiscated.

So why, if such progress has been made, do I feel pessimistic about what is happening? The first edition of *Dirty Dealing* was published at the end of 2000. In the final section of the book I concluded that, at its dark heart, money laundering and everything related to it is an ethical issue. I observed that it is one of the most corrosive social and business problems of the new century, quoting the United States 1998 International Narcotics Control Strategy Report, which observed that:

> *Money laundering has devastating social consequences and is a threat to national security because money laundering provides the fuel for drug dealers, terrorists, arms dealers, and other criminals to operate and expand their criminal enterprises. In doing so, criminals manipulate financial systems in the United States and abroad. Unchecked, money laundering can erode the integrity of a nation's financial institutions... Organized financial crime is assuming an increasingly significant role that threatens the safety and security of peoples, states and democratic institutions. Moreover our ability to conduct foreign policy and to promote our economic security and prosperity is hindered by these threats to our democratic and free-market partners.*

These prophetic words were published in February 1999. I concluded the original edition of this book with the following words:

> *Crime can only succeed if the funds generated can be utilized without their true source being known. Moreover, criminal activity continues to expand because the washed funds are then reinvested in the business. Money laundering is the critical tool to enable this. It is a dynamic and robust circular process. It will only be stopped when the legitimate business world implements strong coherent anti-money laundering procedures in a serious way and when drastic action is taken by relevant authorities against the jurisdictions, people and institutions that make the washing cycle possible. This is a severe problem – a business and financial apocalypse – that now merits such draconian action. If, as I fear, this will not occur then the future looks very grim indeed.*

No one – certainly not me – could have exactly predicted the cataclysmic occurrences of 9/11. However, as the quotation from the 1998 US report shows, there were more than enough warning signs that existed for a number of years to allow one to speculate that something of a horrendous nature would occur, probably earlier rather than later. The only part that virtually everyone got wrong is that it was assumed that the perpetrators of any outrage would be one of the numerous transnational organized crime factions rather than terrorists.

This revised edition of *Dirty Dealing* has as its basic premise that money laundering remains one of the key unresolved global issues. The laundering of dirty money is so important because it is the engine that drives all of the planet's corrosive and destructive activities, such as crime, terrorism, drugs, prostitution and human trafficking. Whilst we may now realize that this is a serious problem, I have severe doubts as to whether we have even begun to tackle it. Most – if not all – of the topics I wrote about in the first edition of this book are just as prevalent as then. In fact, there are various pieces of evidence to suggest that we have learnt very little and the problems are getting far worse.

Immediately prior to the publication of the first edition of *Dirty Dealing*, the US administration were seeking to widen the definition of money laundering to encompass fiscal crimes. Then, as now, I argued that this was a mistake: equally it is erroneous to merely think now that money laundering is only important when it relates to terrorism. Thus, *Dirty Dealing* attempts to tell the story of money laundering in all of its guises, and suggests what can be done to control the washing of this soiled money. Above all, we should never forget that money laundering does not take place in a vacuum: somewhere along the line there will always be real human suffering as a result of this dirty dealing…

He is of South American origin and has homes in London and Switzerland. For good measure he has a chalet in Gstaad (winter skiing) and a villa in Cap d'Antibes (where he spends all of August). He has an adoring Italian wife who shops at expensive designer stores and three children who are educated privately and, as befits their parentage, speak at least three languages fluently. He sits on the board of various reputable companies across Europe and is known to be independently wealthy. He is kind to animals and makes sizeable donations to charity. He is universally admired and his probity is never questioned. Which is a shame because his wealth is generated by drugs from South America and associated organized criminal activities.

As befits his status and influence he has contacts all over the world: or at least the managers of his empire do. The majority of these contacts would not be welcome at the top restaurant tables that our man dines at across the world. Some would be though, and frequently are invited: lawyers, bankers, accountants, professional advisors. The money that pays for those extravagant meals begins in the coca fields of Colombia, or the red light district in Amsterdam or some other salubrious location. The coca from Colombia becomes cocaine and is shipped to the United States. The funds generated are banked in an obliging financial institution in Brazil. From there money goes to Eastern Europe where numerous investments are made in local industries. Further investment and running capital is provided through an International Business Corporation (IBC) in the Bahamas that pays no tax and is owned through bearer shares. This in turn is linked to an offshore bank in the Pacific that is wholly owned by our man. For good measure some of the Eastern European companies set up joint venture companies in Vienna and open bank accounts at prestigious Austrian financial institutions. The joint venture companies in Vienna don't actually do much business apart from issuing invoices for professional services rendered to other parts of the empire, which transfer funds into the relevant Viennese bank accounts. A United Kingdom company has been bought off the shelf and shows nominee directors and shares being held by the Bahamas IBC. The Vienna companies transfer funds to the British company as it has billed them for even more professional services. The UK company then buys copper ingots, which are given a certificate of ownership and are traded on the London metal markets. The money generated is then invested in the United Kingdom and Swiss commercial property market, thus generating rental income that is in turn managed by professional advisors so that tax liabilities can be minimized. And this is just one part of our man's financial empire.

Olga was a quite attractive young(ish) postal worker in a former Eastern Bloc country, struggling to scrape together a living on a meagre wage. When she was offered £1,000 a month to work in a German restaurant she jumped at the opportunity, bragging about it to her family. Once across the border she was raped by the man who had offered her this wonderful chance and then given her new uniform: shoddy lingerie and stilettos. First she worked in a brothel in Berlin, servicing up to 20 men a night, with instructions to let them penetrate her without a condom as that meant that her customers would pay more. The money she made – usually £30 for half an hour – went straight to her pimp. Eventually these funds will emerge cleaned through the world's banking and business systems with no connection whatsoever to the sordid inhuman way that they were generated. She was kept virtually under house arrest during daylight hours. When her attraction faded to the punters in Germany she was sold for £1,500 to a pimp in Amsterdam and forced to work in one of the city's red light districts for 12 hours a day.

Olga is just one of thousands of similar women lured and then entrapped in a modern version of the slave trade that generates sizeable amounts for those controlling it, who usually go undetected and uncaptured. And when Olga is no longer of any use there are many others who will be 'persuaded' to take her place.

IN THE BEGINNING...

If you want to steal then buy a bank.

(BERTOLT BRECHT, PARAPHRASED)

The perception that still endures of money laundering is that of a suspicious character turning up at the counter of a bank with a suitcase (probably helpfully labelled 'swag') overflowing with used notes. Until recently even more sophisticated analyses of the problem have attempted to reduce the process to a neat three-stage technique (placement, layering and integration). It is perhaps only now that it is becoming clear that money laundering is a robust, corrosive, all-consuming and dynamic activity that has far reaching consequences and effects.

Traditionally, money laundering has been viewed (in isolation) as the cleaning of dirty money generated by criminal activity: in the collective mindset these crimes are probably associated with the drug trade. Of course, money laundering is this, but it is also a whole lot more. To understand and appreciate the all-consuming power and influence of money laundering one needs to go back to the purpose of crime. The vast majority of illegal acts are perpetrated to achieve one thing: money. If money is generated by crime, it is useless unless the original tainted source of funds can be disguised, or preferably obliterated. The money laundering dynamic lies at the corrupt heart of many of the social and economic problems experienced across the globe:

- Laundering is obviously a natural by-product of financial fraud; but simultaneously fraud is also a continuance, in some cases, of laundering where the fraud itself is financed by the proceeds of an earlier crime.
- Terrorist groups need to launder funds, but parallel to this are the claims that such groups are active in widespread organized criminal activity (predominantly drug running) sometimes in league with more recognized criminal groupings. Such claims have been made about the PLO, KLF, ETA and the IRA to name just a handful.
- Entire countries have been brought to their knees by criminal activity and the requirement to convert the resultant ill-gotten gains into a universally acceptable currency (which is predominantly US dollars). Colombia is an obvious example; Mexico is fast approaching the same situation. Elsewhere in South America, in Bolivia 300,000 citizens are involved either indirectly or directly in the coca business, and elimination of half of the producing fields in recent years has significantly contributed to unemployment and poverty. In Russia the influence of criminal groupings is all pervasive from street level to the upper echelons of the Kremlin itself. In Burma it is widely believed that the military junta itself is involved in drug trafficking – and this country is merely one of a group of suspected 'narco states'.
- The fall of the Berlin Wall and the ending of the cold war has given rise to more localized outbreaks of warfare; many such conflicts have direct links to organized criminal activity.
- Money laundering is an essential follow-on from such activities as human trafficking, the sex trade, extortion and blackmail: but more crucially, once the funds have been cleaned, they are reinvested in such activities, thus perpetuating the most vicious of circles.
- Money laundering is the dynamic that enables criminal activity of all descriptions to grow and expand. This process – the delivery channel of cleaned funds – is now so embedded in the 'normal' business environment that we may well have little chance to control it, never mind eradicate it.

The rise of organized crime is now an accepted, if regrettable, fact of global business life. The massive sums of money generated by such activity need to be legitimized by inserting and washing them in international banking and business systems. Running parallel are the globalization and internationalization of markets; the sophistication of information technology; and the uncertain political and economical environments in such regions as the former Soviet Union. Criminals are exploiting all of these trends and are operating at the cutting edge to ensure that the funds that they illegally generate are laundered. For example, it has been estimated that the illicit drugs industry is worth $400 billion per annum – making it larger than the world's oil and gas industry. It has 400 million regular customers. $200 billion is successfully laundered across the world each year. And that total is merely one part of the global money laundering process.

There has been a convergence in the last two or three years of key factors that have encouraged, facilitated and sponsored the explosion in money laundering. Some of these ingredients are:

- The globalization of markets and financial flows, most evident in the dizzying rise of the Internet. The creation of a single market means that money (of any pedigree) can move across the world in nanoseconds, thus making multiple jurisdiction leaps in a day commonplace. Virtual money laundering is a reality. As an advertisement for a recent conference (not about money laundering, I hasten to add, but about the new global economy) proclaimed, 'New rules. No borders. Are you ready to go global?'
- In fact it could be argued that there are no new rules because, put simply, in respect of global money laundering, there are no rules at all. Deregulation has brought with it no consistency or coherence in respect of anti-money laundering regulations; simultaneously the global marketplace has brought with it very few, if any, restrictions.
- This period of competition, consolidation and collaboration has created immense pressure to deliver on organizations and their employees. Delivering is all about money: everyone is looking to make a fast buck in booming new industry sectors or geographical regions. The proceeds of crime are so massive that they, and the people who control them, can yield great influence in relationships with legitimate businesses hungry for profit.
- Simultaneously the technological advances that appear to be made daily have been exploited to the full by criminals and launderers. The rapid pace of change and the volatile business environment that it creates is an ideal environment for criminals and their associates to operate in.

- Concurrent with these events has been the widespread criminalization of politics. Organized crime is so influential because it buys influence. Politicians, in numerous cases, are the criminals themselves and the funds that they have removed out of the typically fragile economies of their native countries have been laundered. Corruption and money laundering go hand in hand.
- Moreover, many small countries riddled with poverty and debt have looked to new economic alternatives to save them. Typically these include tourism and now the provision of offshore financial services. The redeployment of resources into the latter has created a myriad of opportunities for criminals to both disguise the origins of funds and place them out of reach of western jurisdictions.

Whilst money launderers have adapted and flourished in the new global economy, governments and regulatory authorities have fared less well. Although the Financial Action Task Force has promoted best practice principles to be adopted by all countries the simple truth is that there is no uniformity across the world in relation to anti-money laundering regulations and legislation. One of the major effects of this is that legitimate business and banking organizations operating internationally end up being caught up in differing systems and regulations. The most voiced comment we hear is that if an organization tries to rigorously apply and enforce all money laundering regulations then the time involved is exorbitant and it becomes almost impossible to do any business.

One of the reasons for this is that the application of money laundering regulations can disadvantage all customers – rather than achieving their aim of highlighting and exposing the small percentage of dishonest or questionable ones. In the end, however, each organization must ensure on-going regulatory compliance, as the penalties for not doing so – both in terms of criminal action against both corporate bodies and individuals, together with loss of reputation – are massive.

Money laundering and the underlying world of organized crime is a daily feature in the news across the world. Our world is one where millions of dollars can transverse the planet in a 15th of a second and over $2 trillion is moved across the globe every day. Thus money generated from drugs manufactured in South America can travel from a Caribbean island via New York through Austria to London quicker than it takes you to read this paragraph. Whereas in the early days of money laundering the concern was with low level peddlers of drugs arriving at banks with their apocryphal suitcases stuffed with notes (if for no other reason than such a concept was easy to comprehend), now it seems that even the high and mighty, the great and good have been implicated in some form of dirty dealing. Moreover, money laundering is no longer perceived – or prosecuted – as merely money from drugs but the proceeds of all serious crime and then some more. The cyclic process of money laundering can also be used for activities that have only recently been grouped together under the same banner such as:

- The payment of bribes or 'inducements' by major national and multinational corporations where for obvious political, public relations or fiscal reasons such payments need to be hidden.
- Governments themselves are not immune or exempted from effectively laundering state funds: a prominent example of this is the claim that Russia moved state funds out of the country through offshore jurisdictions.
- Politicians, it will perhaps not surprise you to hear, form a large (dis)honourable subclass of money launderers with an ever growing list of offenders. Either they are attempting to disguise funds they have stolen from their home country or they are looking for anonymous and discreet homes for bribery payments (sorry, gifts) they have somehow come by.

The term money laundering appears to have originated in the United States in the 1920s. Criminal gangs then were trying to do much the same as today: disassociate the proceeds of their criminal endeavours from the activities themselves. To do this they took over businesses with high cash turnovers – such as launderettes and car washes – and then proceeded to mingle the cash generated from nefarious activities with legitimate income, thus simultaneously creating a logical commercial reason for the existence of large sums of cash. Whilst the term laundering is today stressed for the word's association with washing and cleaning, the original criminal link was because of the use of laundering businesses.

In essence then, as cash rich businesses are still high on various warning lists issued by regulatory authorities (particularly in the United States), little has changed in the intervening 80 years. The money laundering world is based on a subversion of the old maxim, because in the twilight and murky environment of this dirty dealing, evil is the root of all money. The well-used phrase 'money laundering' has become almost meaningless as it does not adequately convey the method by which the vast amount of funds involved across the world have been generated.

This book is not about money laundering or organized crime per se, but about their effect, influence and ramifications on global business activities, the world's economies and infrastructure. All this money is produced as a direct result of criminal activity. Such crimes are not 'victimless' in the sense that financial fraud against large organizations is sometimes incorrectly perceived. The billions that are continually washed around the globe come from the suffering (and quite often deaths) of real people. Whilst money laundering is forever viewed as solely a result of the drug trade, in reality this is but one part of the pan-global business that generates such funds.

> *BCCI had 3,000 criminal customers and every one of those 3,000 customers is a page 1 news story. So if you pick up any one of those accounts you could find financing from nuclear weapons, gun running, narcotics dealing and you will find all manner and means of crime around the world in the records of this bank.*
>
> (SENATOR JOHN KERRY (1992), *THE BCCI AFFAIR*, ALSO KNOWN AS *THE KERRY REPORT*)

Laundering is the method by which all proceeds of crime are integrated into the banking systems and business environments of the world: black money is washed so it ends up whiter than white (hence the descriptive French terminology *Blanchiment d'argent*). This is the process whereby the identity of dirty money that is the proceeds of crime and the real ownership of these assets is transformed so that the proceeds appear to originate from a legitimate source. Criminal amassed fortunes held in unstable locations and/or currencies are metamorphasized into legitimate holdings in centres of financial respectability. In this way the origins of the funds disappear forever and the criminals involved can reap the benefits of their hard work. Money is the lifeblood of all criminal activities: the process of laundering can be viewed as the heart of the process as it enables the money to be purified and pumped around the body to ensure health and survival.

Organized crime is assuming an increasingly significant role that threatens the safety and security of peoples, states and democratic institutions.

(FINCEN, *MONEY IN A BORDERLESS WORLD: THE GLOBAL FIGHT AGAINST MONEY LAUNDERING,* WEB SITE PAGE)

This global problem is not about minor criminals but such powerful transnational organized groups as:

- the Italian Mafia and their second generation follow-ons in the United States;
- the Japanese Yakuza;
- Colombian cartels such as the Medellin and Cali;
- Russian and Eastern European mafia;
- Nigerian and West African gangs;
- South African organized crime groupings;
- the Juarez, Tijuana and Gulf cartels in Mexico.

These groups and other similar ones are far from amateurs. Like any other pan-global, multimillion dollar business they are well financed, highly organized and at the forefront of new technology. More crucially they are elusive and continually masking their insidious activities in cloaks of respectability. Such organized criminal groupings have tremendous power. In Colombia, drug lords have driven government forces out of large areas of the country. But it is not only power in a raw physical sense but increasingly in the political world at the very highest level through infiltration and corruption of weak officials and politicians.

This subversion of political processes combined with adept manipulation of financial and business systems means that in affected countries (with a ripple effect all across the world), democratic institutions are corrupted, confidence in the country is eroded, the integrity of financial systems is destroyed and honest enterprise is undermined and thwarted. Even allowing for the widespread coverage this appalling problem has received, the threats and ramifications of money laundering have almost certainly been under-exaggerated rather than the commonly perceived opposite.

When the 'Foreign Money Laundering Deterrence and Anticorruption Act' was introduced in the US Senate it came with seven key findings from the Congress. All seven of them are damning indictments of the scale and ferocity of the predicament. These are just two of them to give perspective:

1. Money laundering by international criminal enterprises challenges the legitimate authority of national governments, corrupts officials and professionals, endangers the financial and economic stability of nations, diminishes the efficiency of global interest rate markets, and routinely violates legal norms, property rights, and human rights.
2. In some countries such as Colombia, Mexico and Russia the wealth and power of organized criminal enterprises rival the wealth and power of the government of the country.

Such proceeds of crime come from a vast and growing assortment of oppressive yet extremely profitable activities such as:

- The drugs trade – and we are not talking about low level street operations but the manufacturing of illegal substances on a highly organized and commercial basis. If money laundering was only related to income derived from illegal drugs that would be catastrophic enough in itself. It has been estimated that the knock on effects of drug usage in the United States cost $67 billion annually. This figure includes drug-related illness, crime and death. In the United States, 16,000 citizens die each year because of illegal drugs.
- Sales of arms – although recent media coverage has focused on the illegal sale of nuclear material and weapons from the former Soviet Union the more mainstream illegal dealing in weapons of death and destruction continues unabated: from hand grenades through small arms to high tech weaponry.
- Prostitution – again we are not referring to isolated incidents such as one girl on a dark street somewhere but the trade in women and children where they are effectively permanently kidnapped or 'sold' and forced to perform sexual acts for money until they are effectively too exhausted or ill to be of any further use. This isn't only happening in far flung locations: Russian pimps and girls, for example, are active in all major European cities. The United Nations estimate that over 500,000 women and girls are entrapped in this modern version of the slave trade each year.

- Terrorism – virtually every week brings news from some outpost of the globe concerning the latest terrorist outrage. All of these groups need money – and the ability to use it – to support their infrastructures and buy weapons and equipment.
- Corruption – one of the money laundering favourites is where heads of state or political leaders of countries after their physical or political demise are accused of, or found guilty of, accepting corrupt payments or bribes.
- Fraud – every type of successful financial crime and other fraudulent activity generates amounts that need to be infiltrated into the banking system, such as mortgage fraud, advance fee fraud, credit card fraud, pyramid schemes and insurance fraud.
- Forgery.
- Large scale theft of money – one of the first major cases that showed how easy laundering was to achieve was the Brink's Mat robbery in the United Kingdom, where, on 26 November 1983, £26 million worth of gold bullion was stolen from Brink's Mat warehouse near London's Heathrow Airport.
- Blackmail and extortion – activities that, if successful, usually result in payments being made that the criminals hope, or ensure, will be untraceable.
- Art and antique fraud – theft, forgery and resale through the major auction houses and dealers of the world.
- Smuggling of historical icons or works of cultural importance – which has been particularly prevalent from the former Soviet Union.
- Smuggling – of illegal alcohol and tobacco, which invariably results in
- Customs and/or VAT fraud.
- Large scale theft and illegal exportation of new or used vehicles.
- The heinous crime of trafficking in human beings.
- Tax avoidance – yes, I hate to tell you this, but at the time of writing tax avoidance is coming to the forefront of money laundering investigations and regulation. In the past there has been a gaping loophole in the reporting of suspicious transactions and persons: the money launderers and/or their professional advisors could claim a 'fiscal excuse' – that their funds and transactions relate to tax matters only. Increasingly this control gap is being closed with a vengeance.

It is also wrong to think that criminal activities can be neatly segmented as I have done above; most criminal groups are involved in many different nefarious activities: as long as it makes money for them they are there. As an example, in 1997 2,000 people were charged in the United States with money laundering: but 40 per cent of that total were also charged with other white collar crimes. There is also a broadening or switching of activities: so that groups previously solely involved in narcotics are now pursuing less hazardous (but still criminal) activities such as financial fraud or vehicle crime. From a law enforcement and legal viewpoint it is very often difficult to establish whether a strand of criminal activity is the first one that generates the proceeds of crime or whether it is a second or further stage that is being enacted to launder the proceeds of earlier crimes.

Interestingly and again a subject of confusion when attempting to identify money laundering is the issue of capital flight. This is where individuals (or companies for that matter) remove funds from their home economy and invest them abroad, usually avoiding domestic tax in the process. This activity has become more prevalent since the fall of communism and the catastrophic difficulties in post-Soviet economies. Is this money laundering? The logical answer is that if the money involved was earned legitimately then it is not. However, if by evading taxes criminal offences are being committed does this make the process the same as money laundering? If it isn't how can one distinguish the two – particularly as the techniques and channels used by both processes are strikingly similar?

So if the way money is generated is so despicable then presumably we, as a civilized world, will have done all that it is possible to make it as difficult as possible for funds generated in these ways to be laundered...

Not quite.

The fundamental precepts of all international money laundering prevention regulation and legislation are:

- that banking and business in general will not knowingly deal with the proceeds of crime;
- that the business world will take steps to identify their customers and the source of their funds;
- if there are any suspicions of money laundering and/or organized criminal activity they will be reported to the relevant official body.

Leaving aside, at least for the moment, the possibility of complicity by banks and business in the laundering process, let's take an initial look from the launderer's point of view as to how easy or difficult it is to disguise both your identity and the source of funds. What follows could be read as a 'do it yourself' guide to successful money laundering. Many years ago it was suggested to me that one could not prepare an organizational manual to prevent money laundering as by doing so you would tell people not only how to prevent it but how to do it. That, however, is not the point. In my experience there is a universal lack of knowledge and perception as to just what can be achieved quickly and cheaply if you really want to in this area. Moreover, every example I quote can be obtained (and bought) for real by the flick of a mouse click on the Internet. At the back of this book is a Web Directory of useful Internet sites: sadly if you are a money launderer the types of sites that offer the services you will be interested in (and detailed below) are not listed; but that doesn't mean they don't exist – they do in abundance.

Credit cards at the ready to pay for the services offered – let us see just how easy it is to become a successful money launderer by achieving anonymity, or another identity, and leave no paper or money trail:

Do your background research...

The first port of call should probably be an actual or on-line bookshop for a spot of background research. Here you will find a vast array of titles giving detailed advice on 'asset protection', 'tax havens', 'anonymous banking' and 'offshore companies', all of which offer detailed information to manage your personal financial affairs. Taken at face value such books have a legitimate purpose concerning tax and asset planning. However, if your intentions are somewhat more dubious then they are an ideal start point.

Just waltz into the banking system...

The first key to the money laundering world is to get yourself a bank account or at least get into the banking system. The Austrian Sparbuch (from the German *Sparen* meaning save, *Buch* meaning book) account has long been a *cause célèbre*, and until 1 July 2002 was the bank account of choice for would-be launderers. In basic terms this was a savings book opened under a code name that enabled you to deposit and withdraw cash. Just turn up in person (or send somebody) with the book and the code word and access to the money is yours. (Whilst you are there you can also empty or fill your anonymous safe deposit box handily located in the foyer of the bank.) It has been estimated that there are 26 million such passbooks in existence in a country with a population of 7 million: the total balances are said to exceed $50 billion.

There is no limit to the amount that you can invest – and no correspondence such as interest statements are ever sent out by the bank because they haven't got a clue who you are. And a Sparbuch was available on the Internet for a $200 set-up fee. One Web site stated that when you open this type of account even the bank doesn't know who you are. You give the account any name you like. If there is any type of investigation, even if it is conducted by a very powerful agency, the bank cannot turn you in – because the bank does not know who you are. Neither does the bank know who makes deposits and withdrawals. As an initial concession to international pressure the Austrian Government restricted closures to cash only, whereas previously these accounts could be closed in the form of a bank cheque.

The Austrian Sparbuch could only be opened in Austrian Schillings but in the Czech Republic, until recently, their version could be opened in Deutschmarks or US dollars. The Austrian Sparbuch became so infamous that in February 2000 the Financial Action Task Force (FATF), which is the intergovernmental body set up in 1989 to combat money laundering, threatened to suspend Austria's membership of the FATF in June 2000 unless the country eliminated these anonymous passbooks. On 1 July 2002 Austria did just that – no new accounts can be opened, and existing accounts must be identified through the account holder producing the passbook, password and photo identification. Similar steps have been taken in the Czech Republic, where, from the end of 2002, Sparbuch holders cannot deposit any more funds in these accounts and have until 2012 to transfer their money to a different type of account.

However, all is not lost for the potential laundryman or woman because a quick search on the Internet will produce numerous different offers and products that claim to provide anonymous banking facilities. One example we found stated its product benefits as:

- an anonymous bank account in any name of your choice;
- Internet banking;
- a valuable *no-name* ATM card;
- available in just days to you;

- withdraw unlimited cash anywhere in the world;
- have customers send money safe with your knowledge of being totally anonymous.

Credit for life...

Both the Internet and small box adverts offer anonymous credit cards. Many are 'for life'. The process involved is to buy a Panamanian off-the-shelf company that then sets up a bank account on which a credit card is issued. Only the lawyer setting up the corporation knows who you are: the banking relationship is with the Panamanian entity (which has absolutely no reporting requirements). The bank then issues a credit card on the account, which can be used on a worldwide basis. Another alternative of this is, but along the same lines, an account operated in the name of a Panama Corporation by remote-banking technology through a PC. Rather worryingly it is claimed that one bank offering this service 'is the fourth largest in its country'.

Follow Bertolt Brecht's advice (literally)...

If this is all slightly low key for you then why not buy a bank? Whilst there are always adverts appearing in various reputable broadsheet newspapers across the world offering banks and banking licences for sale you can now purchase an offshore bank over the Internet by credit card for as little as $25,000. Presumably the ideal way to achieve complete anonymity is to buy your bank using your anonymous credit card.

Who would you like to be today?

Of course you may be put off by obscure offshore jurisdictions and feel that the best way to integrate your criminal cash into the banking system is through a more mainstream centre. Most, if not all, of such centres have 'know your customer' requirements and thus, at the bare minimum, require sight of your passport. A 'camouflage' passport is thus a wise acquisition. These real looking passports issued in the old name of a retitled country are easily acquired. So choose a name, age and even sex of your choice and become a citizen of: the USSR; Rhodesia; Burma; New Hebrides; British Guyana; British West Indies; and various others...

Again, of major concern are Web sites that are not only offering these documents (ostensibly suggesting that if you are a US citizen this document gives insurance/protection if you are hi-jacked and/or kidnapped) but suggesting that you can use them as ID when you open a bank account. One Web site even goes as far as suggesting that if you do not know of a foreign address you want to use they will make up a fictitious one. One level up from these passports are Diplomatic ones from the same defunct nations. But remember: these documents are available to anyone over the Internet for minimal cost. Once again if you are entering into this in a big way you will find out a corrupt official from as reputable a country as possible and 'persuade' him that you need a passport from that country.

The stage in the middle of these two methods is where countries (particularly in Africa) openly advertise that genuine passports will be issued when an investor pays a fee and/or places money in the country. One such African nation advertises, via a middle man on the Internet (there are probably many more), a legitimate passport available for less than $5,000 and available in 14 days or less. For even greater privileges, the UK *Daily Telegraph* reported that full diplomatic passports have been offered by African nations for less than £18,000. Such a passport offers immunity from arrest and prosecution – and unlimited use of diplomatic bags when entering or leaving countries. Also on offer were positions such as honorary consuls that carry privileges under the Vienna Convention on Consular Relations.

There are also many other ways in which one can change identities. It has long been suspected that a proportion of Jewish emigrants from Russia to Israel were not in fact Jewish, but gentiles (for whatever reason) trying to escape. Confirmation of a further criminal side to this topic was reinforced by the arrest in 2001 of two managers of a company, Vesta, in St Petersburg. Tamara Timofeeva and Eric Suomalinen were accused of fabricating Jewish identities for clients in return for fees of up to £2,500. For this the company would:

- teach potential emigrants about Jewish traditions, customs and manners;
- teach clients to speak Russian with a Jewish accent;
- create false documents to support the claims of the client. Fabricated documents included passport office documents and birth certificates.

The company apparently also specialized in manufacturing 'evidence' that clients' lives were under threat. Anti-Semitic letters were created with phrases used such as 'Jews, go to Israel' and 'Suitcase, railway station, Israel'. The company appears to have been almost always successful in obtaining the emigration to Israel of its clients. No one knows how many clients were assisted by this company – but the potential market for such services is seemingly massive, as 19,000 people emigrated from Russia to Israel in 2000 and between 1988 and 2000 900,000 people emigrated from Russia to Israel. To add to the confusion it is not known how many real Jews there are in Russia: official estimates put the total at about 1 million, but it is entirely possible that this figure is actually much higher due to Jews hiding their national identity to avoid discrimination.

Alternatively you can combine a change of identity with nautical ambitions by applying for a ship's officer certificate in Panama, which has the largest number of ship registrations in the world. The Secretary-General of the International Transport Workers' Federation applied for, and was given, a Panama Maritime Authority Certificate for first officer. As a first officer you are the second most important person on the ship after a captain, and are able to take over from the captain. The certificate cost $4,500 and all that was needed was a form and a passport photograph. The only problem was that the successful applicant had no seafaring experience whatsoever – apart from crossing the Channel to France as a passenger.

The Seafarers International Research Institute has uncovered more than 12,500 cases of certificates forged by criminals or maritime authorities; it is estimated that 40 per cent of basic safety training certificates are false and a very substantial number of qualifications for officers using emergency equipment are false. Moreover a further worrying trend is the use of false certificates then to obtain legal qualifications from authorities that do not check or confirm the provenance of the documents submitted to them to support applications.

However, there are problems with such schemes. The Caribbean island of Dominica has reviewed its economic citizenship programme. In simple terms this scheme enabled you to buy a passport. Not unsurprisingly the scheme was reviewed because, in the words of the island's prime minister, 'it is giving Dominica a bad name as a number of people who hold Dominican passports were discovered to have criminal records'. Over 1,000 people have already become 'economic citizens' of Dominica. However, as of early 2003 the scheme still operates – and is sold by hundreds of providers on the Internet.

Neighbouring St Vincent has recently scrapped a similar scheme there. Ralph Gonsalves, the prime minister of St Vincent, commented that 'The citizenship of this country will no longer be for sale. We are not selling our citizenship to vagabonds and rogues.' However, the economic downside of this decision is that the previous administration had forecast revenue of $4.4 million from this scheme. More crucially if you hold such a passport, St Vincent intends to revoke them.

True anonymity (by phone)...

To communicate with your colleagues and banks you will need an anonymous phone. Whilst such devices are advertised on the Internet, if you live or are visiting the United Kingdom there is a far easier and cheaper way. Go into any phone shop (or supermarket, or anywhere that sells phones). Buy a prepaid phone with cash. You do not have to give any name or ID. There are no bills to be sent and no address required. My own phone is like this (don't read too much into that) and can be used virtually anywhere in the world. When you need to top it up you just go and buy vouchers with cash. So spend £50 and you get an anonymous phone for an hour, day, week or month: use it for what you need to then throw it away (or really confuse things by giving it to someone else).

Your address? C/o anywhere you fancy...

You will probably also need some form of business address – particularly for correspondence from your bank (whilst having the bank hold your mail has some advantages it does mean that you might have to physically visit there at some stage and thus risk potential compromise). This can also be easily used as a residential address. Multitudes of companies in every city on this planet provide serviced office and mail drop facilities. Recent technology has made it easy to redirect phone and fax lines from the office location to anywhere in the world (your anonymous mobile phone, for example). Whilst I am certain that I am doing many legitimate providers of this type a disservice I know that you can sign up for such facilities without providing identification and making all payments in cash.

Any company name you like anywhere Ltd...

Should you need a corporate entity the world is awash with offshore locations offering complete secrecy and anonymity. The International

Business Company (IBC) is another *cause célèbre* in the money laundering prevention world: an anonymous façade with little or no reporting requirements. We will address these issues later in the book. However, two other alternatives that have been offered to me recently are equally as intriguing and useful. In Switzerland, it is possible to buy a dormant company that has a track record and originally invested share capital for a relatively small amount (a few thousand Swiss Francs, if that), and then install nominee directors. Alternatively much the same is available in the United States where you can buy legally registered former multi-million dollar corporations. The drawback of both, which is normally not present in offshore jurisdictions, is that there are reporting requirements. However, should you actually want to trade so that laundering can be achieved through the company's accounts it is far better to have a corporate entity in a credible jurisdiction.

www.letskeepitanonymous.com

Various Web sites have also been offering totally anonymous securities trading accounts, based in a European Union country. All that is required is a minimum investment of a few thousand dollars and a password. No ID needed!

Money laundering by mail order

There are many other aids to money laundering available by mail order or across the Internet. Most are of secondary value (however amusing and ego enhancing). They include but are definitely not limited to:

- various international driving licences;
- a multitude of university degrees (beware PhDs – available for less than $2000).

However, by now you probably have got all that you need to successfully launder money. If it sounds too easy to do that's because it is. Even so, all of the techniques described above are very much the 'do it yourself' end of money laundering. That having being said, an afternoon on the Internet with your credit card at the ready will probably give you all you need to start on the laundering process. Where the process becomes simultaneously both more insidious and effective is when and where professional advisors become involved. We will keep returning to this topic, as the deep entanglement of such groups give criminal activity the sophistication and facade of respectability that is needed. Obviously bankers become involved but now it is also just as likely that representatives of the following professions are implicated:

- lawyers;
- notaries;
- accountants;
- fiduciaries;
- insurance brokers;
- securities/commodities brokers.

Whether these groups become entwined in these dirty dealings innocently is an issue we will consider in other parts of this book.

One other critical and continuing facilitator of money laundering, and one that is increasingly being recognized as such, is the extensive use of offshore business entities by criminals. As briefly referred to earlier in this chapter, such companies and structures are – in simplistic terms – corporate entities that have the facility to conceal the real directors, beneficial owners or true state of financial affairs (in fact they usually do not have to show any financial reporting). For those not familiar with this extensive and profitable commercial environment such entities are known by a variety of different terms such as IBCs (International Business Companies), Offshore Companies and Shell Companies. Amongst the locations where such anonymous entities (to varying degrees) are readily available are: Anguilla; Bahamas; Belize; Bermuda; British Virgin Islands; Cayman Islands; Cyprus; Delaware; Gibraltar; Hong Kong; Hungary; Republic of Ireland; Isle of Man; Jersey; Liberia; Liechtenstein; Madeira; Malta; Marshall Islands; Mauritius; Nevis; Panama; Seychelles; and the Turks and Caicos Islands.

The firms that offer to form and manage these companies for you also masquerade under a multiplicity of titles such as Offshore Formation Agents, International Company Formation Agents, Corporate Service Providers, and Offshore Financial Services. All of them, without exception, stress the strict confidentiality they provide. Whereas before these companies usually advertised extensively in broadsheet newspapers, many of them now have an extensive Web presence. In some form of double irony the primary 'legitimate' use of offshore vehicles is tax minimization: thus in the case of funds generated by crime and washed through such entities the process is also tax free. We shall examine the role of these 'professional advisors' in greater depth in Chapter 5.

Money launderers are clever – thus they are constantly looking for new business opportunities. The regulatory spotlight that has been shone on banks means that they have sought out other types of businesses where anti-money laundering regulation is either non-existent or not as advanced as in the banking environment. Moreover, in such areas of business activity either the knowledge of money laundering is poor or business owners/employees can be enrolled in the process of washing. Money laundering is migratory: it will be attempted where, at any given time, there is least resistance. Obviously this involves staying a few steps ahead of the law regulators and enforcers.

Commercial activities such as those that involve insurance companies, stockbrokers, surveyors, estate agents, precious metal dealers, antique dealers, car dealers and casinos are already being used to wash funds – sometimes on a very large scale. Of increasing importance are seemingly credible trading companies, who on the surface appear to have no connection whatsoever with the world of finance, that are being specifically set up and run solely to launder funds. Banks are no longer the primary target for criminals: their sights are set on the global world of business in general.

Money laundering is a massive, well-organized and – regrettable though it is to admit – very successful global activity. By its very nature the whole point of a successful laundering operation is to convert dirty funds in one part of the world into clean money in a respected and respectable financial centre. There exist many services, structures and professional advisors who ensure the success of this insidious world.

Five rules of money laundering

1. The more genuine the money laundering transactions and process look the less likely they will be detected.
2. To achieve respectability the funds must ultimately end up in a bona fide financial centre. Whilst the launderer may have to start the process offshore, full success will only be achieved when the proceeds are in a mainstream reputable location.

3. Launderers are constantly researching and identifying new opportunities. As US drug czar Barry McCaffey has commented, 'Money will flow to whatever market is willing and available.'
4. Globalization is far more advanced than international regulation or cooperation. Money launderers would be well advised to make sure their funds pass through as many jurisdictions as possible – particularly useful in delaying and frustrating any possible future official investigation.
5. If you have taken much effort to launder money successfully don't leave it all in the banks of one location: you may have spread it around different financial institutions but if anything went wrong at one of them you have put all your eggs in one basket.

Oh, and finally: you have obviously worked hard for it, so now you can spend it on those little luxuries you have promised yourself.

THE INTERNATIONAL GROUPINGS OF ORGANIZED CRIMINALS

Organized criminals are more organized than we are.

(DAVID BLUNKETT, UK HOME SECRETARY, NOVEMBER 2002)

Organized crime does not somehow operate in glorious isolation. All of these 'gangsters' (much as I hate the term because of its glorified connotations) are actively attacking businesses – and operating as a business – across the world:

Colombian cartels

These cartels are highly organized, well equipped, well financed, formidable and totally entrenched in their country of origin. The US Government commented that 'the leaders of these international drug organizations have built powerful financial, transportation, intelligence and communications empires that rival those of many small governments'. The Cali cartel is said to be worth $206 billion. Its two leaders, the brothers Gilberto and Miguel Rodriguez, were sentenced to 10 years' imprisonment in January 1997 but allegedly continue running their operations from jail. Cocaine and heroin trafficking into the United States is their main business but they also do a nice sideline in contract killing. The country has been in a state of permanent civil war for the last 35 years, and allegations abound that link together the drug cartels, far right paramilitary groupings and the Colombian army itself. Colombia, to all intents and purposes, appears to be in a permanent state of national emergency. All of this has meant that the drug cartels have broadened their operations geographically, both to neighbouring South American countries and to Western Europe itself. One unforeseen by-product of the United States' war on terrorism is that the previous unremitting focus on Colombia has decisively shifted, with unpredictable future consequences.

Mexican cartels

Drug trafficking and organized criminal activity are viewed within Mexico as a threat to national security. Mexican cartels have learnt from the Colombians but also have the added advantage of a 2,000-mile-long border with the United States. Just as with the Colombians, the drug gangs have made sizeable inroads into corrupt politicians and political structures. There is a variety of different groups, all of which are extremely violent: the Tijuana cartel; the Juarez cartel; the Miguel Caro-Quintero organization; and the Gulf cartel, aka the Juan Garcia-Abrego organization.

As at 1 March 2000 one of the FBI's 10 most wanted fugitives was Ramon Eduardo Arellano-Felix (aka Ramon Torres-Mendez, El Comadante Mon, El Walin, Ray or Gilberto Camacho Rodriguez), who is somewhat incongruously given the occupations of 'policeman, rancher and physician'. The FBI describe the reasons for his inclusion as 'One of the leaders of the Arellano-Felix organization, also known as the Tijuana cartel, is being sought in connection with the importation of controlled substances. The cartel is known for its importation of large quantities of controlled substances and its propensity for violence.' Ramon Eduardo Arellano-Felix made a somewhat fitting (in the circumstances) exit from the FBI list, as he was killed in a police shoot-out in February 2002.

In Tijuana itself two police chiefs were killed between 1994 and 2000; a presidential candidate was assassinated there; in 1999 five ordinary police officers were killed; and in the first two months of 2000 70 people were murdered. All that having been said, there is something grimly comic in one of the police chiefs, Federico Benitez, being killed in 1994 after he informed his drug cartel friends that their bribe of $100,000 was not large enough.

Russian mafia

The Russian mafia were previously the flavour of the month, if for no other reason than the quarter-million stolen cars per year they are responsible for. But of course there is much, much more to them than that. Membership figures vary widely from 100,000 to in excess of 300,000. In St Petersburg, as an example, it is estimated that 230 criminal groups operate there with five extremely influential gangs. Such an extent of criminality led to 33 contract killings in the city in 1999. In Moscow in 1999 the crime rate increased by 38.7 per cent on the previous year: registered crimes in the areas of economic related, drug related and arms related grew by 64 per cent, 39 per cent and 13 per cent respectively.

It is now clear that much of the criminal activity in Russia itself existed under, and was 'tolerated' by, the Soviet authorities. After the fall of communism the influence of organized crime in Russia was all-pervasive, with estimates running as high as 80 per cent of all Russian businesses being mafia controlled. What has been staggering is the spread of Russian organized crime since the dismantling of communism. There are said to be between 2,000 and 8,000 stratified crime groupings that are alarmingly active all over the world: the United Kingdom (sex trade, drugs and fraud); Holland (sex trade and drugs); the United States (drugs and fraud); Belgium (stolen cars); France (drugs, fraud and the sex trade); Switzerland (dummy businesses); Italy (drugs and human trafficking from Albania); Germany (the sex trade, drugs and stolen cars); Poland (drugs and fraud); Austria (dummy companies, the sex trade and drugs); former Yugoslavia (the black market and illegal supplies of arms); Israel (drugs and extortion); Canada (drugs, sex trade and fraud). It should be taken as read that these groups are involved in money laundering in all of these countries and anywhere else where it is possible. The two largest groupings are Dolgopruadnanskaya and Solntsevskaya, alleged to be headed by the now infamous Sergei Mikhailov.

On 29 January 2001 the deputy chairman of the Russian State Duma's Security Committee, Alexander Kulikov, told the official RIA Novosti news agency that:

- Organized crime structures control approximately 40 per cent of Russia's private businesses and 60 per cent of state run enterprises.
- Revenues from 'shady businesses' make up 40 per cent of Russia's gross domestic product, with nearly 9 million citizens involved in these activities.
- Between 50 and 85 per cent of banks are under the control of organized crime. (This is apparently based on Interior Ministry figures, but we think they are historical and not necessarily a reflection of the current situation.)
- Over the last five years the number of organized crime groups rose 17 times while the number of groups with corrupt links rose 170 times.

A classified UK police report on the impact and threats posed by post-Soviet crime groups, published in 2001, together with various other recent research projects, has thrown some new light on this topic, although, in all honesty, the material that we have seen confirms what was already known rather than radically altering it. Typical criminal activities attributed to these groups are:

- money laundering;
- tax and excise fraud;
- illicit drug trafficking;
- prostitution;
- human trafficking;
- counterfeiting/forgery.

However, as always, the problem of how to disentangle and differentiate between capital flight and money laundering remains ever present. Current intelligence suggests that the major criminal threats to Western Europe come from criminal groups in Lithuania, Russia and Ukraine (as opposed to groups from other republics). But this does not mean that individuals from other post-Soviet republics are not involved in criminal activities, but rather that the threat from organized groups in these areas is less than in the three countries named.

It is now becoming clear that the proliferation of Internet sites offering 'escorts', partners, future wives and sex tours is almost certainly – to varying degrees – a front for organized criminal activity and human trafficking. This is specifically happening in Russia, Ukraine and the Baltic states.

One key element facilitating criminal activity that reappears regularly is the continued prevalence of corruption in the post-Soviet republics. Combined with this is the willingness of different criminals and groups to collaborate, which could imply a network structure (which is obviously difficult to identify and break down) or alternatively that individuals/gangs are weak in some areas of their activities and thus must rely on others.

Interestingly, comments have also been raised concerning the exaggeration and distortion that are prevalent concerning post-Soviet crime groups, such as:

- the overuse of the term 'organized crime' to include many topics that may not be criminal;
- the overuse of the term 'Red Mafia' (or similar), implying that there is one all-powerful 'gangster gang';
- overemphasis on the threat posed by post-Soviet criminal groups, which may blind organizations to other threats from equally dangerous groups such as those originating in Colombia, Mexico, Turkey and Italy (to name but a handful).

There is a common public misconception (fostered by press coverage) that all criminal activity from the post-Soviet republics is 'Russian', rather than being attributed to its exact country of origin.

Japanese Yakuza

The influence of the Yakuza on Japanese business and banking was perhaps underestimated until the last couple of years when their activities finally came out of the woodwork as a result of the Far East financial turmoil. The Yakuza are estimated as being responsible for almost half the bad debts held by Japanese banks. However, it has been suggested that the banks themselves courted Yakuza groups in the 1980s when large corporate borrowers defected to international markets. When the bubble burst the Yakuza borrowers were saddled with massive debts, but the banks were too scared to foreclose on them, fearing retribution. Estimates as to their membership hover around the 100,000 mark with a turnover of up to $90 billion per year. These estimates make them by far and away Japan's biggest individual business. They have cornered the market in Japan for property and loan fraud together with prostitution, debt collection and extortion rackets. The downturn in the Japanese economy has also led to the Yakuza spreading out from their traditional family/national base and looking for investments and business opportunities in Hawaii, other US states, the Philippines, Australia and other areas of South East Asia. It is suspected that the Yakuza have invested $50 billion in financial markets in the United States alone.

Italian Mafia

Read the book, seen the films: membership of 20,000 but should not be underestimated or overlooked. To be strictly correct, as outlined below, the correct term is 'Mafias' in the plural as there are at least four (possibly five) major groupings. Having said that, it has been estimated that there are only 2,000 active members in the United States and that the Russian mafia achieved more in the United States in the last five years of the 20th century than the Mafia did in decades. They are still hugely influential in Italy where it is still estimated that they control about 20 per cent of the country's commercial activities, notwithstanding the on-going governmental purges on their activities. The various groups have a heavy presence in arms, gambling, loan sharking, extortion, disposal of toxic waste, European Union frauds, animal trafficking, fraud centred on government tenders and increasing the infiltration of legitimate companies to launder funds. The Italian Mafia have adapted and survived by entering new dynamic business areas and realizing when it is prudent and/or sensible to leave behind their more traditional activities. The Cosa Nostra is still active all across Italy with 6,000 active member families. It was one of the first groups to cooperate with criminal groups in Moscow. It now focuses on large scale fraud against the EU and Italian Government together with bank fraud and computer related crime. The 'Ndrangheta is the richest Mafia in Italy with a propensity for international drug and arms trafficking. There are 150 cells each solely comprised of blood relatives together with 6,000 families and affiliates in Northern Italy and the rest of the world. It has formed links with Albanian groups to run arms trafficking, prostitution, money laundering and illegal immigration. The Camorra are particularly active in Campania with over 100 clans totalling 7,000 affiliates. It is believed to be the largest Mafia group, preferring waste management activities, public tender frauds and shenanigans with EU money. The Sacra Corona Unita, whilst its strategic control has now decamped to the former Yugoslavia, is heavily present in the contraband tobacco market, prostitution and money laundering.

Chinese Triads

This intricate network of Chinese criminals has its roots in the 19th-century opium trade; some commentators date its origins back even further to the 17th century. The Triads now operate in every major centre of the world with a Chinese population, and have an estimated turnover of $200 billion per annum. Membership figures vary widely but a minimum figure is estimated as being 20,000 with a maximum exceeding 100,000. There are six main gangs (but over 50 in all) who are essentially rivals at local level but cooperate globally. These include the Sun Yee On (also known as the San Yee On), the 14k, the Wo On Lok and the Wo Sing Wo. The Sun Yee On is the largest group with cells in North America, Western Europe, Asia and Australia and a membership of more than 25,000; the 14k is based in Hong Kong with outposts in the Netherlands, North America, the United Kingdom, Canada, Australia and New Zealand. Amongst other businesses that the Triads are involved in are gambling, illegal prostitution, human trafficking, extortion, fraud, loan sharking, counterfeiting, drug trafficking and money laundering.

Turkish and Kurdish gangs

These are very important in the drugs market in the United Kingdom where they supply 80 per cent of the heroin smuggled into the country each year. This group is becoming an increasing concern to the relevant authorities. Turkish is a generic term covering Cypriot and Kurdish members; the groups are extremely tight knit, very efficient and highly secretive. They are also moving into illegal immigrants and stolen cars, utilizing the supply and distribution channels they have established to such good effect in the drug trade.

Nigerians

Often underrated because of the pure volume of the infamous 419 letters (Dear Sir, We have stolen $400 million from the Nigerian Oil Company and would like to give some of it to you, etc), the Nigerians are a highly organized and effective criminal grouping. Bear in mind that the US Secret Service receives about 100 telephone calls per day from victims or interested recipients of these letters together with 300 pieces of correspondence. In the United States alone it is estimated that Nigerian crime groups generate $100 million each year, solely from 419 letters. It is not uncommon for individual victims to lose more than £1 million through such frauds (this observation is not an exaggerated one, as I have dealt with various cases with losses of this level). In the UK it has been estimated that Nigerians generate £3.5 billion per annum through their many and varied criminal endeavours. The areas that they are involved with include drug trafficking, banking fraud, stolen and fraudulent financial instruments, housing and benefit fraud, shipping fraud, oil and gas fraud: you name it. The groups operate in a cell structure across the world with members having specific roles. Ignore this group at your peril.

Hell's Angels/biker gangs

Heavily tipped to be the up and coming organized crime group, these originate in the United States and have approximately 2,000 members worldwide. They are heavily into drugs and extortion. They have been most prominent because of various violent confrontations between individual groups in Scandinavia. It is a subject of keen debate as to whether groups in various countries are just biker gangs or organized criminals. The country that appears to have the biggest problem – and has done the most work in this area – is Canada. In that country Hell's Angels are involved in narcotics trafficking, tobacco and alcohol smuggling, prostitution, theft and extortion. The 1999 Criminal Intelligence Service of Canada's Organized Crime Report commented that 'The Hell's Angels are one of the most powerful and well-structured criminal organizations in Canada.'

Balkan gangs

The UK National Criminal Intelligence Service (NCIS) highlighted gangs originating from the Balkans as being growing players in organized crime activity in the United Kingdom. The key groups comprise ethnic Albanians from Albania and Kosovo. Although involved in drug trafficking, their specialization is human trafficking for prostitution. Official estimates are that such groups now control about 70 per cent of the vice trade in Soho and other parts of London, using 'kidnapped' women. A secondary specialization is the facilitation of illegal immigrants from Moldova, Romania, Iraq, Turkey, Iran, Pakistan, Afghanistan, Sri Lanka and China through the western

Balkans and on to Western Europe. The Albanians have also made inroads into organized crime activities in New York. In Italy they expanded from controlling vice activities to drugs, murder, robbery, theft and illegal arms dealing. In 1988 573 arrests were made in Italy relating to Albanian criminals; by 1998 it had reached 27,247. The Italian Interior Ministry has noted 'the criminal capacity shown by the Albanian groups and their operational ruthlessness'.

Because of the individual and combined scale of the crimes perpetrated by the above groups it is naturally (and correctly) assumed that each of them is involved in large scale and widespread money laundering. It should also be noted that the summary above includes only the major generic groups of organized criminals: don't forget that there are many more domestic units in each country (such as traditional crime families and Yardies in the United Kingdom, and domestic 'mafia' groups, which are particularly prevalent in former Eastern Bloc countries).

At an international conference on transnational organized crime in Tokyo at the end of January 2001, a senior United Nations official claimed that 'Internationally organized crime is now a bigger threat to security for ordinary people than war.'

Pino Arlacchi, the Undersecretary-General at the United Nations Office for Drug Control and Crime Prevention, also made the following points:

- The fight against the organized criminals behind human trafficking, corruption and cyber crime must be a genuinely global effort.
- Organized criminals can cooperate across borders with greater ease than law enforcement officials – that is why international cooperation is so vital.
- The level and intensity of international crime has gone beyond what governments and the general population are prepared to accept.
- As many as 1 million women and children are trafficked each year across national borders by criminal groups.
- The profits from corruption, drug trafficking and other crimes have become so big that the numbers are difficult to grasp, while money laundering is estimated by the US Government to be equivalent to as much as 5 per cent of the world's gross domestic product.

THE NTH LARGEST GLOBAL BUSINESS ACTIVITY

Globalization opens many opportunities for crime, and crime is rapidly becoming global, outpacing international cooperation to fight it... [it is] estimated to gross $1.5 trillion a year – a major economic power rivalling multinational corporations.

(UNITED NATIONS HUMAN DEVELOPMENT REPORT, 1999)

You are standing in the downtown area of any major city of the world. Towering above you is a regional office of one of the major multinationals. You are gazing in awe at Organized Crime Inc (you can check them out at organizedcrimeinc.com) – although the name above the door will probably not be that. The trading style shown will probably be something innocuous and vacuous to reflect the global omnipresent scope of the business. The building is high tech, opulent and up market. At five o'clock every afternoon you need to take cover to avoid the rampaging army of employees released from their daily toil. The company pay their taxes, treat their employees well, contribute to local charities and are an all-round good corporate citizen.

You may wonder why at street level (dependent on local customs and laws) you are confronted by girls who, resplendent in their neon-lit cubicles, are offering sexual services of all descriptions. However, like everything else in this building they are merely part of a greater whole: either creating illegal funds or helping to metamorphose it into something approaching respectability. Just like any other multinational corporation, security of the building is tight: however, once you have signed in and got your security pass you can take a chance and wander about.

This is a highly organized, employee friendly operation; everything you can possibly expect is here:

- operations;
- sales;
- marketing;
- research and development;
- legal;
- quality assurance;
- communications;
- transportation and logistics.

What may surprise you is the sheer scale and extent of their involvement and investment in worldwide business: from football clubs to casinos, from fruit machines to real estate, from washing machines to sports equipment, from car dealers to launderettes. What won't surprise you is the army of bankers, professional advisors and consultants they employ. You almost wish you worked for them yourself.

Somewhat surprisingly there are many reliable indicators as to the true scale of money laundering from internationally accepted sources. Why these staggering figures are not accepted and acted upon will be considered later in this chapter; but for now let us ponder upon the following:

Firstly, at an individual country level

- Drug sales alone in the United States are estimated by the Office of National Drug Control Policy to generate $57.3 billion annually (and these are 1997 figures). Research has shown that 90 per cent of banknotes in circulation in the United States are contaminated by narcotics – and in London an analysis in 1999 showed that 99 per cent of all banknotes circulating in the Capital are tainted with cocaine, with 1 in 20 exhibiting high levels of the drug, suggesting handling by dealers or actually being used to snort the drug.

- The black market peso exchange system in Colombia is estimated to launder $5 billion per annum in drug profits.
- French official regulators put the value of dirty money laundered through the country in excess of 14 billion francs per annum.
- It has been estimated that each year $15 billion flows out of Russia – and it is almost impossible to determine how much of this is capital flight and how much is money laundering. However, the Russian Ministry of Internal Affairs' calculation that 25 per cent of Russia's gross national income is derived from organized criminal activities does not inspire confidence.
- In 1994 in the United Kingdom a House of Commons Select Committee was told by the Bank of England that the country laundered £2.4 billion every year.
- Official Russian sources suggest that in 1998 a figure of $70 billion passed through bank accounts on the Pacific Island of Nauru (where?).
- Press reports suggest that the illegal grey economy in the Czech Republic amounts to about 10 per cent of the country's Gross National Product.
- A 1996 report published by Chulalongkom University in Bangkok estimated that a figure equal to 15 per cent of the country's GDP ($28.5 billion) was laundered criminal money.
- In 1998 the National Bank of Poland reported that more than $2 billion is laundered in the country per annum.
- In Belarus it has been estimated that 30 per cent of the country's GDP is money laundering.
- Mexican drug cartels (now more powerful than their contemporaries in Colombia) are conservatively estimated to generate profits of more than $9 billion per year – that is approximately 5 per cent of Mexico's GDP.
- The Canadian Solicitor General commented in 1998 that the illicit funds generated and laundered in Canada each year were between $5 and $17 billion.
- Also in 1998 the Swiss Finance Ministry confirmed that the country was implicated in $500 billion of money laundering each year. Although no official figure exists it has been reliably estimated that between $40 to $50 billion of Russian money resides in Swiss banks – with realistically little way of knowing whether it is flight capital or laundered money.

- In 1999, official figures placed the annual value of organized crime activity in the United Kingdom at £50 billion – making it the country's third largest industry.
- Whilst it is not considered at the forefront of the money laundering problem, in July 1998 the Egyptian Federation of Banks estimated that each year $3 billion is laundered in the country.
- In Indonesia, which has a rapidly escalating money laundering problem, one US law enforcement agency states that $500,000 is washed on a weekly basis by West Africans and Southeast Asians using West African couriers.
- The Republic of Ireland, with its growing financial centre of Dublin, estimates that in 1998 $126 million was suspected of being laundered through the country.
- Informal estimates voiced in 1997 were that yearly money laundering activity in Italy totalled over $50 billion.
- Meanwhile, the head of the Lebanese Bankers' Association has denied that any money laundering takes place in the country.

And then at a global level...

- The United Nations Human Development Report of 1999 commented that organized crime syndicates grossed $1.5 trillion per annum – which is more than many developed economies and multinational corporations.
- In March 1998, *Dow Jones News* reported that money laundering amounted to between 2 and 5 per cent of world GDP: in other words between $1 and 3 trillion.
- It is estimated that there are in excess of 200 million drug users in the world and in 1995 the world's illegal narcotics trade was calculated at $400 billion. This total is equivalent to 8 per cent of the world's trade – that is more than motor vehicles, iron and steel and about the same as the gas and oil industry. In 1999, a Congressional hearing was told that up to $48 billion per year in profits were generated by illegal drug sales, which was laundered.

If you accept – and I think you should – that the scale of global money laundering each year is at least $1.5 trillion then either the staggering, horrifying scale of the whole problem suddenly snaps into place or you are so bemused that you still don't really believe it.

In real and comparative terms $1.5 trillion is:

- $1,500,000,000,000 – which, when put like that, is even more astounding.
- The estimated GDP of the United States in 1998 was $8.511 trillion – thus the annual money laundering figure is 17 per cent of this. Or to put it another way the GDP of the United States is only just five times that of Global Organized Crime Inc. In fact the figure of $1.5 trillion is only dwarfed by three individual countries' economies.
- The largest corporation quoted in the Fortune 500 as at February 2000 is General Motors with a turnover of $161,315,000,000, which is about a tenth of the amount laundered each year (or money laundering per annum is 10 times the annual turnover of General Motors).
- The GDP of Switzerland is $191,000,000,000 – just an eighth of the annual money-laundering figure.

One could just go on – and the comparisons would become even more overwhelming. Normally when such a staggering financial value is placed on money laundering the normal reaction is one of incredulity and extreme scepticism. Combined with this is the claim that all such figures have no basis in actuality – that essentially they have been plucked out of thin air. The Australian John Walker has addressed these problems in his work on *Modelling Global Money Laundering Flows*. The bad news for the sceptics is that output from the research and modelling process has produced a global money laundering total of $2.85 trillion per year. Rare for someone who introduces a new economic model, Walker actually admits that he is not claiming that the model is yet producing accurate estimates of money laundering flows. That being said, the critical fact is that the total produced is almost twice as much as official estimates or calculations. The basis of Walker's model is as follows:

> *[It] uses a range of publicly available crime statistics to estimate the amount of money generated by crime in each country around the world, and then uses various socio-economic indices to estimate the proportions of these funds that will be laundered, and to which countries these funds will be attracted for laundering. By aggregating these estimates, an assessment can be made of the likely extent of global money laundering.*

In other words for simple folk like me, you take the national crime figures and estimate what of this is laundered and where. Thus we have estimates that place the value of global money laundering between $1.5 and $2.85 trillion each year. Such staggering totals raise a variety of issues, but surely the two fundamental issues are:

1. Where on earth (literally) is all of this money?
2. Why do the reports of suspicions of money laundering filed by financial institutions and professionals to relevant official bodies across the world represent merely a minuscule percentage of this estimated total?

And once again, at the risk of stating the obvious, these total figures relate to one year alone. Presumably this is newly generated criminal wealth to be added to the amounts produced in previous years. Thus even basing it on the lower estimate, the last five years of the 20th century must have produced a figure in excess of $7.5 trillion. Because even if the figures for previous years in that time span were lower than $1.5 trillion per year, we must not forget the interest that would be generated.

So prior to the anti-money laundering initiatives that followed 9/11 why were the suspicious transaction reports filed by civilized countries across the world so pitifully short of anything approaching this total?

- In Switzerland in 1998 there were 160 suspicious transaction reports with a financial value of 330 million Swiss francs (roughly equivalent to $210 million). This compares with about 30 to 40 previously. With typical Swiss understatement, Daniel Thelesklaf, the director of the office responsible for tracking money laundering, commented that 'the number of reports is still low, given Switzerland's importance as a financial centre'.
- In Belgium between December 1993 and June 1998 there were 1,416 cases of money laundering sent to the judicial system with a value of $3.92 billion. In 1997 there were 476 suspicious reports filed with a value of 42.5 million Belgium francs (approximately $1.1 billion).
- In most other countries the financial value of reported suspicious transactions relating to money laundering is hard to come by. Nevertheless the number of reports does not inspire confidence that across the world we are doing nothing more than scratching the surface. In the United Kingdom in 1998 there were 18,000 suspicious transactions reported. In the Netherlands in the first

> half of 1997 there were 5,683 reports: but in the previous year only 0.5 per cent of such reports led to arrests and prosecution. Hong Kong appears to be particularly vigilant: in 1996 there were 4,124 reports and from January to mid-November 1998 there were 4,700 reports of suspicious activity. In Cyprus between 1997 and late 1998 there were 125 referrals – but half of them were from other governments. In the first nine months of 1998 Greece had approximately 200 cases of suspicious activity. And finally in Hungary between 1994 and 1998 there were about 2,000 relevant reports.

If this is just scratching the surface, it is not the law enforcement agencies that are at fault: these reports are generated by banks, professionals and business. In the United Kingdom in 1997, the NCIS (National Criminal Intelligence Service), the relevant law enforcement body that receives notification of suspicious transactions, dealt with 14,000 such tip-offs. Legal and regulatory obligations mean that banks, other financial institutions and various professionals have to report suspicions. Of these, 7,000 came from banks; 3,000 from building societies. But, here is the rub, 44 came from accountants – and there are 100,000 such professionals in the country; 236 came from solicitors – of which there are over 40,000 practising in the UK. Insurance companies (3.7 per cent of total reports), financial advisors (3.8 per cent) and bureaux de change (17.5 per cent, that is 2,000 reports, double that of the previous year) all succeeded where accountants and solicitors so patently failed.

It could of course be argued that solicitors and accountants reported large value cases (because that is what they predominantly deal with) and thus the number will be lower than volume markets such as those inhabited by banks and building societies. Such a case could be argued – but I am not going to. I suggest that almost the opposite is true: the sums involved in money laundering are so huge that you cannot miss them (unless of course you want to). How can anybody ignore:

- The $500 million stashed away in Swiss banks by Ferdinand Marcos.
- The various Russian money laundering stories where figures of $15 billion washed through accounts have surfaced.
- The former dictator of the Congo, Joseph Mobutu, who is believed to have transferred up to $5,000 million from the country.

As for where the funds generated by money laundering reside I suggest that the best place to start is offshore. Conservative estimates place the funds controlled by offshore centres at $5 trillion – which increases by $500 billion each year. $3.5 trillion has been shipped there since 1989. Added to this there exist well in excess of one million International Business Corporations (IBCs). On 11 June 1998, Jack A Blum, a partner in the Washington DC law firm of Lobel, Novins & Lamont, testified to the US House of Representatives Committee on Banking and Financial Services. He was the co-author of a United Nations International Drug Control Programme report on money laundering published in that year. His testimony is a chilling indictment of the nefarious use that offshore facilities, services and providers supply to the international organized crime world:

> *The International Business Corporation – a corporation with anonymous ownership which can do no business in its country of incorporation – has no legitimate place in the international arena... while a substantial portion of [assets held in IBCs] are legitimate – a very substantial portion is not. The portion that is not is the bank for the international criminal community. It is where most of the world's drug money is laundered. It is home to the proceeds of crime from around the world.*

The opposite side of the argument can be neatly summarized by the comment of Prime Minister Lester Bird of Antigua who has claimed that more money is laundered in Miami in a month than is laundered in the entire Caribbean in one year. However, that surely is not the point. The issue is not the amount of money but the relevant proportions of clean versus dirty money being transmitted through financial centres. By their very nature, Offshore Financial Centres (OFC) attract criminal money and thus the percentage of dirty money as part of the total of all funds flowing through such centres is high. Obviously this percentage varies from OFC to OFC, dependent on such factors as reputation and anti-money laundering controls in place. In some obscure OFCs the percentage of dirty money accepted as part of the whole is very high indeed. Whereas in traditional financial centres (such as London, New York and Frankfurt), however good money laundering controls may (or, for that matter, may not) be, the sheer volume of money passing through on a daily – if not hourly – basis logically means that a certain proportion must be dirty cash. Because of the volumes, that proportion – even if it is a minute percentage of the total – can in financial value be large. The role of offshore financial centres in the process of money laundering will never be far from our mind in the remainder of this book, particularly in Chapter 5, where we consider them in some depth.

There is a very simple answer to why professional groups assist money launderers, whether willingly, by turning a blind eye or in a state of stupidity or ignorance. The answer is of course money. In the mid-1980s, the average fees paid by criminals to those who laundered their money was 6 per cent; now it can be 20 per cent. So the professional advisors who are likely to make in excess of $30,000 by setting up a string of IBCs or similar structures in offshore financial centres can afford (in their eyes) not to ask too many penetrating questions about the wealth and activities of their client. Money laundering is good business for those professionals who become involved in it: bankers, lawyers, accountants, company formation agents, tax advisors, fiduciaries and various other groups all benefit handsomely from washing the proceeds of crime.

At a second stage the benefits are also available: let us say that you are an estate agent selling an expensive property in the heart of London. Do you care how your Russian buyer has accumulated his wealth? Is it your place to risk offending him by asking such questions – particularly when the person who will lose out is you if the prosperous Russian is offended by your impertinence, pulls out of the purchase, and you lose your hefty commission on sale?

Sometimes the stance of 'wilful blindness' by professionals slides into something more insidious altogether. Raul Salinas, the brother of the former President of Mexico, Carlos Salinas, was arrested and jailed on murder charges in February 1995. He was also accused of various incidents of money laundering. In December 1998, US congressional investigators released a report that analysed the relationship between Salinas and Citibank. The report concluded that:

> *Citibank, whilst violating only one aspect of its then policies, facilitated a money management system that disguised the origin, destination and beneficial owner of the funds involved.*

In simple terms, this is what the report says happened: cheques drawn on a Mexican bank were deposited in Citibank Mexico by the wife of Raul Salinas – using an alias name. The cheques were wired to New York where they were 'commingled' (in plain English, mixed up) with other funds before being transferred to Citibank in London and Switzerland. It has been stated that one private bank employee in

Citibank London had dealt with the Salinas account for years – but did not know it was his because the account was only referred to by a code, CC2. The funds dealt with in this manner were between $90 million and $100 million.

The above example also gives a graphic archetype of how easy it is – with a little help, admittedly – to transfer tainted funds from Mexico, through the United States to London and Switzerland. Underpinning the boom in successful money laundering is globalization. It is also globalization that is the driving force behind the rapid, all-embracing spread and influence of organized crime. Whereas previously organized crime could (to some extent) be contained within its country of origin, now such gangs are increasingly engaged in transnational organized criminal activities where geographical borders are irrelevant – next stop cyberspace. The facilitators of such activity are:

- Free movement of capital: such as the removal of exchange and currency controls.
- Free transit of goods across borders: in Europe it is perfectly feasible to drive large sums of cash across borders with no problem whatsoever.
- The breakdown of traditional orders can in certain countries create a deprived dislocated underclass who can be exploited by organized crime.
- The speed of new technology: faxes, the Internet, on-line banking, advertising of anonymous banking facilities by the Internet, and encrypted global mobile phones.

What is clear is that transnational organized crime groupings are now active on a pan-global basis, turning up in the most unlikely places. Not only are such groups demonstrating their agility by moving with the technology, they are also forming alliances with each other (just like normal business: as in strategic alliances between airline companies to provide a seamless service). One could argue, taking a devil's advocate's position, that such organized criminal groups are cooperating with each other far more effectively than politicians, bureaucrats and law enforcement agencies of different countries:

- In January 1998, Colombian cocaine valued at $32 million was seized on the French side of the channel tunnel. The value makes this one of the biggest smuggling rings seen to date. How was this massive haul identified? The smugglers were stopped in their Land Rover because French customs officials thought it appeared heavy. How right they were: each wheel of the 4[bl]4 contained approximately 30 kilograms of cocaine. The drug originated in Colombia, was taken to Brazil and then shipped to Italy hidden in imported vehicles. Once in Italy it was put in wheels of cars that would appear to be owned by holidaymakers returning home to England.

- The on-going fight against the Colombian cocaine cartels by the US Government continues: but the criminals themselves are now both targeting the heroin market in Europe and utilizing even more European financial and banking channels to launder money. In the United States itself, the Colombians have been fighting a war with Chinese, Asian and Turkish heroin suppliers. The Colombians appear to have won, as it is now estimated that they supply over 60 per cent of the heroin in the country. Crucially they have achieved this by undercutting the price of their competitors and supplying heroin with a 95 per cent purity level. Various arrests across Spain late in 1999 highlighted a major Colombian money laundering operation that involved a group of individuals of various nationalities washing dirty money through the Spanish banking system. One key element of the process was Spain's strong historical and contemporary links with South America. It is now believed on the drug trafficking front that London's Heathrow Airport is emerging as a vital gateway from South America to Europe. Drugs are being carried in hand luggage on flights from South America that have a connection to mainland Europe through Heathrow. They are then handed over to English couriers who transport the drugs to European cities, particularly Amsterdam and Madrid. English couriers are less obvious than South American or Spanish ones. Police at Madrid Barajas Airport have targeted flights from Latin America for a considerable amount of time but are now also increasing surveillance on flights arriving from London. However, no arrests have yet been made at Heathrow, Madrid or any other European airport that we are aware of.
- Colombia is now a byword for the catastrophic effects that illegal drugs and organized crime can have on a country. The good news though is that the situation is improving – at a price. Today the power base for drugs has moved to Mexico – specifically the US/Mexican border town of Tijuana, which is within easy reach of Los Angeles. The Tijuana cartel makes liberal use

of both corruption and the latest technology (satellites, the Internet, and encrypted phones). It is estimated that 70 per cent of the world's heroin is sourced through Mexico. This agility in the face of hostile action by the authorities and the ease with which geographical borders are crossed does not end in Mexico. Argentina seems to be the next port of call as both United States and Argentinian authorities are worried both about the rise of drug related crime and the growth of money laundering. Allied to this is the ever present scourge of corruption. Back in Colombia it is alleged that organized crime factions in Dublin have built up connections with both Colombian and Russian organized criminals to speed up the flow of cocaine and heroin into Europe.

- Argentina has in fact become the next port of call rather quicker than anybody imagined. In December 1999 it was claimed that the Juarez cartel, based in the Mexican city of Ciudad Juarez (a city just across the US border from El Paso), had laundered about $25 million through Argentinian banks – admittedly after it had originally gone through banks in the United States. Argentinian police raided a bank in Argentina, Mercado Abierto, as a result of the allegations. Mercado Abierto acted in a somewhat unique manner, as instead of seeking to hush up any rumours of their involvement in money laundering they took out a series of advertisements in newspapers denying any involvement whatsoever. Perhaps the most apt comment on the situation in Argentina was made by a senator to the daily newspaper *Clarin*. The subject under discussion was anti-money laundering legislation: the senator commented wryly, 'We have to recognize that there is a black economy, and that under such a law half of all Argentinians would be under arrest.'
- Colombia of course does not share a border with Argentina. But the former does share a border with Brazil; Brazil borders, amongst others, Argentina, together with 1,500 miles of borders with Colombia itself, Bolivia (third largest potential producer of cocaine in the world) and Peru (once the world's largest coca producer). And guess what? Organized crime linked to the illegal narcotics trade has come to be an influential force in Northern and Western Brazil. Brazil borders the three largest cocaine producers in the world and it has been estimated (although this figure, to be fair, is disputed) that 40 per cent of the world's cocaine production goes through Brazil. Particular attention was

drawn to the Bolivian border town of Mato Grosso where a local judge, Leopoldino Marques de Amarai, was murdered in September 1999. Prior to his death Amarai had publicly claimed that 16 of the 20 state judges were involved in various narcotics related crimes such as prostitution and drug trafficking.

- And running the risk of this sounding like a South American geography lesson, Brazil also borders Guyana where it has been claimed that 20 per cent of the country's output of gold is being siphoned off and also Guyanan gold is being used for money laundering.
- The free movement of persons across Europe under the Schengen agreement, which effectively has done away with border controls, has enabled a motley crew of individuals to move with impunity throughout the area. Amongst this varied collection are: Turkish and Kurdish drug smugglers; traffickers in migrants; the Italian Mafia; Kosovo Albanian gangs; even the Nigerians have attempted to get in on the act through Athens Airport, which they have considered to be a soft touch. Little wonder that Belgium in late 1999 decided, albeit temporarily, to withdraw from the Schengen agreement because of the problems being experienced with illegal immigrants. The Observatoire Geopolitique des Drogues observed in their Annual Report for 1998/99 that 'the Schengen area has become the largest drug consumer market on the planet in recent years'.
- Turkish, Bulgarian and Kosovo Albanian organized crime groups have linked with couriers based in Prague to supply British based drug dealers with heroin. Bulgaria is now a major drug trans-shipment point for Western Europe, whilst the Czech Republic is being used as a cross point between East and West. In 1998 the Czech National Drug Squad Chief commented that his country had now become 'the centre of the heroin and cannabis trade in central Europe'. Turkish organized crime is ultimately responsible for 80 per cent of heroin smuggled into the United Kingdom each year – additionally these groups major in money laundering throughout Europe.
- Triad groups from Hong Kong are active in Britain, Holland, Belgium and France. They are involved in such activities as counterfeit currency, loan sharking and money laundering. One of their notable business areas is prostitution rings in Holland and Belgium. At its extreme they imprison young girls as sex slaves.

- The world of art is another not impervious to the global activities of organized crime groups. In 1996 it was claimed in an Italian court that Caravaggio's 'Palermo Nativity', stolen in 1969, was passed between Italian Mafia bosses as collateral for financial deals. Whilst not perhaps generally known, banks across the world hold numerous works of art as collateral for loans. In 1996 a London bank received an old master worth £500,000 as collateral for a loan. The work was in fact stolen in 1993 from a Milan Gallery, a year after it was sold to it by Christies in London.
- The ubiquitous and omnipresent Nigerian organized crime groups are active at virtually every point across the globe. The infamous 419 letters are a phenomenal earner – in the United Kingdom alone they are estimated as generating £3 billion each year. In another example of global cooperation, Nigerians are reported as keen to travel to Japan and marry there, thus confirming their immigration status. Once that has been achieved they ally themselves with Yakuza members who have extensive knowledge of how to perpetrate successful advance fee fraud.
- Elsewhere in the United Kingdom not only traditional family based Anglo Saxon organized criminals are active but also Turkish gangs, Chinese gangs, Colombian groups, Indian and Pakistani criminals and Yardies. In Italy there are 20,000 Russians amongst whom are various organized criminal groups dealing in drugs, arms and money laundering. Also in the country are Nigerians specializing in drugs and prostitution together with Chinese and Albanian gangs that are involved in arms and illegal immigration rackets.

And I have only mentioned Russian organized crime briefly so far. I think it is about time to remedy that obvious omission.

In the years after the fall of communism, Russian gangsters have achieved at least one remarkable feat. Nowadays when organized crime is written about, commentated on, or discussed, the natural association is with Russia and not, as was 10, 20 or 30 years ago, Italy, Sicily and Italian families in New York. One of the major problems with writing about Russian organized crime is knowing where to start. One of the problems with researching Russian organized crime is knowing what to believe. What is now accepted is that organized crime and corruption have been part of the fabric of Russian society for a considerable period of time: it just did not simply appear overnight with the dismantling of communism. However, previously it was to a large extent regulated by the state (or at least the Communist Party, which in effect is one and the same thing), moreover organized crime went about its business with the connivance of the state. This was effectively a form of regulation. What has occurred in the 'brave new world' of a free market economy is that one of the first groups to embrace capitalism, unrestricted travel and technology are the criminals.

Being realistic it is doubtful whether there would be so much concern about Russian organized crime if, as was the case in the communist years, the problem was a localized and contained one in the country itself. What has prompted the continuous scare stories is the ease with which Russian organized crime factions have infiltrated the West. In a cynical outside world no-one is really concerned whether Boris Yeltsin and members of his family took massive bribes; no-one is really bothered if the country is run by oligarchs such as Aven, Potatin and Berezovsky; no-one is truly concerned by the large number of prostitutes and willing Russian girls in Moscow; no-one is actually bothered by what really went on in the nationalization programme and who was made mega-rich because of it. The outside world only becomes concerned when the problems land with an almighty thump on its doorstep. Even then it is a double-edged sword: capital flight is effectively encouraged by the West as it provides good business for banks and the western economy in general. Various estimates have all hovered around the amount of $15 billion per year being the total of capital being taken out of the country. This figure is only slightly less than Russia's trade balance. The most ominous factor of capital flight for Russia itself is that it is an ongoing process. Normally capital flight occurs for a short period of time after economic collapse: this flow of money has been going on since 1992 and shows no signs of abating.

The spread of organized crime from Russia itself to all points on the globe has set the alarm bells ringing. Switzerland, for example, has a problem with Russian organized crime that is probably similar to that of London, insofar as both locations are being used extensively to launder Russian crime funds and also for prosperous individuals to take up residence.

Other countries and locations have rather more pressing and loathsome problems in that Russian criminals are perpetrating the actual crimes there. In Switzerland the (then) Attorney General Carla del Ponte was quoted in 1999 as stating that Russian organized crime gangs had infiltrated some 300 Swiss companies and were using Switzerland as a 'piggy bank'. These comments reinforced a Swiss

Federal Police Report released two years earlier that observed that in the coming years Switzerland could be increasingly hit by the expansion of organized crime structures, particularly Russian. The use of Switzerland by Russians started in the early 1990s with large flows of money from the former Soviet Union as the wealthy tried to secure the value of their wealth by moving it to a safe haven. Swiss authorities estimate that in total $40 to $50 billion is deposited in Swiss banks and other financial institutions. Switzerland welcomed the original influx, as its banking sector was under competition both from offshore centres and global mainstream banks muscling in on the traditional Swiss domain of wealth management and private banking. There is no way of knowing how much of this early torrent of money was tainted with crime: just as there is no way of calculating what percentage of the entire amounts deposited is dirty money.

The Russians then decided that not only should their wealth be in Switzerland, but their families should be too. Russians bought property, moved their families and started contributing to the local economy. In 1996 Switzerland issued visas to approximately 70,000 Russian citizens. In the 1970s it was roughly 4,000 per year. Various high profile cases, scares, fears and ultimately the possible involvement of Boris Yeltsin, his family and close associates in a Swiss-related money laundering process has dampened the Swiss enthusiasm, or at least made them more careful.

The pattern described above does, to a large extent, fit what has also happened in London. Certainly any claims that single out Switzerland as the only major haven for Russian money is a substantially flawed argument. One only has to look at the Bank of New York case to see that. Without going into the personalities involved – or alleged to be involved – in what the *New York Times* has described as possibly the largest money laundering operation ever uncovered in the United States, the pivotal factors are the amounts involved and the global reach of the relevant activities. The case has just about everything:

- the possible involvement of bank employees;
- allegations that IMF loans could have formed part of the money laundered;
- possible links with Yeltsin himself, his family and inner circle;
- money transfers involving London, the United States, China and Australia;
- companies in Russia, London, Switzerland and the Isle of Man;
- accounts in London, New York, the Channel Islands and many other locations.

Forget the personalities: look at the Byzantine structures that have been created, the global reach and the amount involved ($10 billion plus). These are the important factors in a case that seems to prove beyond doubt many of the arguments forwarded in this book about the influence and abilities of organized crime groups.

The magnitude of such cases as this once again throws the spotlight back on Russia itself and the origins of the organized crime nexus that has been exported so successfully. The facts are staggeringly frightening:

- In 1994, the Russian Ministry of Internal Affairs estimated that 25 per cent of the country's Gross National Income was derived from the activities of organized crime.
- The same ministry concluded that over 5,500 criminal groups were involved in money laundering, the illegal drug trade and extortion.
- Intelligence reports suggest that there are over 100,000 members of the Russian mafia with over 8,000 individual groups who control up to 80 per cent of all private business and 40 per cent of the country's wealth.
- Organized crime controls 50 per cent of Russian banks and 80 per cent of joint venture companies with foreign capital.

But that is not enough for these highly organized, non-political, closed environment groups that are organized in a cell structure. In fact it almost seems as if the world is not enough:

- In Israel, traditional Israeli underworld structures are being decimated by Russian criminals who are benefiting from the mass immigration from the Soviet Union that began in the 1980s and are now muscling in on the country's drug running, prostitution and gambling rackets.
- In Germany, Holland and the United Kingdom, Russian gangs are involved in everything from prostitution, drugs, stolen cars and fraud.
- In Sri Lanka, Russian criminals are elbowing their way into the existing profitable business areas of prostitution, gambling and drugs.
- In Canada, Russian organized crime groups are involved in financial crime, extortion, drug smuggling, tobacco and weapons smuggling and immigration fraud. Just to confuse things many such criminals have set up legitimate businesses to

give their operations a facade of respectability. Yet the financing of such businesses invariably comes from organized crime activities: thus it can be said that they are at least partially laundering their own criminal proceeds. Canada is also a large centre of organized vehicle theft – as cars exported to Russia can be sold for twice their value back at home. The Russians who have emigrated to Canada then provide letters of invitation to other Russian 'investors' so they can visit the country. In December 1999, 35 suspects were arrested and charged in part of what was termed 'the largest crackdown on Eastern European criminals' operating in North America. The Royal Canadian Mounted Police (RCMP) stated that the suspects had been charged with a comprehensive range of offences including drug trafficking, credit card fraud and various immigration related crimes. However, the activities of this group were much wider: prostitution, money laundering, human smuggling, smuggling of goods and the counterfeiting of computer software. Inspector Ben Soave of the RCMP commented that Canada 'was becoming a sanctuary for organized criminals' as they had identified and targeted 'a peaceful, tolerant and perhaps naive Canadian Community as their prey'.

- Where are the Russians not active? Certainly not the following countries: United States (drugs, money laundering and fraud); Belgium (stolen cars); Spain (the sex industry and prostitution); France (prostitution, money laundering, fraud and drugs); Italy (just in case you thought it was all sewn up by some other groups – drugs and illegal immigrants); Poland (fraud, money laundering and drugs); Austria (money laundering and rumours of nuclear material smuggling); Former Yugoslavia (basically anything to profit from domestic warfare and particularly arms sales).

In the new freedoms of the technologically advanced 21st century, the Russian mafia have achieved in less than ten years what the Italian Mafia took decades to perfect. And that of course is not even allowing for the fact that the Russians and Italians (and Colombians, Mexicans, Bulgarians, Nigerians, etc) have not at some stage – or on an on-going basis – pooled resources and expertise.

However, the success, for want of a better word, of post-Soviet organized crime groups may actually originate back in the past, where there existed a traditional code of conduct that, if broken, is punishable by death. A free translation of the Thieves' Code is:

1. Forsake all relatives: mother, father, sister, brother.
2. Do not have a family of your own: no wife, no children. However, this does not mean that you are precluded from having a lover.
3. Never, under any circumstances, work. This may cause severe difficulty, but live only from the profits of crime.
4. Help other thieves – both through moral and material support and through the community of thieves.
5. Do not disclose secret information about the whereabouts of accomplices, safe houses, hideouts, etc.
6. If placed in an untenable situation you should take the blame for someone else's crime – this buys that person invaluable time.
7. Demand an assembly of inquiry to resolve disputes between thieves.
8. If necessary take part in such inquiries.
9. Carry out the punishment of the offending thief as determined by the assembly.
10. Do not resist carrying out the punishment of the offender.
11. Ensure that you have good command of the thieves' language and jargon.
12. Do not gamble unless you can cover your losses.
13. Teach your trade to young beginners.
14. Cultivate informants from the rank and file of thieves.
15. Do not lose your reasoning ability when under the influence of alcohol.
16. Have nothing to do with the authorities. Do not participate in public activities. Do not join any community organizations.
17. Do not take weapons from the authorities. Do not undertake military service.
18. Always make good on promises to other thieves.

The Nearest Thing to Alchemy

As wealth is power, so all power will infallibly draw wealth to itself by some means or other.

(EDMUND BURKE)

The alchemist's theory that base metals could be transmuted into gold is a fitting analogy for the process of money laundering. For the latter succeeds in transforming tainted and base materials into a far purer substance. The classical model of the money laundering procedure presupposes that the base component is cash. Increasingly, as money laundering is not just drug related, but encompassing all proceeds of serious crime, this may no longer be the case.

Consider, for example, an intricate advance fee fraud that is targeted at 'sophisticated' investors. It is very unlikely that payments into such a scheme would be requested or made in cash because by their very nature large cash payments would raise suspicion. Equally, one of the simplest (and most effective) cases of money laundering I have witnessed turned the classical model on its head. This involved the fraudulent negotiation of stolen financial instruments by physically taking them to Vienna and using them to open a Sparbuch account (as this was the very early 1990s these accounts were not quite as infamous – or as widely known about – as they are now). When the instruments were cleared the perpetrator just walked into the bank, passbook and code word in hand, and withdrew the cash. If he had wished to commit the perfect fraud he would have then gone to another bank – or preferably banks – in Vienna and opened a series of further Sparbuchs. As the original bank recorded no details of the customer then the money trail effectively died there.

If you would like another example of how easy it is to launder money then why not overpay your tax bill. It is rumoured that money launderers in the United Kingdom, and possibly elsewhere, have hit upon a novel scheme to wash funds. This involves making a substantial overpayment to the Inland Revenue (or relevant domestic tax authority) due to a 'clerical error'. When the overpayment is discovered the criminals are (eventually) presented with a refund cheque from the tax authority, which of course can be paid in at any bank or financial institution without any questions being raised.

For another example of how simple it is we should focus on a small bureau de change in Notting Hill, London – totally nondescript, and resembling many hundreds, if not thousands, of almost identical shops in London and the millions around the world. You even had the impression that changing foreign currencies couldn't be too profitable as the shop also listed on its fascia 'Theatre Tickets; Photo/Film and Jewellery'. It is somewhat of a shock then to learn that this small shop managed to launder £70 million and has been described as the biggest money laundering operation in Europe.

The owner of the shop, Yussama El-Kurd, provided an unparalleled service to criminals across the United Kingdom by turning their cash into foreign currency, mostly guilders. This was hardly a complex method then. In fact his money laundering activities found such popularity with his clients that the shop regularly ran out of money and thus had to request additional large amounts of guilders from local Thomas Cook branches, Barclays and various Arab banks. From November 1994 to November 1996 currency transactions for the bureau increased 10 times. El-Kurd made £3 million from this activity and ended up being jailed for 14 years in February 1999. At the time of his arrest, El-Kurd was laundering £7 million a month – mostly from drug dealers in the north-west of the country.

Money laundering is frustratingly and simultaneously clear-cut in some cases, and obscurely complex in others. Certainly it is not quite as uniform and linear as perhaps text book examples would like to have us believe. For if it were it would presumably be extremely easy to identify and stop. It should also not be forgotten that there are some methods of money laundering that do not need to involve the banking system, such as dirty dealing in cash based economies, the African barter trade, which revolves around the trading of cannabis, and the elementary system of barter that remains in various outposts of the former Soviet Union. The three normally quoted stages of the process in traditional money laundering are placement, layering and integration. The fact that terrorist funding rarely follows this pattern is considered separately in Chapter 7.

If we now accept that funds that need to be laundered are not all cash, the overriding principle still applies that money laundering must begin with funds that can be identified as proceeds of crime. Drugs are heavy: $1 million worth of cocaine weighs 44 lb. Cash of $1 million in $100 bills (the largest available) weighs half this. But to reduce this physical mass even further, $1 million in Euros weighs just 5.2 lb. Yet these funds are still difficult to conceal and have an inherent risk of being stolen.

The first thing to do with all proceeds of crime is to get it into the world's banking system but simultaneously arouse no suspicion by doing this. As criminals have become more adept at this initial stage they have, for example, invested in businesses that in the normal course of events have a high physical cash flow. Examples of these cash intensive businesses are casinos, bars, retail outlets, art dealers and restaurants. If they can utilize a business type where it is accepted that cash forms the major proportion of their takings and therefore bankings, then where cash is the base metal, it can easily be inserted in the banking system. Criminals can make use of existing businesses of this type, create their own – where a trading concern is merely a front – or they can establish a totally fictitious concern that never trades but simply launders cash.

There are other ways to achieve placement of criminal funds: buy high value goods such as works of art, aeroplanes, property, precious metals or diamonds that can then be sold to a legitimate purchaser and thus the criminal is banking the proceeds of a business transaction. If the money is in cash then the free movement of capital in Europe, as an example, means that cash can be transported from the country of its origin into one where it is gratefully received. In the United States the cash is smuggled out of the country through a range of ingenious methods principally to South America where it is banked and then wired back to the States or other reputable financial centres.

Whether the profits of crime are in the form of cash or not, placement is the most dangerous stage for the criminal. It is here that there exists a direct connection between the profits and the crime. From here on in the money is not cash, merely numbers on a piece of paper or computer screen. This is of course why all legislation, regulation and training to counter money laundering is focused on account opening procedures. These normally comprise:

- verification of the identity of the new customer (KYC – Know Your Customer);
- reporting to official bodies when the initial investment is over a certain limit;
- training staff who deal with account opening to recognize suspicious transactions.

In the United States and elsewhere this has led to reporting procedures where the amount used to open an account exceeds $10,000 in cash (in the case of the United States). The equally logical response from the criminal world to this has become known as 'smurfing'. This is where an army of smurfs visit multiple banks, or bank branches, making payments just below the reporting threshold. In actuality the typical smurfed amounts are now way below that threshold (as it became obvious that transactions just below $10,000 were probably more suspicious than amounts of that level or more) at a sum of $3,000 or less. The reporting procedures control has also forced the smurfs to look for opportunities outside the banking system: by buying goods such as cars, white goods and jewellery and then shipping them out of the country for resale. Such a technique has the additional advantage of a 'legitimate' business cover – and additional profits from the goods exported!

Thus countries or financial institutions that offer true anonymous banking – where the owners of the funds do not have to identify themselves or prove their identity by the production of official documents – are naturally a target – and a soft touch – for money launderers: hence the strong official antipathy towards the Austrian Sparbuch, to offshore financial centres that offer similar services, and to International Business Companies that hide the true owners – bearing in mind that IBCs open bank accounts, not disclosing who is behind them. However, one common fallacy ought to be corrected: numbered accounts are not a serious problem as banks know who the customer is and have satisfied themselves as to his/her probity before disguising that ownership by allocating the account holder a number. Numbered accounts are, therefore, not anonymous accounts. Of course the one arena where all of the control procedures in the world could be redundant is the offering of anonymous banking facilities through the Internet.

The next stage in the process is most commonly known as layering but is also referred to as Agitation or Commingling. As each of the terms implies, unless this stage is completed, the criminal money may have been placed in the banking system but it is still in one block and can be identified as such. The trick at this stage is to move money around: within the same financial institution; to other financial institutions; to other countries; into other currencies; to other types of investments (bonds, stocks and travellers' cheques); or by investment in real estate. Additionally at this stage the ubiquitous International Business Company may make an appearance as an appropriate vehicle. The whole purpose of these moves is to break the money up, create as much paperwork as possible to confuse and frustrate any active surveillance or future investigation, and, at the end of the day, create a false provenance for the source of the funds. However, by the very nature of layering it is possible to identify certain traits that can indicate that money laundering is taking place:

- financial transactions that just do not make sense – and appear to be done just for the sake of the transaction with no underlying reason;
- frequent sales and purchases of investments – particularly where fees and commissions are taken by professional advisors;
- numerous account balances being consolidated in a far smaller number of accounts – particularly where the original series of accounts are apparently unconnected;
- lack of concern over losses on investments, bank charges or professional advisor charges. The money launderer is only interested in profit as a secondary issue – the sole motive is to obscure the origins of the funds.

The final stage – where the winning post is in sight and passed by the criminals – is Integration. The original proceeds of crime have now been washed and spun dry so that they can be introduced into a respectable financial environment. The money can also be taken out of the banking system for 'legitimate' purchases without too many awkward questions being raised.

Whilst the final stage of integration is often perceived in terms of massive windfalls becoming available to the criminal, probably the most effective method is to copy a normal on-going business relationship. Thus a launderer operating onshore can bill his own offshore entity on an on-going basis for professional services provided and thus 'legitimately' be paid on this basis. Taking this logical business arrangement one stage further you can then have your offshore entity make a business loan to your onshore operations; apart from having domestic tax advantages this transactional set-up means that you can legitimately ship more money offshore as you 'repay' the loan.

One interesting lateral link with money laundering is the availability, in the United States particularly, of books about asset and wealth protection. These books and seminars offer 'legitimate' strategies to guard your wealth from the IRS, creditors, lawsuits, divorce, etc. In many of these books hundreds, if not thousands, of wealth protection tips and 'secrets' are provided. Below is a compilation of the top ten tips offered in such volumes to ensure that your financial transactions are private. Strangely, or perhaps not so strangely, it resembles a money launderers' charter. It is vital to note that these books are widely available and extremely popular, and the list below, although in my own words, is based directly on the advice given:

1. Incorporate a company to deal with sensitive transactions.
2. Do not use cheque account transactions: cash, money orders or credit cards are safer to use.
3. Take care when investing money abroad: watch the particular country's currency reporting limits.
4. NEVER involve a US bank in cash transactions over $10,000: split the transactions into various smaller amounts. Then put them through on separate dates – so that your bank cannot add them together and make a suspicious transaction report.
5. Conduct as many transactions as possible as bearer transactions – as your name does not appear.
6. Use only professional advisors who will keep your information totally private. This includes lawyers, accountants, investment advisors and banks. You should get them to confirm that they will tell you immediately if they receive a request for information or a subpoena.
7. Use a post office box or mail drop service to receive legal, financial or confidential documents and correspondence.
8. Use private vaults for your cash and valuables.
9. Do not give out personal and financial information unless you have to: borrow from and establish business relationships with those who ask the least possible information about you.

10. If you incorporate, do it in a state or jurisdiction that gives you and your corporation as much privacy as possible.

Shall we just go home and give up now?

Work carried out by, amongst others, the IRS and the US Customs Service – in line with the suggestions made in Chapter 1 that there is now a high level of broadening, switching and intermingling of criminal activity – confirm that money laundering is just as likely to be a self-perpetuating cycle or continuum as opposed to a definable process with a discernible beginning and conclusion. This alternative or additional model is specifically related to the South American drug trade but can almost certainly be abstracted and amended to profile other related money laundering flows. The six-stage cycle is:

1. The drug cartel boss in Colombia, Mexico or the Dominican Republic ships a load of cocaine to New York.
2. The wholesaler in New York sells the drugs to various distributors and gives the illegally generated money to a money launderer. Cash is also smuggled back to the drugs boss who banks the funds in South American banks, which are then laundered, ultimately being invested in the United States in property, stocks and bonds.
3. The money launderer converts the criminal profits into untraceable low level financial instruments such as travellers' cheques, vouchers and money orders. These are then used to buy cars and white goods on behalf of a major foreign buyer.
4. The goods that have been purchased are shipped by road (to Mexico) or by boat to further afield.
5. The foreign retailer sells the goods on the open market and pays off a loan to a local currency broker.
6. The currency broker skims off 3 per cent handling fee and gives the rest to the cartel boss to finance further production and transportation of drugs.

This cycle is in itself a variation (or extension) of the Black Market Peso Exchange system in Colombia. As US authorities claim that this system is 'the single most efficient and extensive money laundering scheme in the Western Hemisphere' and equates to 30 per cent of the illegal cash of the Colombian drug cartels ($6 billion per year), it merits explanation:

1. A Colombian drug cartel ships drugs to the United States.
2. The drugs are sold in the United States for dollars.
3. The Colombian cartel sells its profits in US dollars to the Colombian black market peso broker's representative in the United States. This amount is sold at a discount below its face value because the representative and his smurfers must take the responsibility for placing the dollars in the US banking system and evading the US reporting requirements ($10,000).
4. Once the peso broker's representative in the United States has received the dollars, his boss, the peso broker in Colombia, deposits the agreed amount in pesos in the cartel's account(s) in Colombia. At this stage the drug cartel has successfully laundered its proceeds of crime, as the currency it was in (dollars) has been converted into pesos.
5. The dollars – the direct proceeds of sale of drugs – are now placed in the US banking system by smurfing.
6. The Colombian black market peso broker has now created a pool of 'clean' dollar funds that he can sell to Colombian importers who in turn use the washed dollars to buy goods from the United States or other markets.
7. Finally the purchased goods are imported to Colombia – with a final irony of them frequently being smuggled in order to avoid Colombian laws and duties.

In September 1999, as a result of the three-year undercover 'Operation Cashback', 24 grand jury indictments were made against 60 defendants. This total of 60 included 16 Colombian nationals, peso brokers or business owners, and 9 more were Colombian couriers living in the United States. But 35 were US employees of 16 separate businesses, mostly located in South Florida. The key to this successful operation was a 'storefront' set up by Florida police. The storefront helped to move drug money and told its customers there would be no paper trail. The cash was put in banks by smurfing techniques: it was then withdrawn by money orders, wire transfers and cashiers' cheques. These funds were also utilized to purchase goods from US businesses: who in turn were told that the money given to them was from drugs – but they agreed not to report the relevant large cash transactions.

The international community's response to the global money laundering explosion began in 1988 with the United Nations; the role of financial institutions in preventing and detecting money laundering has been most notably commented on by the Basel Committee on

Banking Supervision; the European Union adopted a directive on money laundering in 1991 that then cascaded into domestic legislation of member countries. Finally the main international body concerned with the on-going prevention of money laundering is the Financial Action Task Force (FATF), which has issued the keynote 'Forty Recommendations' that details the countermeasures that should be adopted by countries. These initiatives establish the framework, ground rules and benchmarks for national anti-money laundering legislation and regulation. It is, therefore, worth examining each of these responses to money laundering for an assortment of reasons. Primarily because it is very clear by reading each document separately and then collectively what has to be done to stop money laundering, it becomes blatantly obvious that some countries and their financial and business systems have taken not a blind bit of notice of any of these efforts and carry on regardless.

The 1988 'United Nations Convention against Illicit Traffic in Narcotic Drugs and Psychotropic Substances' mercifully also has the shortened title of the Vienna Convention. With regard to money laundering it stated the following important principles that the UN urges all member states to implement:

- Establishment of a comprehensive legislative framework to criminalize money laundering related to serious crimes and to prevent, detect, investigate and prosecute money laundering by:
  - identifying, seizing and confiscating the proceeds of crime;
  - including money laundering in mutual legal assistance agreements to ensure assistance in investigations, court cases or judicial proceedings.
- Establishment of an effective financial/regulatory regime to deny access to national and international financial systems by criminals and their illicit funds through:
  - customer identification and verification requirements, in order to have available for competent authorities the necessary information on the identity of clients and the types of financial movements they carry out;
  - financial record-keeping;
  - mandatory reporting of suspicious activity;
  - removal of banking secrecy impediments to anti-money laundering efforts.

- Implementation of enforcement measures to provide for:
  - effective detection, investigation, prosecution and conviction of criminals engaging in money laundering activity;
  - extradition procedures;
  - information sharing mechanisms.

Remember: this was adopted in December 1988. The declaration unequivocally calls for Know Your Customer procedures (as they later became known), mandatory reporting of suspicious transactions, and most tellingly – in view of the massive problems that still exist in offshore financial centres – the principle that domestic bank secrecy provisions should not hinder anti-money laundering endeavours.

The Basel Committee on Banking Supervision issued their statement of principles on the 'Prevention of Criminal Use of the Banking System for the Purpose of Money Laundering' in the same month (December 1988). Banks of member states are expected to comply with the tenets listed. Even then the dangers of international organized crime was recognized and referred to in the document's preamble. The best-practice guidelines contained in the report, which aims to 'encourage vigilance against criminal use of the payments system', are:

- Banks should institute effective procedures for obtaining identification from all new customers – and identify ownership of accounts. The principles state that it should be an explicit policy that significant transactions will not be undertaken if the relevant customers have not proved their identity.
- Banks should run their businesses to high ethical standards, and comply with relevant laws and regulations. Banks should not offer services or provide assistance in transactions that 'they have good reason to suppose are associated with money laundering activity'.
- Banks should cooperate with law enforcement agencies, not assist customers who are trying to deceive such agencies, and should take appropriate measures to frustrate money laundering if it is suspected that a bank is involved in such activities.
- Banks should adopt the principles together with training staff and retaining internal records. They should also test general compliance with the statement.

In June 1991 the Council of the European Communities adopted a directive on the 'Prevention of the Use of the Financial System for the

Purpose of Money Laundering'. The directive, which came about primarily as a consequence of the liberalization of cross border money movements and financial services in the European Union, had these fundamental requirements:

- Member states are obligated to outlaw money laundering.
- Member states must ensure that financial institutions establish and maintain internal systems to prevent money laundering, to obtain identification from customers and to retain proper records for five years.
- Member states must also require financial institutions to report suspicious transactions, simultaneously ensuring that by making such reports no liability is experienced by the relevant institution or its employees.

The only facet of this directive that in hindsight was badly thought out is that customer identification was only required when the institution entered into transactions with that customer of more than ECU 15,000. Immediately there was a limit under which smurfing could be achieved. Moreover, if the directive was applied literally, the internal procedures of financial institutions with regards to taking identification – and ultimately relationships with customers – would end up confused and confusing. The European Union returned to the fray in October 1999 at their summit in Finland, where a 10-point plan was agreed to tackle various issues including organized crime and money laundering. One of the agreements involved easing banking secrecy to 'trace, freeze, seize and confiscate the proceeds of crime'.

The Financial Action Task Force on Money Laundering (the FATF) was set up by the G-7 Summit in Paris in July 1989. Its brief was to examine measures to combat money laundering. At the time of writing it comprises 26 governments and two regional organizations (listed fully in the glossary section). The FATF has been the most active international body in the area of trying to prevent money laundering, together with attempting to define the problem and encourage the adoption of effective counter measures. It issues a comprehensive annual report together with a yearly report on money laundering typologies. The foundation stone of the FATF response to money laundering is their 40 recommendations that were originally issued in 1990 and updated in 1996 to reflect developments in the intervening period. The recommendations are segmented into four areas:

1. the general framework of the recommendations;
2. the role of national legal systems in combating money laundering;
3. the role of the financial system in combating money laundering;
4. the strengthening of international cooperation.

The key issues addressed by the 40 recommendations are:

- Each country should ratify and implement fully the Vienna Convention.
- Somewhat crucially, the 40 recommendations state that 'Financial institution secrecy laws should be conceived so as not to inhibit implementation of the[se] recommendations.'
- The importance of multilateral cooperation, mutual legal assistance and extradition is stressed.
- There are copious common sense recommendations in respect of taking customer identification and the uncompromising statement that 'financial institutions should not keep anonymous accounts or accounts in obviously fictitious names.'
- Necessary records should be maintained for five years so that any transactions can be reconstructed.
- Recommendation 13, both tellingly and somewhat prophetically, advised countries to pay special attention to threats contained in new or emerging technologies, particularly those that may encourage or facilitate anonymity.
- There are various recommendations that outline the importance of financial institutions applying increased diligence to customers and transactions. Policies, procedures, controls, ongoing staff training and compliance testing are all recommended.
- Financial institutions should be particularly wary of business relationships and transactions that involve countries that do not apply the Recommendations.
- Recommendation 25 takes another bull directly by the horns: 'Countries should take notice of the potential for abuse of shell corporations by money launderers and should consider whether additional measures are required to prevent unlawful use of such entities.'
- The final set of recommendations promote international cooperation through the exchanging of intelligence, and bilateral and multilateral agreements facilitated by common legal concepts. The tools to achieve this aim should include financial

institutions producing records, identifying, freezing, seizing and confiscating criminal proceeds together with extradition and prosecution.

After these four documents what more is there to say? Both individually and collectively these papers spell out the risks of money laundering together with outlining exactly what needs to be done (particularly in the financial sector) to control and hopefully eradicate the predicament. Without wishing to appear either presumptuous or facetious a top 10 of money laundering preventative measures should look like this (in no specific order):

THE TOP TEN MONEY LAUNDERING PREVENTATIVE MEASURES

1. Governments must criminalize money laundering.
2. Money launderers must be prosecuted and convicted. To achieve this bilateral and multilateral treaties must be established and offenders must be extradited.
3. The proceeds of crime should be frozen and ultimately confiscated.
4. Countries, law enforcement agencies and institutions should share intelligence.
5. Banks should cooperate with law enforcement efforts and enquiries and should not assist money launderers.
6. Banks (and similar entities) must install vigorous identification procedures to verify that people opening an account are who they say they are.
7. Banks must keep records to assist law enforcement efforts.
8. Banks must report suspicious customers and transactions.
9. Banking secrecy must be removed if it facilitates money laundering.
10. Banks must install systems, train staff and monitor how they are doing.

It is worth pausing here for a moment just to consider and expand upon the verification of a customer's identity as this is one of the central principles in the fight against money laundering. In the United States (and elsewhere) this has been christened KYC ('Know Your

Customer'). There are some very good reasons for banks (and increasingly all types of business) to validate the identity of their customers:

- It is the first line of defence: a business can stop money laundering in its tracks before it has started.
- By doing so effectively your organization is achieving the necessary compliance.
- Such a procedure protects the reputation of your business.
- If carried out effectively it is a powerful deterrent: criminals (more so than governments or even law enforcement agents) communicate with each other. If an institution is identified that is simply paying lip service to identification procedures the word will soon be spread around and the floodgates forced open by a substantial number of eager new customers with large, tempting deposits.

However, there are practical problems with the implementation of a KYC policy such as:

- On various occasions I have been asked to formulate a list of acceptable identification documents that will always be totally genuine. My final lists have always been a blank piece of paper – there is no document that cannot be purchased, forged, copied and altered, fabricated or stolen.
- Just because a client is who he or she says s/he is does not mean that s/he is not attempting to launder funds.
- Just because a client is who he or she says s/he is does not mean that s/he isn't a known money launderer/drug dealer/illegal arms trader/supplier of pornography/trafficker of humans, etc.
- The ease with which fraudulent documents can be obtained – and the excellent quality of such forgeries – mean that it is not too difficult to pass the KYC test with flying colours.
- If you are determined to launder then you can always find compliant bank staff (in plain English that means pay them enough and they will turn a blind eye).
- Because many business people are commission orientated, make your initial deposit sufficiently enticing and they will do all that they can to accommodate you. You do not need to pay them directly – money talks.
- What about postal deposits? For a start photocopied identity documents can hide a multitude of sins – you may be able to isolate an original forgery but with a photocopy it is very difficult.

We will return to these issues in Chapter 8 by providing preventative strategies in this area. It is also worth mentioning at this juncture, concerning the procedures, that however logical and well meaning KYC regulations are they are never universally welcomed or appreciated. Claims of invasion of privacy, Big Brother tactics and eroding basic freedoms are common from groups claiming that their basic civil liberties are being eroded. Examples are trotted out of honest, down to earth people who have saved for years by keeping cash in the house being accused of money laundering when they try and use it as a deposit to buy a house, or open a bank account with it. Scorn has been poured on the suspicious traits that money launderers are supposed to exhibit as they could well be signs of other legal activities or simply erratic behaviour.

Providers of offshore services have been quick to jump on this bandwagon by trying to assure us that the facilities they provide are being offered to all individuals so that we can still have the fundamental right of financial privacy that is being stolen from us by the money laundering prevention nanny state. In a word, all of this pompous rhetoric is claptrap. No government or international body is remotely interested in the funds of honest law abiding citizens who pay their taxes. Without jumping on as equally high a horse as the protesters against money laundering regulation, it would appear to me that the people whose basic civil liberties have been removed are the direct or indirect victims of organized crime. If once in a while a 'genuine' customer is mistakenly reported as carrying out suspicious activity then I think that this is a fairly small price to pay in the attempt to starve criminals of their lifeblood.

Another slant on the KYC phenomena was provided by Senator Carl Levin in his statement to the Permanent Subcommittee on Investigations Hearing on Private Banking and Money Laundering. This must be an example of knowing your customer but not quite as intended:

> *The legal counsel for Bankers Trust private bank asked the Subcommittee not to make public any information about an account of a certain Latin American client because the private banker was concerned that the banker's life would be in danger if the information were revealed. The Bankers Trust counsel, when describing one of its clients, told our staff words to the effect that 'These are bad people'. If the bank thinks they're 'bad people' why are they seeking them as customers of the private bank? In the Bankers Trust case it appears the bank does know its client; but what it knows is that its client is bad.*

Which neatly brings us to the concept of 'wilful blindness', although I am not sure there is very much to say about it. Essentially, wilful blindness occurs when bank or business staff have been trained to recognize telltale signs of money laundering, yet do not report suspicious transactions or customers even though they know that they should. Normally – although not, it should be said, exclusively – this occurs because the relevant employee will receive some form of financial reward from his employer such as commission for the business. Whilst, as far as I am aware, very little research has been carried out on it, a far more interesting and relevant concept is corporate wilful blindness, when organizations themselves fail to report red flags of money laundering and instruct their staff (either explicitly or implicitly) to do likewise.

If all of the various recommendations of the international accords (which are variations on common themes) had been implemented by each country across the globe, the scale of money laundering would be substantially reduced and effectively the proceeds of crime would have to be washed without using the banking system. However, it hasn't quite worked like that.

And of course the point is this: whilst there are numerous countries that have taken strident and continuous steps in the fight against money laundering, the enterprising criminals who are behind the laundering have already identified and utilized the nations that have lagged behind in enacting anti-money laundering legislation. At the risk of becoming boring that is why offshore financial centres – and specifically those with no anti-money laundering regulations – are so dangerous.

The launderers have also moved on to a jurisdiction where international regulations are even more difficult to agree upon and implement – cyberspace. If the world's nations have found it demanding to both construct a common legal and regulatory system and then execute it on *terra firma*, what hope is there for regulating money laundering on the Internet and related platforms?

In February 2000 the FATF published a report on countries and territories that were 'Non-Cooperative' with anti-money laundering regulations. Whilst this report did not provide a list of such jurisdictions (this was issued in June 2000), the focus once again fell on offshore financial centres. Amongst the problems that were identified across the world that undermine anti-money laundering progress were:

- Lack of or inadequate regulations and supervision of financial institutions.

- Inadequate rules for the licensing and creation of financial institutions – particularly in offshore jurisdictions. In this respect the FATF draw attention to organized criminal groups taking over or buying banking licences.
- Problems with customer identification caused by anonymous accounts, accounts in fictitious names and non-retention of relevant records.
- The increased number of territories offering bank secrecy.
- Countries with no effective system for reporting suspicious transactions.
- Inadequate or non-existent requirements for the identification of beneficial owners or corporate entities.
- Lack of resources in business, law enforcement and other relevant areas.

The FATF report concludes with an admittance that as long as these glaring loopholes exist, money will be washed by launderers entering the international financial system through such jurisdictions or using such lax territories to escape and evade investigation in more mainstream and regulated environments. The publication of this report led to some interesting reactions – particularly from France. That country's Justice Minister, Elisabeth Guigou, commented that European states should coordinate their fight against international money laundering more effectively, as criminals found it too easy to operate in Europe. European countries must agree on a common definition of money laundering, coordinate their investigations and encourage inter-state cooperation. Somewhat dramatically (but totally logically as will be seen in later chapters) Minister Guigou called on states to 'stop all financial relations with tax havens'. She estimated that up to $8,000 billion were hidden in such offshore centres and of that up to $700 billion were the proceeds and profits from organized crime. She also confirmed that the FATF list of non-cooperative jurisdictions, when compiled, could be made public in an effort to 'name and shame' such countries and force them into compliance. In Appendix I we consider money laundering risks on a country by country basis and detail the various nations that have appeared on the FATF blacklists since June 2000.

There is also a rudimentary failing in all of the four seminal international accords detailed in this chapter. That is they – quite correctly – perceived that the primary mechanism for laundering the proceeds of crime was the banking system. Because of the very nature of banks this is patently logical. As the methodologies of money laundering became more advanced the preventative regulations of enlightened and active countries were extended to encompass ancillary services such as financial institutions that are not banks: lawyers, accountants, independent financial advisors, casinos, bureaux de change, insurance companies and suchlike.

The guile and agility of the dirty dealers spotted this oncoming and tightening net and moved on. What is now becoming clear is that it may be perfectly possible to launder money successfully by utilizing the banking system in a secondary manner or only in passing. This can be achieved by either exploiting and infiltrating business sectors that are cash based or creating companies and entities whose sole *raison d'être* is to launder money. In Northern Italy, and specifically Milan, there are, at last estimation, 20 'Ndrangheta groups, 10 Cosa Nostra gangs, 3 Camorra units, 1 Sacra Corona cell and other organized criminal groupings from at least 10 other countries. Their three favourite money laundering processes only touch upon the traditional banking environment in one aspect: firstly they favour investments in stock and real estate; the second alternative is to plug into informal money changing systems of less developed and highly cash intensive economies in countries with a lower level of financial sophistication; the third alternative is to utilize the financial system through compliant banking institutions.

In this fashion the criminals have jumped outside (at least for the present) the regulatory straightjacket. And it is to that free for all environment we move to in the next chapter.

LOST IN THE WASH: THE BUSINESS OF MONEY LAUNDERING

When bad men combine, the good must associate; else they will fall one by one, an unpitied sacrifice in a contemptible struggle.

(EDMUND BURKE)

Question: what do the following have in common? English horse races; the Hatton Garden jewellery and goldsmiths quarter of London; the Amish sect; City of London law firms; the Antwerp diamond trade; the Lloyds insurance market; a sports company in Chicago; property developers; the car trade; suppliers of white goods.

The answer is probably all too obvious in the context that the question is placed. All of them have been accused of being involved in money laundering activities. It has been suggested that alongside money laundering – which is viewed as occurring in the banking system – there is a similar process termed merchandise laundering. In essence this is where cash is used to purchase goods that can then be sold, thus effectively avoiding the banking system until the money to be deposited is totally clean, as it can be shown that it is derived from a legitimate business transaction.

Calling this something other than money laundering misses the point: money laundering is not confined to banks and financial institutions. The greater the international regulatory efforts aimed at banks to prevent and identify laundering, the more criminals will look for other market opportunities that either will not involve banks or arouse suspicion, or preferably both. Money laundering based on barter and not the banking system occurs across the world in such diverse transactions as those involving agricultural produce, arms, white goods and non-ferrous metals/gems.

There are many business areas and industry types that still would not know what money laundering is even if it came and introduced itself. It is exactly this ignorance that criminals are exploiting. Moreover, any business is run to make a profit: so if a large order comes in, most companies would not ask too many questions even if the relevant invoice was settled in cash. This presumes that the business people 'involved' are innocent accomplices: just imagine what can be achieved when the accomplices are willing and receiving a percentage of the money laundered. The business world in its entirety, not just banks, launders the proceeds of organized crime activity. The more that we get used to this concept – and expand anti-money laundering guidelines from banks to all business areas – the greater the success of reducing the flow of funds will be.

Criminals can no longer solely rely on the banking industry to launder funds and thus they have infiltrated many other business areas. Starting, rather like the launderers themselves, with banking facilities and related services, we will then consider businesses and services perhaps not traditionally associated with dirty money.

CORRESPONDENT BANKING: A GATEWAY TO MONEY LAUNDERING

On 5 February 2001, after a year-long investigation, 'The minority staff of the permanent subcommittee on investigations report on correspondent banking: a gateway to money laundering' was issued in the United States, under the auspices of US senator Carl Levin. This 380-page report gave various graphic illustrations as to how launderers could exploit weaknesses in the banking system or areas that had not previously been examined by the authorities (or banks themselves) in relation to relevant risks. The key elements of the report were:

- Many banks in the United States have established correspondent relationships with high risk foreign banks.
- Such foreign banks are shell banks, offshore banks with licences limited to doing business with persons solely located outside the licensing jurisdiction or banks licensed by weak jurisdictions.
- Because many of these foreign banks complete virtually all of their transactions in correspondent banks, the US financial system has become a gateway to money laundering.
- Many US banks rely on the fact that a foreign bank is 'licensed' and are ignorant of the true status, lack of controls, and activities of the foreign bank.
- US banks' on-going anti-money laundering checks on their correspondent accounts are 'often weak or ineffective'. In particular US banks are not enquiring into what correspondent facilities are being offered by direct correspondents – thus in one example an offshore bank was allowing at least six offshore shell banks to use its US accounts.
- One critical failure of US banks is the difference they make in due diligence procedures enacted where a foreign bank seeks credit as opposed to establishing a correspondent relationship. The report concludes that 'under current practice in the United States, high risk foreign banks in non-credit relationships seem to fly under the radar screen of most US banks' anti-money laundering programs'.
- Ten case histories were examined in the report. These examples include instances of:
  - laundering funds that the high risk foreign bank knew or should have known were associated with drug trafficking, financial fraud or other wrongdoing;
  - high yield investment scams;
  - advance fee fraud;
  - facilitating Internet gambling (which is illegal under US law).

The high risk foreign banks examined in the report were:

- American International Bank (licensed by Antigua);
- British Bank of Latin America (licensed by Bahamas);
- British Trade and Commerce Bank (licensed by Dominica);
- Caribbean American Bank (licensed by Antigua and Barbuda);
- European Bank (licensed by Vanuatu);

- Federal Bank (licensed by Bahamas);
- Guardian Bank and Trust (Cayman) Ltd (licensed by Cayman Islands);
- Hanover Bank (licensed by Antigua and Barbuda);
- MA Bank (licensed by Cayman Islands);
- Overseas Development Bank and Trust (licensed by Dominica);
- Swiss American Bank (licensed by Antigua and Barbuda);
- Swiss American National Bank (licensed by Antigua and Barbuda).

The shockwaves generated by the report immediately reached Argentina and the Caribbean. In Argentina serious concerns were voiced about Federal Bank (licensed in Bahamas), which served Argentinian clients, and MA Bank, which was licensed in the Cayman Islands but operated in Argentina. The incipient scandal escalated when it was rumoured that US investigators had found that as much as $9 billion had been laundered in Argentina between 1992 and 1999. The crisis then proceeded to snowball when the Central Bank chief in Argentina was accused of withholding information from the country's lawmakers on cases that had been reported in the Senate report.

In the Bahamas on 13 February 2002, as a result of the report, the Central Bank governor froze the accounts of Federal Bank and the British Bank of Latin America together with ordering their liquidation. The Bahamas also suspended licences held by five International Business Companies that operate investments such as offshore mutual funds. The five are:

- Chase Bank of Texas National Association;
- The Bank of Virginia Bahamas Ltd;
- Apax Banks and Trust Company Bahamas Ltd;
- United Overseas Bank and Trust Companies Bahamas Ltd;
- Bank One Oklahoma NA.

In Dominica the licence held by British Trade and Commerce Bank was revoked on 15 February due to 'poor financial status'. And in Antigua and Barbuda the licence of Hanover Bank has also been revoked.

Ultimately the report findings led to section 313 of the US Patriot Act of 2001, which generally prohibits US financial institutions from maintaining a correspondent account in the United States for a foreign shell bank; that is, a foreign bank that does not have a physical presence in any country. The provision also generally requires financial institutions to take reasonable steps to ensure that foreign banks with correspondent accounts do not use those accounts indirectly to provide banking services to a foreign shell bank.

However, the risks inherent in corresponding banking arrangements are on a global basis: thus until all of the world's mainstream financial centres adopt and enforce similar measures, the problem still exists.

LAUNDERING THROUGH SECURITIES

In January 2002 Carl Levin shifted his focus to securities firms through a report that warned that US securities firms have tens of thousands of clients based offshore who channel billions of dollars into their US accounts. Levin suggested that these customers included drug kingpins, foreign politicians and terrorists. It was slightly unfortunate that the relevant report was short on hard evidence for these claims, but did reveal that, in the 22 securities firms that were examined, there were 45,000 offshore clients with an estimated $140 billion in assets – $137 billion of which came from offshore corporations or trusts.

LAUNDERING THROUGH CREDIT CARDS

The United States General Accounting Office report on money laundering using credit cards (published in August 2002) rather removed the need to read the full 56 pages of the document by subtitling it 'Extent of money laundering through credit cards is unknown'. That having been said, the report made some interesting observations – and highlights the fact that the use of credit cards for laundering may be yet another compliance weak spot:

- There is a perception that credit cards are not used in the placement stage of money laundering but might be used in the layering or integration stages.
- Most law enforcement officials interviewed were unable to cite any specific cases of credit card facilitated money laundering in US financial institutions.

- There are very few money laundering Suspicious Activity Reports filed in respect of credit card usage.
- However, there is evidence that 'credit card accounts accessed through banks in certain offshore financial secrecy jurisdictions could be vulnerable to money laundering'.
- Credit card industry representatives said that they did not have AML policies and programmes focused on credit cards because they considered money laundering using credit cards to be unlikely. Whilst the credit card industry believes fraud prevention methods used in credit card applications and processing will help identify launderers and laundering, the US Treasury believes that these systems are 'a starting point for appropriate anti-money laundering safeguards, but alone they are not sufficient'.
- The average value of a US credit card transaction is $70, whilst Fedwire and Clearinghouse Interbank Payment electronic payment averages are $3.5 million and $4.9 million respectively. Thus the argument is that credit card transactions pose far smaller risks.
- Examples of how credit cards could be used in the laundering process include: the launderer prepays the credit card using funds already in the banking system, creating a credit balance in the account, and then requests a refund, presumably in the form of a cheque, which further obscures the origins of the funds; the launderer uses illicit funds already in the banking system to pay a credit card bill (thus integrating the funds).
- The report highlights the risks of the use of credit cards associated with banks in offshore jurisdictions to launder money but comments that the extent of this activity is unknown.

My own take on this is that one of the advantages offered to launderers by credit cards is that such pieces of plastic are a global currency. Thus if you can obtain a card in a jurisdiction (or a particular financial institution) that has non-effective fraud prevention and AML systems, then you can use your card anywhere in the world and on the Internet. Thus the launderer can purchase anything anywhere (and withdraw cash) and then pay off the monthly bill without generating any red flags. This type of usage would be particularly attractive, for example, to a terrorist or an individual planning a terrorist attack. Information concerning the 9/11 terrorists suggests that they made numerous transactions and cash withdrawals with debit cards, which are not a million miles away from credit cards. Certainly, solely the use of credit cards would not facilitate a successful money laundering operation: but as one part of a complex and well thought out methodology, credit cards could be a valuable tool.

LAUNDERING THROUGH STOCK EXCHANGES

It was Al Capone who observed that he was surprised that so many people turned to crime when there are so many legal ways to be dishonest. Mr Capone would have been familiar with both the theory and practice of money laundering. The financial world has moved on substantially in the intervening years; however, it is open to question whether the response to (or understanding of) money laundering has developed at the same pace. The London Stock Exchange is, just like any other international financial forum, a magnet for money laundering. The very simple reason for this is because it is an effective vehicle to wash funds. Examples are: criminal funds transferred into alternative financial instruments, ownership of shares and bonds; and brokerage firms taking washed or partially washed funds that are then used to buy shares or other financial instruments.

Research has shown that 80 per cent of all money laundering transactions involve an international component: certainly criminals have fully embraced the new global marketplace. This creates additional problems, as criminal money arriving to be invested in the stock exchange is more likely to come from another reputable financial centre than a country with discernible links to organized criminal activity. The increased globalization of financial marketplaces also throws up other difficulties, such as criminals establishing a trading account in the office of a financial institution in one country and then having it transferred to London.

Another more extreme method to utilize the stock exchange as a money laundering vehicle is through listed companies being nothing more than a laundering operation themselves. The now infamous YBM Magnex International Inc was delisted by the Toronto Stock Exchange in December 1998. A US class action suit claimed that YBM's 'only successful business is the laundering of criminal proceeds'. Red flags were also retrospectively raised about the money laundering possibilities inherent in the listing of dotcom companies that had no track record and unsustainable market valuations.

The current regulatory regime that highlights identification procedures, record keeping, internal reporting systems and staff training can effectively combat money laundering only if it is applied on a coherent basis in a serious and effective way with a true understanding by those in the market of what they are trying to fight and why. Critical to the success of the UK anti-money laundering regime is the disclosure of suspicious transactions (and clients) to the National Criminal Intelligence Service (NCIS).

In 1999, of 271 member firms of the London Stock Exchange, 18 made disclosures – 6.6 per cent of the total. This compares unfavourably with almost 77 per cent of building societies that made disclosures in the same period but favourably with the 0.1 per cent of accountants in the United Kingdom who made a disclosure.

But disclosure of suspicious transactions and/or clients can only be successful if relevant staff are trained to identify 'red flags' of money laundering activity. The use of shell companies (such as International Business Companies registered offshore) is now a very common money laundering tool. Moreover it is one that is being targeted by both regulatory and law enforcement authorities. Variations on this theme include transfers of funds from offshore banks; loans to and from offshore banks; and a high level of transactions with offshore entities or companies in geographical high risk areas.

'ILLEGAL' BUSINESSES

All crime is based on money, and most organized crime relates to providing goods or services in return for payment. At the most extreme end of the spectrum is illegal drug trading; then there is the sex trade (which, dependent on the country, may or may not be illegal, or may be at that halfway house stage of toleration); also don't let us forget arms dealing and such like. All of these activities are run as businesses (and very profitable ones) by organized crime groups and produce the endless flow of funds to be laundered.

Apart from the drugs trade it is of course possible that legitimate business companies are present in such areas as the respectable end of the sex trade (sex shops, magazines, videos, etc) and legal arms dealing. One consequence of organized crime expansion into such business sectors is that legitimate operators will be squeezed, threatened, infiltrated and targeted. Certainly one consequence of high levels of organized crime activities in individual countries is that the reputation of that entire nation is tarnished, if not decimated.

Prostitution – although legal in some countries and tolerated in others – is a vicious breeding ground for organized criminal activities: tying together the lucrative financial rewards of sex for sale and the misery of human trafficking. One of the more hideous side effects of the Kosovo crisis is the Albanian mafia trafficking in women and girls. The route is simple: women flee Kosovo to Albania. Once in Albania (usually at a refugee camp), they are 'persuaded' by criminals that a better life awaits them in Italy. Some women actually pay to be taken out of Albania for this better life; others are continually in debt to their transporters and thus told that the only way that the debt can be repaid is through prostitution. Once in Italy that better life is essentially to be kept as a prisoner during the day, being let out at night to walk the streets picking up men and having sex for money – which they have to hand over in full to their Albanian captors.

In mid-1999 it was estimated that you could 'buy' a Kosovo girl for £1,300. This problem is not confined to Italy; it is widely assumed that women from Kosovo have been 'exported' to work as prostitutes in Hamburg, Amsterdam, London and other Western European cities. It is vital to realize that these women are not volunteers: they are prisoners who have been trafficked as pieces of meat, then forced to have sex with anyone that comes along against their will. It is in business deals like this that the proceeds of crime that are then laundered in respectable banks and businesses are generated.

But it would be wrong to single out the Albanian mafia as the only group behind this nauseating industry. In April 1999, three Russians who in turn were linked to Lithuanian criminal factions were jailed for trafficking women to Britain and forcing them to work in brothels. The four women were lured with the promise of great wealth: but when in Britain they were kept prisoners, charged ludicrous sums in 'rent' and told that if they attempted to escape their families back home would be attacked. It has been estimated that 60 per cent of the flats used by prostitutes in the Soho area of London are occupied by women of Eastern European origin.

In the United Kingdom, and elsewhere in Western Europe, this is a growing problem. And it is not just capital cities that are targets: increasing police surveillance and vigilance mean that girls are being used in less regulated provincial towns (who would have thought that, as an example, Cheltenham and Northampton were breeding grounds for such activity). Other organized crime groups such as the

Chinese Triads are also doing exactly the same thing. Moreover, as crime begets crime the proceeds of this abominable trade are being used to finance further criminal activity such as financial fraud, illegal arms dealing and anything else that is profitable.

Because the relationship between criminal activity and money laundering is a complex one, it is also important to appreciate illegal activities that can both give rise to laundering and be used to invest funds from other criminal activity. Two prime examples of this are counterfeit goods and cigarette smuggling. The Anti-Counterfeiting Group estimates that the global market in counterfeit goods is worth more than $250 billion each year and may be as high as $1 trillion per annum. It is now accepted that the major players in this trade are organized criminal groups. Worldwide cigarette smuggling (and the trade in counterfeit cigarettes) facilitates money laundering for drug dealers and terrorists, who buy cigarettes with their funds. The sellers then launder these funds. The purchasers resell the cigarettes on the black market for an additional profit, thus creating additional amounts that are either reinvested or laundered (or more probably both).

BUSINESSES THAT ARE IDEAL FOR LAUNDERING CASH

There are certain businesses that have naturally occurring high levels of cash such as:

- casinos;
- bureau de change shops – it is rather telling that after the Netherlands installed a robust regime for these outlets in their country almost half of them closed down. That is the good news: the bad news is that in many countries their activities remain uncontrolled;
- international money transmitters;
- retail outlets;
- to a certain extent art, antique, jewellery shops and dealers;
- restaurants (ever wondered why it is that so many seemingly empty restaurants operated by ethnic groups survive in major European cities? – you will probably find that their cash turnover bears little relation to the minimal number of bums on seats);

- hotels;
- bars;
- night-clubs;
- dry cleaners – in a return to the origin of the problem;
- video rental companies;
- vending machine operators;
- fair grounds and attractions;
- parking lots.

If cash in its raw form occurs naturally then organized crime will seek to maximize their use of such a laundering channel by:

- attempting to launder funds without any involvement of the business and/or its staff;
- attempting to launder funds with the complicity of the business and/or its staff;
- setting up real businesses that trade but are fundamentally a front for money laundering – and probably a very cheap way of doing it.

BUSINESS AREAS THAT HAVE NOT TRADITIONALLY BEEN USED FOR MONEY LAUNDERING BUT ARE NOW

What is now being experienced is that genuine businesses, that historically have not been involved in money laundering, are being targeted and utilized by launderers. There is no finite list of such firms or industry sectors, nor will there ever be. Any commodity that can be bought in sufficient volumes in cash and then sold on at a profit (or even a loss will do) is a target. In the United States the following businesses and industries have been targets:

- sports equipment companies – large orders paid for by cash or money orders;
- real estate developments;
- computer software and hardware;
- car dealers;
- washing machines and other white goods;
- televisions and hi-fi equipment.

And as organized crime utilize more and more legitimate businesses and trade routes a certain problematic ambivalence enters the equation. Firstly, if you are running a business without any anti-money laundering regulations, trying to make a living, do you really care about – or question – a buyer who places a large order and pays for it in cash? Secondly, if so much criminal money is being washed through legitimate businesses can any government risk the social and political consequences of trying to stop it if the direct result will be business failures, bankruptcies and unemployment?

It could be argued that all of this talk of organized crime infiltration of wide ranging business sectors is a vast over-reaction to a small problem and this is just scare mongering. It could be argued – was it not for the fact that there already exists at least one country where the pervasive effects on business of organized crime activities can be evaluated and measured. That country is Colombia, and the penetration of criminal activity and resultant money laundering into seemingly unrelated fields is frightening.

The United States Treasury's Office of Foreign Assets Control (OFAC) administers the list of Specially Designated Narcotics Traffickers (SDNTs), which is essentially a list of companies and individuals who are involved in Colombian drug dealing. This list is the practical implementation of President Clinton's Executive Order 12978, which was signed on 21 October 1995, and applies economic sanctions against the Colombian drug cartels. In June 1998, when the list was increased to 496 blocked businesses and individuals, James E Johnson, Treasury Under Secretary for Enforcement, commented that 'This list of companies shows the extent to which narcotics traffickers' illicit proceeds have infiltrated various commercial sectors as the traffickers attempt to legitimize their drug profits.' Is this official hyperbole? By examining the list the reality of the pervasive influence and spread of organized crime is brought sharply into focus. Detailed in the list are:

- the América soccer team (determined to be owned or controlled by Cali cartel leader Miguel Rodriguez Orejula and others named on the list);
- various pharmaceutical and drug companies;
- various radio-broadcasting companies;
- investment companies;
- construction companies;
- real-estate firms;

- a large drugstore chain;
- the wholesale purchaser for a chain of grocery stores;
- a plastics manufacturer;
- agricultural firms;
- several hotel and restaurant service companies;
- a clinic;
- supermarket chains.

Another crucial pattern is that some companies named on the list have reorganized themselves under new names and claimed new ownership: which was probably an expensive waste of effort as such firms got on to the list again in their new incarnations. Such entities have been termed successors or transformers and by June 1999, 27 such companies had been named on the Specially Designated Narcotics Traffickers List.

Is this example an extreme? Or is it just the tip of the iceberg? We know that Mexico is now more important than Colombia for drug exports to the United States. We have also seen in Chapter 2 that the Colombian connection has spilled over dramatically into Brazil and Argentina. How many companies in Mexico are controlled by organized crime gangs? How many companies across the world are fronts for Russian and other Eastern European crime gangs? Moreover, in the SDNTs list there are some companies and activities listed that come as something of a surprise to be linked to organized crime and thus laundering undertakings. A football team for a start: then a clinic, a plastics manufacturer? These are not traditional businesses linked with criminal groupings, never mind full control. It has been known for many years that Colombian drugs money has been used to purchase white goods and automobiles. General Electric, for example, has had an awareness programme since 1993 for their employees to identify money laundering. The *Dallas Morning News* reported in November 2001 just one small example of how such a company could be used for money laundering. Dwayne Kahl, a GE employee, received an order for $40,000 worth of air-conditioning units. The customer then paid for his purchase with 35 money orders – which luckily threw up a red flag to Mr Kahl, who stopped the transaction. However, a transaction that was not stopped was a $1.5 million helicopter bought from Bell Helicopter Textron, based in Fort Worth, Texas. Ultimately the helicopter was seized by Panamanian authorities at the request of the US Government. The US Customs Service had discovered that the purchase was made by 25 third-party wire transfers from 16 different bank accounts – all of which could be traced directly back to Colombian drug traffickers. Quite possibly the only difference between these front organizations in Colombia and those elsewhere in the world is that because of the concerted campaign against Colombian drug barons by the United States, we actually know about these companies – whereas the real danger is the thousands, possibly millions, of similar entities elsewhere, of which we are ignorant.

In fact, it is not only football clubs in Colombia that are popular with criminals. Drug traffickers are known to have invested their funds in several Scottish football clubs including Celtic (it should be stated without any of the clubs' knowledge). In the period 1996–99, law enforcement investigators in Scotland have tracked the finances of 43 prime criminals and of those 6 had funds invested in football clubs. There are also investigations in the United Kingdom that have suggested similar links between organized crime and some of the major English clubs.

Allegations have also surfaced concerning organized criminal activity in horse racing. One of the claims is that as many as one in ten jockeys in England have been corrupted by criminals operating from the United Kingdom itself, or enjoying the sun in Spain. The scam is to rig a race and then bet dirty money on the outcome. A particular focus for such betting activities are illegal betting clubs that have surfaced in various locations along the Costa del Sol. You do not have to win large amounts of money from small bets – in fact that would defeat the object as you would end up with more cash. However, by placing each way bets on a rigged race the criminals can clean the dirty cash.

BUSINESSES WHOSE SOLE RAISON D'ÊTRE IS TO LAUNDER MONEY

As the negotiation of criminal money through banks becomes more hazardous and anti-money laundering regulations spread out from the financial world to other business sectors, the obvious solution for the professional launderer is to do it yourself. Whereas in the past cash-rich businesses like those listed previously found favour, now it may be more prudent to operate front companies whose sole raison d'être is to launder funds. Whilst it would be logical to operate entities that are known to have a high cash throughput there is an equal logic to set up firms that deal in intangibles. Consultancy firms, for instance, can operate on a global basis and receive large wire transfers from 'clients' all over the world for services rendered. By setting up such firms criminals can operate legitimate businesses, pay relevant taxes and bill other entities that they control for non-existent services.

Disreputable professional advisors

What has become crystal clear in this murky world of dirty dealing is that the original basic money laundering scams (essentially turn up at a bank with your money) would quickly fail as soon as national regulators put in place anti-money laundering procedures. Whilst we have already noted that this caused the spread of laundering to non-financial businesses it also gave rise to perhaps the most insidious group of washing accomplices: disreputable professional advisors. The increasing power and influence of organized criminals and their skilled running of their affairs as a multinational business has meant that they can afford to use the best professional advisors available. Not only are bankers caught in the honey trap of money laundering but more usually these days lawyers, accountants, fiduciaries, company formation agents, 'middlemen', investment advisors – in fact anyone who is offering a professional service that can be utilized by organized criminals.

What is also clear is that it is difficult and totally impractical to estimate the extent of the involvement in the laundering process by such professionals across the world. To confuse and muddy this already murky area there are a variety of conflicting viewpoints being put forward such as:

- The oft-voiced comments by law enforcement officials concerning the willingness of professionals to be used as laundering conduits and facilitators. In the United Kingdom there is a frequently recurring theme of major London law firms being involved in such activity. The gist of the accusations is that solicitors at major firms are working as a front for Colombian gangs, the Italian Mafia, East European criminals and of course traditional English crooks. NCIS, the National Criminal Intelligence Service in the United Kingdom, have made various comments over the years such as 'These firms are actively working on behalf of organized crime. They know who their clients are and how their clients make their money, and they know it is not from legitimate activity', or 'It is our very strong view that law firms are not meeting their legal or moral responsibilities... the bottom line is that if the lawyers were more honest and diligent, then we would not have the problems that we are having.'

In essence law firms are being accused of providing the respectable interface between organized crime and financial institutions and structures. The oft quoted example is that of accounts being opened for clients by law firms at banks where the latter already have an existing relationship, thus the probity of the law firm's client will not be questioned. Whilst it is obvious that such scare stories do have more than a basis in fact, it is perhaps interesting to note that one of the major complaints that NCIS have is that although lawyers have to report suspicious transactions and customers, the level of such reporting in the United Kingdom is very low. Thus as no United Kingdom lawyers have been charged with money laundering offences (or if any have they are small fry and not on or of the scale that has been alleged in the reports), one does begin to wonder whether the point that is being made by NCIS concerns the justifiable concern about the very low level of suspicious transaction reporting from law firms. And then there is the other side of the coin in that one of the weaknesses in the UK system of money laundering regulation has been the inability of NCIS to keep up with the number of suspicious reports sent to them.

- The role of accountants and similar professional advisors is very rarely out of the money laundering spotlight, for very good reasons: the low level of suspicious reports usually generated by such professions compared with the fact that their core business centres on money and detailed knowledge of financial patterns, structures and systems. It is these complex systems, products and transactions that are ideal laundering mechanisms, particularly when they are established and operated by professionals with a sound reputation. Just as with solicitors, probability suggests that there will be rotten apples amongst any profession, but any professional group's standing is not enhanced if (rightly or wrongly) there is a perception that it is not taking the threats of money laundering seriously.

The most obvious way to demonstrate that this is not the case is reporting suspicions. Whilst on occasions it is difficult to define what it is that you must be suspicious about, on other occasions it is reporting the blindingly obvious. In their report on money laundering typologies 1998–99, the FATF give an example of such an incident, which goes something like this. From the middle of 1994 onwards two clients of an accountancy firm regularly turned up at their offices with cash in plain brown envelopes or shoe boxes (presumably their suitcases were being used for other purposes!). The accountant did not issue a receipt for the money and proceeded to store the cash in his office until he could work out how to place the money into the financial system. His deliberations led him to establish company and trust accounts with his clients as ultimate beneficial owners and additionally personal bank accounts in names of his relatives. He then smurfed the money into these accounts, attempting to avoid any suspicious reporting procedures.

The next stage involved transferring funds overseas – once again in small chunks to avoid suspicions being aroused. This money was used to buy automobile parts that were then imported back into the country and sold at a profit. Additionally, some of the funds – now washed – were used to buy property. The accountant involved is alleged to have laundered about $650,000 – and received 10 per cent commission for his services. Interestingly, three of his colleagues at the same firm were also implicated in the cleaning process.

- As we shall see in Chapter 5, the providers of offshore services, or whatever they would like to call themselves, seem to be continually balancing on a tightrope between what is legal and what is downright disreputable.

Hatton Garden – essentially just one street off Holborn Circus and running parallel with Leather Lane Market in London – is famous as the English capital city's gold and jewellery centre. However, this predominantly cash based business is now gaining notoriety for its involvement in money laundering. As United Kingdom regulations made it more difficult to wash tainted funds through the banking system, the Hatton Garden culture, built on gold for cash, was an obvious avenue to be explored by organized crime gangs. In fact the purchase of gold on a world wide basis is an obvious channel for money laundering; so are other jewellery and precious metals businesses that continue to carry out transactions on a cash basis.

The Antwerp diamond market turns over an estimated £40 billion per year and a large proportion of that sum is cash across the counter. Historically some of the practices of this exchange have been designed and continued to give anonymity to the purchasers: invoices to non-existent people and false export sales. This culture, with its international melting point of traders (Jews, South Africans and Indians), is an ideal channel for money launderers to use: what could be better than converting hard cash into diamonds that can then be sold on legitimately after a suitable intervening period?

Gold is a particularly effective mechanism to launder the proceeds of crime. One of its key advantages is that it can be used in a vast number of ways. The utilization of gold as a laundering vehicle is highlighted by the fact that every major money laundering case investigated by the US authorities in recent years has involved the criminal use of gold. Whether the metal is in the form of ingots, scrap or jewellery it can be bought, transferred across geographical borders and sold on: thus producing cleaned funds. Because of the historical basis of the gold industry as a cash intensive business it is particularly attractive to all types of criminals – and certainly it is now very well used by South American drug cartels.

Freed of the vagaries of currency markets and difficult questions posed by the banking industry, gold is a universal currency that is also a material symbol of the generated funds. Almost ludicrously the gold trade is being abused so much by launderers that some countries that did not previously have a gold industry now, as if by magic, have acquired one (Uruguay for example). In the Netherland Antilles, US gold imports in 1993 were $68,000 – by 1997 they had rocketed to $29 million. Colombians have muscled in on this process and incorporated it into other systems already in operation such as the black market peso exchange. Because gold can be converted into many forms it actually can embody and facilitate all of the separate stages of money laundering.

Although there exist no truly new vehicles for money laundering there are some intriguing variations on old themes:

- The purchase by criminals of winning national lottery tickets whereby the true winner actually collects even more than he has won from the launderer and the latter picks up the winnings, thus having a legitimate source of funds. Certainly in Ireland it is believed that both winning lottery tickets and winning betting slips can be sold for a premium. Both confer on the holder a legitimate reason for having large, otherwise unexplainable, volumes of cash. In the case of lottery tickets in Ireland they are purchased anonymously and winners can elect not to be made public – a situation that also probably exists in many other countries of the world.

- Trafficking in new or used vehicles – either legitimately bought using the proceeds of crime or stolen to generate such proceeds.
- Shipments of tobacco, alcohol, precious metals and textiles: once again either to generate criminal funds to be laundered or as a vehicle to wash the funds that have already been obtained from criminal activities.
- Real estate remains a popular alternative for criminal washers – but with a few new twists. Firstly criminals are raising mortgages on property but the lender is an offshore company owned by the criminal himself; even more cunning is where a criminal does not buy the property but rents it off an offshore registered International Business Company, the ownership of which is anonymous. Of course the criminal owns the IBC and the property – but come arrest, seizure and confiscation time such a link may well be difficult, if not impossible, for the authorities to prove.
- Insurance remains a profitable domain for launderers: purchasing policies by a large single payment being the prime example.
- The use of cash dispenser networks is obviously a prime target for money launderers, as they can be accessed on a world-wide basis. For example, funds can be paid in through machines in the United States and withdrawn almost immediately in South America. Who needs sophisticated financial structures when you can achieve the same end result so much more easily?

To see what can happen to business and financial structures when they are subjected to organized criminal pressures one only has to evaluate the inexorable rise of the Russian mafia. Bulgaria, whose very economy was threatened by the activity of organized crime, is an interesting counter point: the problem in that country is still to a large extent contained within its national borders. That's how it began in Russia. A confidential National Criminal Intelligence Service Report from the United Kingdom written in the late 1990s commented of Russia that:

> *...the normal stable international banking business has become a dangerous place...The economy's criminalization is so pervasive that there is often a fine line between gangsters, corrupt bureaucrats and the new entrepreneurs who find it virtually impossible to operate in Russia without breaking the law or having some contact with Russia's mafia. There is a crude view of business; disputes are settled with guns and the legal system is in a state of collapse.*

The economic and legal meltdown that occurred in Russia was the result of a fairly simplistic process. The criminals infiltrated the fabric of the country's business, either through outright control or protection rackets. Then their ill-gotten gains were deposited in banks. However, that was not enough: their influence then spread into politics and they also re-evaluated their stance in relation to the banks in which they had deposited their funds. Working on Brecht's maxim, the criminals either infiltrated the existing banks or formed their own. At one stage it was estimated that 85 per cent of the country's banks were controlled by organized crime groups and their overall activities contributed almost half of the country's gross domestic product.

The Russian mafia had both subverted the country's banking and business structures whilst simultaneously meted out mob rule to those who resisted: in 1993 alone, 10 Moscow bankers were murdered by organized criminals; in 1995, 10 individuals whose occupation was metal trading were murdered. During this period, and still today, western corporations were investing heavily in Russia – even though the by-products and ramifications of organized crime were readily apparent. It has been estimated that western companies were paying up to 20 per cent of their profits to organized crime groups just so that the former could carry on in business; Microsoft estimate that 98 per cent of its products used in Russia are counterfeits.

If you were a western businessman, after all of the delays getting into the country through Moscow Airport, you could console yourself with the undoubted charms of one of the many attractive young ladies at your four or five star hotel. Prostitution – controlled exclusively by organized crime – has become a lucrative trade. The attractive girls are either forced into this meat trade or do it voluntarily because it pays far more than any legitimate job. Unless I was hallucinating at the time, I am certain that I once read that in a poll of Russian schoolgirls the job that the highest percentage of them would like to do was to be a prostitute.

However, we should not forget that to get to your hotel you would have to fight your way through the chaos that is Moscow Airport, and if you are really unlucky take a cab – in which you are probably charged at least twice the real cost so that the cab driver can pay his protector a service charge. Then when you eat, shop and probably even just walk you are contributing to the coffers of the Russian mafia.

This morally bankrupt environment led to various flights from the country. Principally money started haemorrhaging out – if you were honest would you want your funds sitting in banks of doubtful standing that were presiding over an economy in freefall? Since 1992, it has been estimated that the equivalent of approximately £10 billion per year leaves the country in capital flight. Simultaneously, the collapse of various Russian banks and the organized criminal control of others, combined with a punishing fiscal regime, encouraged normally law abiding citizens to keep their money at home – estimated at some £25 billion.

It was not only money that was leaving the motherland at an unprecedented rate: organized crime was shipping any and everything out of the country that would make a fast buck. On a daily basis copper, zinc, nickel, cobalt, weapons, historical artefacts – in fact anything that moves and could be sold profitably – was 'acquired' and exported. Simultaneously, the organized crime groups established a stranglehold in profitable (or highly subsidized) domestic industries such as automobile, aluminium and oil production. Law enforcement agencies were powerless to stop any of this – underpaid, chronically under resourced and demoralized they were themselves an easy target to corrupt. And as now become clear the political will to combat this pervasive epidemic certainly did not exist – apart from making some suitable noises to facilitate the payment of western aid.

And then the problem started cascading into the West. One early (and still popular) route was through joint venture companies. The accounting principles are simple: the Russian company orders goods or services from its subsidiaries/joint ventures in the West. Either such invoices represent something that never existed or the price is vastly over-inflated. Both methods achieve the aim of getting money out of Russia – to the tune of $1 billion per month. The funds both leave Russia and are partially (if not fully) washed in the process, bearing in mind that their origin may lie in arms, prostitution, fraud or any other serious crime.

The fall of communism also brought the fall of travel restrictions: from 1991 onwards, Russians were free to travel to other countries. As we have already seen, one popular destination was Israel where many organized criminals posed as Jewish refugees and took advantage of liberal money transfer regulations: in 1996 between 3 and 4 billion dollars were deposited in Israeli bank accounts by such émigrés (and remember money laundering is not a crime in Israel). Interestingly at one stage Israel was attempting to expel 33 such immigrants – 32 were Russian gentiles, only one was Jewish. However, whilst Israel provided a fast track solution what becomes increasingly clear is that Russian criminals, perhaps tired of an economy in meltdown or simply frustrated at the lack of opportunities at home, exported their skills and expertise to the West.

In the United States – predominantly but not exclusively in the Brighton Beach area of Brooklyn – the FBI believe that there are at least 15 distinct groups in existence in America comprising 4,000 members. It has been assessed that fuel tax scams alone cost $2 billion in lost tax revenue per annum. That figure is only a minuscule percentage of a total income derived from: automobile theft, smuggling, credit card fraud, contract killing, loan sharking, narcotics trading, telecoms fraud, prostitution and money laundering. Telecoms fraud involving the cloning of genuine phone details became a particularly booming industry in the late 1990s. But the Russians did not exclusively stay in their newly established enclave in Brighton Beach – they have established power bases in Miami, Los Angeles, San Francisco, Philadelphia and Boston. Moreover, the Russian groups in the United States have forged links with the Colombian drug cartels for their mutual benefit.

But it is not only in the United States and Israel that business and financial structures have been subverted, infiltrated and corrupted by the Russian mafia. In the United Kingdom, Russian organized criminals have undermined the international metal market, the art world and the property market. Of more unconventional trades they have substantial influence in prostitution both within the capital and the provinces. And if such criminals tire of their properties and business empires in London they can always retire to their holiday homes in the South of France where as a hobby they can engage in the established trades of kidnapping, extortion, fraud, contract killing and drug trafficking. If France is not to their liking they can always go to Spain where Russian organized criminals are extremely active in all areas of their 'normal' activities together with property ownership.

The funds that are earned from these activities can be washed through Cyprus or Switzerland where, as early as 1997, the Swiss Federal Police highlighted the problem:

> *In the coming years Switzerland could be increasingly hit by the expansion in organized crime structures, particularly Russian. Switzerland must prepare itself for an influx of capital from former Soviet countries and massive amounts of investments of dubious origin in businesses and real estate.*

And if you are wearied by Switzerland there is always Belgium, Germany, Austria, the Netherlands or somewhere new.

The two models of organized criminal obliteration of normal structures in Colombia and the spread of the Russian mafia disease across the West should provide us with all of the signposts that we need. In case the writing on the wall is not big enough to be read yet, consider the following examples, which although presented in an abstract form are real cases.

The Money Laundering Reporting Office in Switzerland quote the case of the disappearing depositor, which is a fairly common trend. This is where a customer from Southern Europe or South America opens a bank account and makes a large initial deposit. Identification is produced and the man who comes to the bank in person confirms that the funds (which can either be in cash or a transfer) are the proceeds of a sale of properties in South America.

A couple of months later the customer returns with another large deposit – he has now sold more of his property holdings in South America and intends to retire from active business life. The bank do not hear from the customer again but his wife suddenly turns up at the bank with a large amount of pesetas in cash. Yet again, explains the wife, this money is from the sale of properties. The woman wishes to open a joint account but the forms she brings are incorrectly completed by her husband, who, she explains, has suffered an accident and thus could not come himself. The bank attempt to contact their customer – the woman's husband – but are unable to. The bank do not open the joint account and the woman leaves, only to return three months later with more money. This time after continued questioning as to the source of funds the woman finally admits that the reason her husband cannot come to the bank is that he has been arrested for drug trafficking offences and is in prison. The bank reports this event – but even in such an apparent cut and dried case there is the possibility (however remote) that even if the customer is a drug trafficker and money launderer the funds in the bank account may not be a direct result of such activities.

Bank accounts operated by high volume cash businesses such as second hand car dealers are ideal vehicles (pun intended) for money laundering transactions. Many such accounts have been identified as being used for this purpose. One way of highlighting such use is to look at the movements and balances on such an account and compare it with similar businesses. Because there are various possibilities for the criminal to utilize (buying cars to launder money, or stealing cars then selling them are two prime examples), this area of commerce will remain a popular option. In Norfolk, Virginia, the general manager of a car dealership was found guilty of money laundering for drug dealers. Also found guilty were various other employees and drug dealers. Guy Amuial repeatedly sold cars to drug dealers for cash; then he wrote receipts, titled the cars and helped get bank loans in other people's names. In one example a car was shown as being bought by a 67-year-old blind man, who not only couldn't possibly drive the vehicle but also knew nothing about it.

Leaving banking behind for a moment, another key territory is where international trade through import/export companies is being used either as a cover for washing dirty funds or as a mechanism of actual washing. For instance, a company that was in effect merely a front for criminal activities paid large regular sums to a supplier in a different country. What was being purchased, however the goods were described on the invoices, was just about worthless, and when they were received they were junked. But that is not the point: a paper trail had been created that showed how money was being spent and more importantly the proceeds of crime generated by the purchasing company had been laundered by their payments to the supplier (which of course they ultimately controlled). A further variation on this theme (and there are many) is where a company in the United States wants to launder $1 million in cash. It uses this money to buy 200 watches at approximately $5,000 each and then exports them to subsidiary companies or associates in Ireland, the Bahamas, France, Italy – in fact, any country you like. The importer in the other country is invoiced for, and pays, $5 for each of the watches and then sells them at their market value of $5,000. Apart from avoiding relevant import taxes, the US company has succeeded in laundering $1 million out of the United States – it reappears as perfectly legitimate business turnover in another country.

Similarly the rise in providers of 'professional services' where what is being billed for is intangible presents a myriad of false billing opportunities to criminals – and many difficulties to official investigators. If, for example, a 'professional advisor' claims that he has provided advisory services to a client at a high hourly/daily rate, and the client is quite happy to pay that and agrees he has been supplied with such services, where does one start to dismantle this simple but effective washing channel?

One important aspect of anti-money laundering regulations is not only the corporate responsibility it places on employers but more pertinently the onus that is put on employees. In the United Kingdom, for example, there are three possible criminal offences that may be committed by staff:

- Assisting a money launderer, which can result in 14 years' imprisonment, a fine or both. This is where a person obtains, conceals, retains or invests funds where the person should have known or suspected that such funds are the proceeds of serious criminal conduct.
- Tipping off a money launderer, which can get you five years' imprisonment, a fine or both. This is where you tell your customer, or any third party, that a disclosure has been made to the relevant authorities.
- Failure to report suspicions – which leads to five years' imprisonment, a fine or both.

One further problem that probably occurs more frequently than is thought concerns the association of your staff with organized crime. Certainly organized crime groups infiltrate key organizations and businesses: we have seen how the Russian mafia infiltrated then took over the banking system in Moscow; Nigerian groups are experts at placing key cell members in relevant organizations that can provide either the know-how to commit frauds, or customer (then victim) information; at a lower yet just as crucial level, Nigerian groups specialize in utilizing the services of office cleaners to steal documents and anything else of value; in the political and administrative world of South American countries it is often difficult to tell who is a puppet of organized crime or not.

Then there are the honest employees, who, for some kind of financial benefit, become the dupes of criminals. Various sting operations in the United States have been facilitated by the employees of organizations 'helping' undercover police officers posing as criminals – even though the employees thought that they were dealing with real criminals who had made no secret of the fact that the money that was being used came from criminal activities. This has happened in a variety of cases, not only in banking but also in the car and white goods business.

And of course the problem for an ethical and law abiding employer – even one with a robust and effective money laundering control regime – is that there is very little that can be done to identify such staff. For example, how do you distinguish between the good, bad and ugly in situations such as:

- You are the senior vice president of a private bank; one of your reliable private bankers has a very important and profitable client who originates from South America. The junior banker has his own suspicions about the source of funds but if you ever ask he assures you that the money is not associated with criminal activity. Your employee does not want to lose a very good customer and the kudos that he brings. Moreover, perhaps he is also somewhat frightened of the consequences for him personally if the true status of his client is discovered.
- You run a large car business: the sole reason for the existence of sales people is to move cars – the more the better. Are you seriously going to question any large orders for cars, perhaps paid for in cash, by a customer you have never dealt with before? More likely you are going to tell the salesman or woman involved to find a few more new customers like that.
- You are an area manager for an insurance company controlling a large number of salespeople. One of your most successful employees comes from an ethnic minority and does a roaring trade in selling policies that require a large initial premium, to people from his own background. His sales figures and commissions simultaneously help you reach your targets. Would you ever think of questioning what may be happening and the true reason for these sales?

Unless the criminal owns the bank or the bank is in a country that is either unsophisticated or where money laundering controls are lax, then the last place that dirty money will be taken to on the first stage of its washing process is a bank. Criminal groups are constantly seeking out new business opportunities, channels and people to launder their funds: no business, however innocuous it may seem, is safe from these omnipresent threats.

Complete anonymity

Own your own bank – it's just like having a licence to print money.

(ADVERT ON THE INTERNET BY AN OFFSHORE SERVICE PROVIDER)

Welcome to the Bermuda Triangle of money laundering. You can almost certainly prove that the money went in – but that is about all you can prove. You have no idea whether the funds are still there, or have been moved out. Welcome to the world of anonymous banking, banks that aren't banks, International Business Companies, and above all, welcome offshore.

They used to be known as tax havens: in the French language they are known by the wonderfully descriptive term *Paradis Fiscaux*. These locations are now increasingly referred to as Offshore Financial Centres or OFCs. But what are they and why are they becoming increasingly pivotal in both the money laundering cycle and the battle to prevent it?

In his book *Behind Closed Doors*, James Hal defines these centres and their utilization as:

> *...conducting business with a financial institution in countries that have laws and regulations more favourable to you than the country you are operating in now. These laws allow you greater opportunity to reach your financial goals... these jurisdictions [tax*

> *havens] predominantly pay interest on your money gross, without deducting taxes from your interest income.*
>
> (HAL, 1995)

There is, in most countries, nothing illegal in corporate entities and individuals making use of offshore financial centres. The illegality occurs when investors do not declare the interest they receive to their domestic tax authorities. On this fiscal matter there are also various shades of grey:

- Lawful tax avoidance is essentially structuring one's fiscal matters to minimize tax to be paid, and maximize benefits whilst observing all relevant laws.
- Illegal tax avoidance is to arrange one's tax matters and by doing so contravene relevant laws.
- Tax evasion is when income and/or principal is mis-stated to tax authorities – usually to the extent that it is not stated at all.

Thus there exists a perfectly legitimate market and customer base for offshore centres. Amongst the customers and reasons for using them are:

- high net worth individuals who are seeking confidentiality, privacy and protection of their assets;
- high net worth individuals or companies whose country of residence is politically unstable. Thus by investing offshore the value of the funds can be maintained and also security of them achieved;
- complex trade financing for companies;
- liability containment for vessel and aeroplane owners;
- structures to maximize the benefits of insurance management.

As an entire market sector, the importance and size of offshore financial centres is neither peripheral nor inconsequential. Again, hard figures are difficult to acquire but it has been estimated that half the world's money goes through offshore centres, about 20 per cent of all private wealth is invested there and 75 per cent of the captive insurance market is located offshore. If you pick up any glossy brochure from the myriad companies that form offshore vehicles there are endless examples quoted of how OFCs can be used legitimately and totally legally. If you are a company or individual with excess funds to invest you want an OFC that will offer you:

1. A secure banking and financial environment with well-established financial institutions – probably offshore arms of high street banks.
2. A bank that has experience in these complex matters.
3. Probably a bank that is not just in a far-flung location but has an international/national presence.
4. Personal service, total discretion and confidentiality.
5. The ability to manage your account by phone, fax or electronically.
6. The ability to transfer funds by SWIFT or similar systems anywhere in the world.

And of course this is where the problems begin, because the money launderer is looking for these attributes as well, with probably just one other requirement: complete anonymity.

Offshore Financial Centres are the result of local government policies in the relevant jurisdiction to attract foreign investment and thus stimulate and in many cases maintain the local economy. Countries that you have never heard of have escaped poverty and debt by providing a panoramic variety of financial services and products. To varying degrees these centres offer, or are based on:

- the maintenance of absolute confidentiality and secrecy;
- the absence of any tax burden in the offshore location;
- non-existence of any treaties to exchange tax information with other countries;
- corporate structures that can be created or bought quickly, easily and cost-effectively;
- excellent communications links;
- predominant use of a major world currency, preferably dollars;
- no exchange controls;
- the ability to disguise the ownership of corporate vehicles through the use of nominee directors and bearer shares;
- the absence of normally accepted reporting requirements for companies such as annual returns;
- the absence of normally accepted supervision of companies such as Annual General Meetings.

It is almost impossible to state with any certainty what comprises a definitive list of offshore centres, as new and even more obscure countries seem to suddenly spring up as an OFC as a result of local governmental initiatives to get the money rolling in. With that caveat the types of locations that are normally perceived to be a tax haven, financial haven or offshore financial centre are: Alderney; Andorra; Anguilla; Antigua; Aruba; Austria; Bahamas; Bahrain; Barbados; Belize; Bermuda; British Virgin Islands; Cayman Islands; Cook Islands; Costa Rica; Cyprus; Delaware (USA); Dubai; Dutch Antilles; Gibraltar; Guernsey; Hong Kong; Hungary; Ireland (Dublin); Isle of Man; Jersey; Labuan; Lebanon; Liberia; Liechtenstein; Luxembourg; Macao; Madeira; Malta; Marianas; Marshall Islands; Mauritius; Monaco; Monserrat; Nauru; Nevada (USA); Niue; Panama; Saint Kitts and Nevis; Saint Lucia; Saint Pierre et Miquelon; Saint Vincent and the Grenadines; Samoa; Sark; Seychelles; Singapore; Switzerland; Turks and Caicos Islands; Vanuatu; United Kingdom; and Wyoming (USA).

This list is of 56 relevant jurisdictions: the actual number of tax havens is higher – dependent on which figures you believe, the total is somewhere between 63 and 70. The most recent entrants are predominantly in remote geographical areas of the world such as the Pacific, but not remote for communications thanks to phones, faxes, e-mail and the Internet. And of course one should not forget, from a tax angle, the substantial funds held in Luxembourg – almost literally at the centre of the European Union – in relation to which it has been reported that Germany loses £7.5 billion per annum in unpaid taxes relating to interest earned on investments held in Luxembourg by German citizens. Moreover, what is striking in the above list amongst the unheard of Pacific islands and other remote locations is the presence of three states of the United States together with such mainstream financial locations as Austria, Switzerland and the United Kingdom.

As can be seen, there are a wide variety of locations with an equally wide range of legislations and regulations. Even within the offshore industry itself there are locations that are perceived as being sound and legitimate and others that have various stigmas attached to them. One cannot help feeling a hint of sympathy for the more regulated and robust financial centres for the guilt they suffer by association with other less salubrious locales. As Anthony Travers, the Chairman of the Cayman Islands Tax Exchange, put it in a letter on tax harmonization to the *Financial Times* on 20 August 1999:

> *The essential issue where there should be common ground between the OECD and legitimate offshore centres is in relation to effective regulation. The hawks of the OECD must not be allowed to smear offshore centres by seeking to assert that low tax regimes somehow equate with fraud and money laundering.*

> *Equally, mainstream financial centres need to put in place proper safeguards against such activities. The Cayman Islands, for example, has suspicious transaction reporting legislation modelled on that of the United Kingdom, which is, at least as good as, if not more stringent, than that in effect in continental Europe and the United States. The Cayman Islands also applies the Basle Convention. By all means let us have some more of this reasoned debate and less of the unjustifiable rhetoric.*

Whilst agreeing with the sentiments expressed, what is interesting is the reference to '*legitimate* offshore centres' and '*mainstream* financial centres'. Unless I am misreading the context, what is clearly being signalled is that there exist rather less valid offshore centres than the Cayman Islands. Peter Crook, the Director-General of the Guernsey Financial Services Commission, has also made similar comments about the stringency of money laundering controls on that island:

> *Anyone who took the trouble to look would realize that we regulate to a higher standard than the [European] Commission requires. Our money laundering guidelines also equal those of any country in the European Union.*

That is not to say that all problems have been eradicated: far from it. Where every other car is a Mercedes, the well-polished and video-surveyed streets of Monaco have long been welcoming to traditional Italian Mafia members. In recent years the principality has also offered a warm welcome to Russian organized crime money. There are no reliable figures as to how much is involved but educated guesses put the total amount washed as hundreds of millions of pounds each year. Certainly, like London, investments in property have been particularly popular. If you buy an apartment overlooking the sea you will pay upwards of £1 million: pay the cash, enjoy the view then sell it on – laundering complete.

Cyprus has also been a haven for Russian organized crime money: in the Greek controlled section of the island, specifically in Limassol, thousands of companies of Russian origin have been registered. An estimated £800 million per month is laundered through banks, trading companies and finance houses. The washed goods then can enter the universal banking system as sparkling Cypriot cash.

Switzerland – which is still one of the foremost world financial centres as well as a tax haven – has done much in terms of money laundering prevention. However, the 1999 first Annual Report of the

Swiss Money Laundering Reporting Office makes interesting reading: both for what is there and what is not. In the introduction the following telling words appear:

> *We have got off to a good start. Only thirty to forty reports were received from financial intermediaries prior to 1 April 1998... in contrast with one hundred and sixty in the period under review. These reports concerned assets totalling over 330 million Swiss francs... In international terms, however, the number of reports is still low, given Switzerland's importance as a financial centre. In the next few years we will have to create the conditions to ensure a greater number of reports.*

The breakdown of where suspicious reports originate from is fascinating: 80 per cent came from banks; 27 out of 160 came from fiduciaries; but only 2 out of the total came from credit card companies and 3 out of the total from lawyers. As with many other jurisdictions in the world, the Money Laundering Reporting Office stresses the need for greater awareness.

In fact many of the legitimate offshore centres are doing all that they can to deter money laundering. At the risk of generalizations the following jurisdictions are all perceived as taking robust action against money laundering and providing cooperation in international enquiries: the Bahamas; Barbados; Bermuda; Cayman Islands; Gibraltar; Guernsey; Hong Kong; Ireland; the Isle of Man; Jersey; Liechtenstein; and Singapore. In other words the 'legitimate' offshore centres are taking their responsibilities seriously whereas the new entrants to this booming market place are a different matter.

The problem with generalizations such as this is that, for example, in the case of Liechtenstein, the US authorities praise the cooperation received from this tiny principality whilst fellow European neighbours do not necessarily share the same view. In February 2000, a German led request to the European Union's executive commission asked that Liechtenstein's implementation of tax and money laundering laws be investigated. Liechtenstein, which is not part of the European Union but is a trade partner in the European Economic Area, was subsequently exonerated by the investigations. Claims involving a former head of government and head of police were also thrown in for good measure. However, what has emerged is not a criminal community, but links with cocaine cartels, and indications of links with the Russian mafia. Liechtenstein's reputation was further damaged in June 2000 when the principality was blacklisted by the

FATF. Following legal and regulatory improvement it was removed from the blacklist in June 2001. Yet problems still remain: Liechtenstein (as at 1 January 2003) remains categorized by the OECD as an 'uncooperative tax haven'.

In all offshore centres the three vehicles that offer the most opportunity to money launderers are:

- International Business Companies (IBCs);
- Offshore Banking Licences;
- Trusts.

One of the key issues here is the ease and speed with which anonymous corporate vehicles can be created and utilized. The International Business Company (or corporation) is a prime example of this. In essence an IBC is a corporate vehicle that can be owned anonymously and does not do business in the country of its domicile (and just for good measure is rarely taxed). The advantages of such a corporate vehicle are:

- can be formed quickly (some in less than an hour);
- costs relatively little to form and maintain;
- minimal (if any) filing and reporting requirements;
- limited liability;
- can virtually do anything in terms of business activities.

Many offshore financial centres offer such companies, with varying degrees of anonymity. When you have an IBC you can then open bank accounts in the name of the company, thus completely shielding the true beneficial owner. During 1997 it has been estimated that 85,000 offshore companies were formed in the Caribbean region. When one adds Pacific and European offshore financial centres this total rises to 160,000 in that year. At that stage it was estimated that at least a further 500,000 such entities would be created before the end of the 20th century.

Implicit in the concept of an IBC is that of bearer shares. There is nothing complicated here: if you physically have the share certificates you own the company, but it is not recorded that you hold them. Bear in mind that the majority of IBCs allow nominee directors, thus meaning that the only officials recorded are hired hands and there is no official record of who holds the bearer shares and thus is the company's beneficial owner.

Offshore banks can be something else altogether – and that something else is certainly not what would be normally perceived as a bank. These are not onshore banks located in an offshore jurisdiction doing legitimate business. Rather they are entities that are domiciled in one jurisdiction and conduct their business with non-residents. In essence, subject to the payment of a fee you can own a 'bank' that probably has very little regulation, no capital requirements and no supervision. You don't necessarily even have to maintain an office in the country of incorporation. These structures can be one of the ultimate 'must haves' for a money launderer – essentially because people (and other banks) are taken in when the word 'bank' is introduced into the loop, when in reality all the bank comprises is an incorporation document in a far flung jurisdiction.

To explain the ramifications of trusts fully (that is even if I understood them myself) would take up an entire book – of which a few already exist. In very basic terms a trust is a legal structure that is created by an agreement whereby the settlor (who can be an individual or corporate entity) transfers the legal ownership of assets to a trustee who in turn owns these assets for the benefit of beneficiaries who can include the settlor.

The types of locations that are making the money laundering alarm bells ring by their utilization of these structures are all in the second or third tier of Offshore Financial Centres such as:

- **Anguilla:** discovered by Columbus in 1493, this long, thin coral atoll of a Caribbean island, with approximately 7,500 inhabitants, is a separate dependency of the United Kingdom. It has been a semi tax haven since 1977 and a full tax haven since 1992. At the last count – and these are rough figures – there are about 300 offshore banks registered here.
- **Antigua:** of which more will be said later in this chapter.
- **Aruba:** another Caribbean island off the coast of Venezuela that is an overseas part of the Netherlands with roughly 70,000 inhabitants. Suspicions of money laundering continue to hover around the island with such vehicles as the Aruban Exempt Corporation, which can be controlled through anonymous bearer shares.
- **Belize:** the Central American coastal country (formerly British Honduras), which is bordered by Mexico and Guatemala, is another prime target for money launderers both in view of the ability to set up offshore banks there and also the possibility of having an anonymous trust.

- **Cook Islands:** an ideal location for an offshore bank, as we shall discover later.
- **Costa Rica:** this Central American country offers International Business Corporations, offshore banks, and on-line Internet casinos.
- **Cyprus:** a target for Russian organized crime funds.
- **Grenada:** another Caribbean island with a population of just under 100,000, which somewhat ironically is heavily dependent on US aid. The pursuit of offshore funds leaves it vulnerable to money laundering as it offers International Business Companies, offshore banks, Internet gaming licences and economic citizenship.
- **Marshall Islands:** there are over 1,250 islands and atolls comprising the Marshall Islands in the South Pacific including the former US atomic testing sites of Bikini and Enewetak. The islands have a population of about 55,000 and have a free association with the United States. Advertised via the Internet, International Business Companies, bearer shares and trusts are all offered. Money laundering may be attracted here because of lack of supervision and the ability to set up virtually anonymous entities.
- **Mauritius:** a commonwealth island in the Indian Ocean, east of Madagascar, with a population of over a million people. Mauritius offers International Business Companies, bearer shares and trusts. As it has declared that it wants to become the major offshore services provider for the area and it has lax money laundering enforcement, the attractions are obvious.
- **Nauru:** what do you do when you think the phosphate is going to run out? In a moment we reveal the awful truth that is almost stranger than fiction.
- **Niue:** one of the world's largest coral islands with a population of under 2,000 people and an area of approximately 260 square kilometres. It is a self-governing territory with a free association with New Zealand and is a British Commonwealth associate member. Most of the small population work on family plantations. It is another high risk money laundering location with its preponderance of International Business Companies and prime bank instrument fraud being perpetrated on the back of its offshore banking industry. In various offshore company formation agent circulars these are some of the advantages put forward for incorporating in Niue:

- no requirement to disclose beneficial owners or to file directors' details with the Registrar of Companies;
- no requirement to file annual returns or financial statements;
- company names can be in Chinese, Cyrillic and other accepted languages with an English translation;
- no maximum or minimum capital required;
- total secrecy and anonymity: I think we get the idea.

- **Palau:** 458 square kilometres, a population of about 18,000 and almost impossible to find on a map (for information, the islands used to be called Belau and are in the Pacific Ocean east of the Philippines). There has actually been some doubt expressed as to whether Palau is offering offshore services. However, courtesy of the Internet you can buy an offshore banking licence in Palau – although you do not apply for a licence you just register a normal company and say somewhere in the objectives of the entity that you are going to become a bank (that's what it says). One to watch.
- **Panama:** next door to Colombia, the second largest free zone in the world, a major financial centre and a dollar economy: what more do you need? Panama's money laundering framework only relates to narcotics profits, which is somewhat problematic when International Business Corporations with bearer shares are available. Panama is actually attempting to improve the situation, as it accepts that it is a drug transit route – but points out that it is not an industrial drug producer and does not grow drug producing plants. Even so, I am not sure that we should be comforted by the statistic that in 1996 a total of two people were found guilty of drug trafficking when the advantages of International Business Companies are listed in many and various places as:
  - total secrecy and anonymity;
  - no requirement to disclose beneficial owners;
  - no requirement to file annual return/financial statements;
  - full exemption from taxation;
  - complete business privacy;
  - no minimum or maximum capital requirements;
  - complete banking privacy;
  - convenient registration of vessels and ship mortgages.
- **Samoa:** an independent state in the South West Pacific with a population of approximately 170,000. Offshore banks and International Business Companies can be bought.

- **St Kitts and Nevis:** British dependent territories, these two volcanic islands have a population of 6,000. The two islands actually have two separate and competing offshore centres. Although they claim that they are 'squeaky clean' the islands offer a full range of anonymous offshore services, including 'citizenship by investment', which means that if you invest enough in Nevis you will get citizenship there.
- **St Vincent and the Grenadines:** a growing vulnerability is present in these West Indian Islands – particularly bearing in mind their proximity to the South American coast and an Offshore Financial Centre that offers International Business Companies, offshore banks and trusts.
- **Turks and Caicos Islands:** a group of 30 islands north of Haiti with a total population of 15,000. Remains extremely vulnerable to money laundering because of International Business Companies and other vehicles offered.

What follows in this chapter is quite deliberately a story of extremes: because it is in these obscure countries with even more obscure money laundering prevention policies, so obscure in some cases that they are invisible, that the new generation of risks from organized crime's dirty dealings are coming from.

Unless you are a student in geography of the former Soviet Union (and even then you may be hard pushed) I doubt whether you will have heard of, let alone know, where Ingushetia is (it isn't even in the list above). To put you out of your misery, Ingushetia is a semi-autonomous republic that is straight next door to what is left of Chechnya. Remote and primitive are not the words for this area in the Caucasus Mountains. However, the area has claimed in the last couple of years that it is one of the fastest growing world offshore centres – so far holding the unique honour of being the only offshore financial centre in the Russian Federation. This new financial trade has been credited with completely regenerating the economy of the Republic.

Operating from the capital city of Nazran, this republic offers their version of an International Business Company in that any offshore entities registered there receive a tax free existence with no exchange controls. In return such companies cannot trade in Russia (it would probably be too easy if they just didn't have to trade in Ingushetia). However, it hasn't quite worked out like that as various companies have used the advantages of registering in Ingushetia and simultaneously were trading in Russia. To complicate matters even further, officials of the International Business Center, which is the organization promoting these facilities, not only have stressed their strict confidentiality rules but have on occasions commented that they have no idea who is behind some companies registered there.

The importance of the embryonic offshore industry to Ingushetia is underlined by the fact that the Republic's President, Ruslan Aushev, 'personally supervises the progress of the International Business Center'. International Business Companies are particularly promoted by Ingushetia because of their 'anonymity of owners and confidentiality of operations'. None of this, of course, automatically means that money laundering is taking place in this obscure outpost of the Russian Federation. There are almost certainly substantial reasons why such a location is not attractive until further development and sophistication has been achieved. The critical fact remains that the potential for infiltration of money laundering and organized crime is there.

The Republic of Nauru is an island in the South West Pacific, 26 miles from the equator, with a population of about 11,000, which live on its 21 square kilometres. Nauru is the smallest and richest republic in the world. It is two thousand miles from Sydney and almost two and a half thousand miles from Honolulu. For many years the island's main trade has been the mining of phosphates that were exported to Pacific Rim countries for the production of fertilizers (their export has in the past provided 98 per cent of the total of the island), which has left the majority of the land as desolate mines. It does have coral cliffs and sandy beaches though, and is a member of the United Nations – and a special member of the Commonwealth.

In the late 1980s the island realized that it could not rely on the income from phosphates forever, as supplies may be exhausted, and thus turned to offshore financial services. It is a zero tax haven – it does not see the need for the following taxes: income; corporation; real estate; capital gains; inheritance; gift; estate; sales; or stamp duty. As recently as 1996, Nauru was not perceived as being a priority location for money laundering. However, things have changed with a vengeance: in October 1999, Victor Melnikov, the deputy Chairman of the Russian Central Bank, claimed that in 1998 70 billion dollars were transferred from Russian banks to banks chartered in Nauru. This claim has two other interesting angles: in 1998 Russia's total exports were only 74 billion dollars and the term 'bank' may be a misnomer as, on various Internet sites, Nauru is touted as the easiest place in the world to get a banking licence – for an annual fee of just under £6,000.

The official Russian line expounded by Melnikov was that this money was to evade taxes but it is now becoming clear that Nauru is being used to launder the funds of Russian organized crime groups.

Nobody can say that they weren't warned: in 1998 the United States' State Department commented that 'Nauru's current offshore banking regime is an open invitation to financial crime and money laundering'. In a rare move in December 1999, four private banks banned all US dollar bank transfers from Nauru together with Vanuatu and Palau, two other interesting locations in the Pacific. This ban by Deutsche Bank, Bankers Trust, Bank of New York and Republic Bank was obviously a step in the right direction but possibly overlooked the fact that the main currency on the island is actually the Australian Dollar. The US International Narcotics Control Strategy Report of 1998 observes that:

> *Russian organized crime is increasingly exploiting Nauru's offshore financial sector. One common scheme is to employ middlemen to open accounts or charter banks in Nauru, to give the perception of legitimate business by non-Russian entities (no Russian names attached to the bank and/or accounts, or front companies). Tracking particular banks operating in Nauru is difficult, however, since all banks have the same post office box.*

No, I couldn't believe the last sentence either!

The problem is not confined to Nauru because these weird and wonderful Nauru banks have accounts at other foreign banks around the world. However, Agence France Presse reported in May 1999 that at one stage there was so much cash in Nauru that government officials flew to neighbouring Kiribati to deposit money in Australian banks. The reaction to the problem (which has been highlighted now by every international money laundering regulatory body) from Nauru itself is interesting to say the least. The previous president, Bernard Dowiyogo, started a complete review of the Offshore Financial Centre and commented that his government 'does not condone registered off-shore Nauruan companies or banking licenses being exploited by unscrupulous people for fraudulent or money laundering purposes'. His successor, Rene Harris, has stated that it was European consumers of Russian mafia-provided prostitution and drugs who created the wealth and if European bodies like the FATF wanted to end the tax haven operation they should stop being consumers for the Mafia. And of course, whilst that reasoning does not excuse the money laundering assistance Nauru is providing, he does have a point.

But probably the wrong point: the crucial point is that at the end of a mouse on a computer screen. Nauru, because of its geographical obscurity, has been able to promote itself effectively through the Internet, where everything and anything is only a mouse click away. Even though I have dealt with money laundering issues for the last 15 years I was sceptical about the shock/horror stories being written about this island – until I searched the World Wide Web. As of February 2000 there exist a vast array of offshore service provider sites offering facilities in Nauru. Amongst the most extreme propositions in a global context are the following statements – which are all from real Web sites, but for obvious reasons I have not attributed them:

- Your bank in Nauru can: take deposits... issue letters of credit... offer credit reports... issue your own bank references[!!!]... set up your own banking instruments, advertise worldwide, solicit funds from the general public, write your own credit ratings, write your own bank references. All for only $6,500.
- The program includes bearer shares so that complete anonymity is guaranteed... we trust that we have clarified the intriguing world of Nauru bank formation.
- Nauru is absolutely the easiest jurisdiction in the world to get a banking licence. The fact that [Offshore provider name] works directly with the government itself to file and register offshore banks enable us to complete incorporations there very rapidly.
- The low capitalization, non-interference in operations, minimum administrative expenses and simplicity of banking laws, rules and regulations provide enough incentives to genuine entrepreneurs to seek banking licences under the laws of Nauru. Yes! Start your own Nauru offshore bank right now!
- The bank can be registered without any paid-up capital... No local directors are required... Management of a Nauru offshore bank may be entirely located outside of the country... there is no detailed business plan required... Correspondent account facilities can be set up for Nauru banks without any significant restrictions.
- Over the years we [the offshore service provider] have established close relationships with government officials and legal representatives in many tax haven venues. Presently some of the best opportunities to charter and licence your own bank can be found in six countries which are attractive low or no-tax haven jurisdictions... the powers described give the beneficial owners of the bank much latitude in their operations not

readily obtainable in other tax havens. This is not just an 'offshore bank' but an international commercial bank with full banking powers.
- If all information is provided as requested by us, the licence applicants do not have a criminal record, and all fees are paid in full, it is almost certain you will obtain a bank licence.

Whilst not wishing to promote these too good to be true opportunities even more, it is relevant (and simultaneously worrying) to point out that the ability to buy an offshore bank is not confined to Nauru. There are at least five other jurisdictions that offer similar services.

For an initial fee of approximately $40,000 and an annul fee of about $15,000 you can own your own bank in Antigua. This is not perhaps the best location for such a venerable institution – as will be shown later in this chapter.

For slightly more (about $65,000 and an annual fee of roughly $17,000), you can set up shop in the Cook Islands. This group of 15 islands are situated in the South Pacific Ocean between Tahiti, Samoa and Tonga. Although money laundering has been identified as a crime, the potential money launderer (and bank owner) will be encouraged to know that the islands have no specific anti-money laundering laws.

Choice number three is more expensive but offers even greater flexibility: welcome to a class one banking licence in Grenada, available for an initial payment of about $100,000 and an annual fee of just $15,000. However, you may be put off by the fact that Grenada has a previous history of being the location of 'phantom' banks – in 1991, 188 such non-existent institutions were identified giving Grenada addresses. Notwithstanding that minor drawback, what is on offer in Grenada is actually a bargain because it gives you all the rights of an onshore banker – not an offshore bank with restrictions – that are predominantly offered in other offshore jurisdictions. Essentially this gives you the same opportunities, products and services as any mainstream bank operating or applying to operate in the same jurisdiction such as:

- investment banking;
- currency exchange;
- commodities broking,
- cash management;
- letters of credit;
- confidential numbered accounts;

- arbitrage;
- issue of financial guarantees;
- third-party loans;
- trust formation;
- sale and exchange of investments;
- export and trade funding.

A similar Class A banking licence is also available in Western Samoa for under $80,000 arrangement fee and an annual payment of just $25,000 – in the same jurisdiction should you want an offshore bank just pay an annual fee of $5,500. In Vanuatu for an initial deposit of $30,000 and a $7,000 annual fee, a banking licence can be yours. And almost certainly by shopping around on the Internet you can get even better prices than this – remember some sites advertise that they will beat any cheaper price on offer!

Antigua and Barbuda comprise three islands in the East Caribbean with a population of approximately 64,000. This independent state, which is a member of the Commonwealth, has also attracted attention for its dirty dealing. Why? Well how about this?

> *The European Union Bank strives to give our European and international clients easy, quick and secure computer access to European Union Bank's complete range of offshore banking services.*
>
> *Incorporated in Antigua and Barbuda under the International Corporations Act (IBC) of 1982 European Union Bank provides multicurrency banking and financial services to clients throughout the world with utmost privacy, confidentiality and security.*
>
> *Under Antiguan law, no person shall disclose any information relating to the business affairs of a customer, that he/she acquired as an officer, employee, director, shareholder, agent, auditor or solicitor of the banking corporation, except pursuant to the order of a court in Antigua. The court can only issue such an order in connection with an alleged criminal offence.*
>
> (FROM THE WEB SITE OF THE EUROPEAN UNION BANK, 1997)

Antiguan International Business Corporation has a perfect privacy tool:

- bearer shares allowed;
- no public share register;

- no shareholder disclosure;
- no beneficial ownership disclosure.

Perhaps if it had kept its original name of the East European International Bank its purpose would have been even more clear, as from its very beginning EUB was rumoured to be a conduit for Russian organized crime money. The Bank of England issued a warning about European Union Bank in 1997 prior to the Bank's collapse in August of the same year and the disappearance of the owners (or apparent owners), who were both Russian nationals, with what was left of investors' funds. At one stage the Chairman of the bank was Lord Mancroft, deputy chairman of the British Field Sports Society and two drug rehabilitation charities, who came out with the telling quote that the financial regulation in Antigua comprises 'literally two men in a Nissen hut. The country is too small and too badly run.'

Antigua and Barbuda licenses offshore banks to do business with anybody apart from the inhabitants of the islands themselves. At last count there are about 50 of these worthy institutions. It has been rumoured that in the last few years eight offshore banks have been struck off the list of licensed institutions because of failure to comply with regulations. It should however also be noted that the offshore banking sector provides the nation's government with over $11 million dollars in fees annually and employs more than 100 people. Whether any of this contributes to some of the following I will let you decide.

Operation Risky Business ran by the US Customs service has been described as the biggest non-narcotics money laundering racket it has investigated. For six years between 1991 and 1997, eight con men working from South Florida managed to relieve over 400 people from around the world out of more than $60 million. This was essentially an advanced fee fraud: by placing adverts in such respectable broadsheet newspapers as the *Wall Street Journal*, the *International Herald Tribune* and the *New York Times*, they offered business loans and project financing. The catch? The lucky applicants had to pay a fee – of between $40,000 and $2 million dollars. The applicants were then told that they had not kept to the terms of the contract they had signed and had thus lost the fees they had paid. The fees went to two offshore banks in Antigua and Barbuda to be transferred back to the United States. One of the 'banks' was part owned by one of those convicted (who incidentally was a paroled murder convict). One of the banks involved, Caribbean American Bank, is now in receivership.

Although the government of Antigua claims they uncovered them in November 1999, offshore bank accounts were discovered there belonging to Pavlo Lavarenko, a former prime minister of Ukraine, who had been charged with corruption in that country, and also was wanted in Switzerland on money laundering charges.

The United States regulatory bodies are of the view that the legal and regulatory environment in Antigua and Barbuda are an open invitation to money launderers. The United States Department of the Treasury's, *Financial Crimes Enforcement Network Advisory*, Issue 11, released in April 1999, spelt it out:

> *Banks and other financial institutions are advised to give enhanced scrutiny to all financial transactions routed into or out of Antigua and Barbuda... the amendment of the Money Laundering (Prevention) Act, combined with changes in Antigua and Barbuda's treatment of its offshore financial services sector are likely to erode supervision, stiffen bank secrecy, and decrease the possibility for effective international law enforcement and judicial cooperation regarding assets secreted in Antigua and Barbuda. These changes threaten to create a 'haven' whose existence will undermine international efforts of the United States and other nations to counter money laundering and other criminal activity, a concern of which the United States has repeatedly made the government of Antigua and Barbuda aware.*

What it is vital to realize is that these Offshore Financial Centres can be utilized together to create an almost impenetrable maze of International Business Companies, trusts, anonymous bank accounts and offshore banks. Many offshore providers advertise 'anonymous' credit cards, for example, in conjunction with an International Business Company so that you can spend your hard earned money in any place in the world in total secrecy. The small ad columns of most of the world's most respectable newspapers carry wall to wall adverts for offshore service providers, mail drop addresses and other aids to 'financial privacy'. These companies do not want their customers just to buy one offshore company: they are trying to provide packages of services and act as ongoing consultants. A real example of such a package could be:

- Register an International Business Company in offshore Country A.

- Customer provided with nominee directors so he is not shown as an official.
- IBC owned by bearer shares – thus totally anonymous.
- IBC is registered at offshore service provider's offices in Country A.
- Open bank account in name of IBC in offshore Country B.
- Obtain credit card from bank account.
- Have mail forwarded from Country A to offices of offshore service provider in Country C; have mail from bank in Country B mailed to offices of offshore service provider in Country D.
- Offshore service provider in Countries C and D re-mail all correspondence to Customer in Country E – but this is in fact just a mail drop address.

And this is a very simple structure. Some offshore service providers even suggest other things you may wish to do to confuse things such as:

> *The use of addresses in prestigious onshore locations enables your offshore company to appear to be domiciled there, thus giving your company an added degree of respectability. For example, your offshore entity could quote our [the offshore service provider's] address in London on its letterhead and documents, thus giving the appearance of being domiciled in the United Kingdom. This procedure is even more attractive if our Hong Kong address is used, as a Hong Kong company is not required to show its registered office address on its letterhead. This means that if an offshore company quotes a Hong Kong address it cannot be distinguished from a normal trading company registered in Hong Kong.*

The annual fee for this service is less than $300 per annum. However, various legitimate financial centres are now cracking down on offshore companies that use an address in a more respectable centre. For example, the Swiss Federal Banking Commission has noticed this trend and taken action against offshore entities (particularly financial services companies) that operate in the country without the necessary permits or licences: 'The Federal Banking Commission has repeatedly had to take action against companies that are based in offshore financial centres but use addresses in Switzerland to accept deposits from the public or act as securities dealers.'

There are a substantial number of problems that I am convinced are inherent in secondary offshore jurisdictions. The anonymity of IBCs and offshore banks are a very suitable vehicle for money laundering; in order for new entrant countries to compete they have to offer more (or less) than existing players: more secrecy, less documentation, lower capital requirements; all such jurisdictions offer an ideal entry point for dirty dealing. What I am not so certain of is how the volume of money washed through such centres compares with traditional, more respectable centres. The focus of the world's money laundering regulatory agencies and bodies is now firmly fixed on offshore financial centres, but is this focus slightly off beam as there still exists a larger washing load nearer to home? I don't know – because there will never be enough information available to be able to conclusively say. However, what is certain is that more well-known locations are also being used in the laundering process.

All of the occurrences described so far in this chapter occurred prior to the rush for AML legislation and regulation that occurred after 9/11 (outlined in more detail in Chapters 8, 9 and 10 and Appendix I). Logically one would suppose that most, if not all, of the anonymous vehicles previously to be found in offshore locations would now be consigned to the waste-paper bin of history. This is the view that has been expressed by various official bodies, and generally accepted. Regrettably, I have some doubts. The reason for my cynicism is based on the credibility and believability gap between the theory and reality of these issues. Thus, as an experiment, I decided to find out (in January 2003) how easy, or difficult, it would be to buy an anonymous offshore bank. And this is merely a small selection of what I was offered:

- A 'Class A' offshore bank, registered in 1991 but never used. The bank has 'full authority' to operate worldwide as a commercial bank. Even more worryingly (after the comments contained in Chapter 4), it was claimed that this entity can 'use correspondent banks for wire transfers and issuance of credit cards'. Ownership – which would be transferred to me – is through registered shares. The bank is fully licensed and paid up. All of this is available for $85,000.
- A bank registered in 2002 in the state of Mwali, Africa. This entity has, it is claimed, authorized capital of $15 million, but I could buy it for just $4,500 and an annual licence fee of $1,500. If I wanted a brand new bank it would cost $6,000 in the first year and $4,000 in following years. And what key advantages would I get for this outlay? No disclosure of beneficial owners, 0 per cent taxation and bearer shares.

- A 'fully integrated e-commerce offshore bank'. For 'reasonable terms' I could buy the relevant banking licence and 'correspondent relationship'.

This final offer graphically illustrates that launderers, having exploited fully what offshore jurisdictions can offer, have now crossed that final geographical frontier and moved into a cyber dimension – which is where we join them next.

WASHED IN SPACE: CYBER LAUNDERING IN THE 21ST CENTURY

The serious problems of life are never fully solved. If ever they should appear to be so, it is a sure sign that something has been lost. The meaning and purpose of a problem seem to lie not in its solution but in our working at it incessantly.

(CARL JUNG)

Space, the final frontier... well at least until a new and even more final frontier comes along. It is estimated that by 2004 the global online Internet population will be anything up to 945 million users. There is a total inevitability about the fact that organized criminal groups are now making the best use possible of advanced technology and cyberspace. At the dawn of the 21st century we operate in a digital, global world where written communication is by fax and e-mail, money transfers are by computer screen and commerce is increasingly transacted through the Internet. Anybody, anywhere can access this global village: just plug in a PC, connect to a telecoms provider and off you go (strictly speaking of course you don't even need a PC – a hand held machine will do just as well, or even a WAP phone).

The pace of this fundamental revolution is forever quickening. Organized crime groups and launderers are at the forefront of harnessing and developing this technology in a variety of differing ways. From pay as you go mobile phones for anonymous communication (bear in mind that there are 80 million mobile phone users in the United States alone) to transacting business through the Internet, all of the tools and techniques that are available to global business are simultaneously available to global criminals.

The new economy is a dynamic marketplace that cannot be ignored by the criminal fraternity. Far from it: they have embraced the possibilities offered and turned them into certainties. The scale of such an unregulated global marketplace makes it very easy for suspicious transactions, processes and actions to be hidden. Seven new users join the Internet every second; in 1998 online retail sales were $7.8 billion – up from $0.5 billion just three years earlier; by April 2000 there were 6.6 million people in Russia with Internet access. The US Department of Commerce comments in *The Emerging Digital Economy II,* published in June 1999, that 'by 2006, 50 per cent of all American workers will be employed in IT positions or within industries that intensively utilize information technology, products and services'. In April 2000, US Treasury Secretary Lawrence Summers, talking of computer assaults, warned somewhat optimistically that within 10 years information security would be 'an absolutely central priority in terms of business risk'. The statement is optimistic because the mounting evidence suggests that it will not take 10 years for hostile nations or organized criminals to master the techniques needed to successfully mount cyber attacks or manipulate the technological infrastructure to further their aims.

The rise of electronic banking and e-payment systems present valuable opportunities for money launderers. Firstly, and hotly disputed by online banking providers, is how an effective Know Your Customer policy can be implemented when your customer could be anybody in front of a computer screen anywhere in the world. The security and confidentiality claimed by all banking institutions online are the very qualities and attributes that money launderers are always seeking in the terrestrial banking world. At the very heart of commerce on the World Wide Web is the international borderless environment in which it is located, together with:

- the cost effectiveness of the medium;
- the Internet's breadth of reach;

- the difficulties with authenticating identity – both of the user and the supplier;
- anonymity;
- novelty.

We have already seen how money laundering regulations across the world differ widely – so if you operate a multi-currency account with an online bank in Finland but you live in Spain, and your main banking relationships are in the United Kingdom, Portugal and Switzerland, which jurisdiction do you fall under? Of course, and once again, what we are seeing is the effective use of international delivery and supply channels by organized criminals, which should evoke the response of greater and on-going cooperation between individual countries. Bearing in mind the differing standards, policies and opinions of countries how likely is this?

The opportunities that are being capitalized upon by criminals are:

- the use of cutting edge technology to evade and frustrate official investigations, particularly by creating anonymous and secure methods of communicating;
- generating income by cyber crime attacks;
- using services offered via the Internet by 'genuine' suppliers to aid money laundering operations;
- advertising their own services (via front companies) on the Internet;
- making good use of international banking and business technological advances and systems to transfer funds and goods across the world.

It has been argued that up until now in the realms of cyber crime, in an offence in which a computer, network or system is a direct and significant instrument in the commission of that crime, that the people with the knowledge (hackers) have not yet teamed up with, or been employed by, those with the criminal intent. The basic argument is that the majority of hacker attacks are carried out for a variety of non-criminal reasons such as:

- to make mischief;
- to prove that it can be done;
- to make a point.

However, there is mounting evidence that this is not always the case. Although it has never been proved it has always been suspected that Russian organized criminal groups were behind Vladimir Levin's now infamous (and successful) cyber raid on Citibank. When he was sentenced on 24 February 1998, in the Southern District of New York, Levin pleaded guilty to stealing $3.7 million from Citibank – but the original documents filed in court accuse him of stealing £400,000 and illegally transferring $11.6 million.

In essence the illegal transfers were of money that Levin managed to steal via his computer attack but Citibank recovered them. If one leaves aside whether 'organized' crime was involved, it is blatantly obvious that there was no other motive behind Levin's activities apart from large-scale theft. The critical question is not was this a criminal act but was Levin working on his own or merely as an operator for a larger criminal group. Levin's attacks took place in 1994: it could be argued that the reason that no other similar cases have come to light is not because they have not happened but because either (heaven forbid) the subject of the attack has not been found out, or, much more likely, the attacked company does not want to publicize its problems. Levin's activities took place in the last century, which makes Lawrence Summer's warning six years later in 2000, that danger lay ahead from cyber attacks in the next ten years, even more optimistic than reality suggests.

If organized crime is active in this area then there are many other methods and subjects of attack that could bring them substantial benefits:

- There have been numerous proven examples of customer details being stolen online: particularly relating to credit cards. In May 1997, Carlos Felipe Salgado was arrested in San Francisco after trying to sell 100,000 credit card data sets to undercover FBI agents for $200,000. Essentially then, each customer's details were being sold for $2!
- Another key target of attack by criminals are government or law enforcement systems – in other words trying to get relevant information on what is being done by the authorities to fight crime and money laundering. There have been millions of attacks on US Government and Defence Agencies in the last few years. Moreover, both on these networks and those of defence companies, secret military and product data can be obtained – to be sold on to the highest bidder, normally a foreign group or nation.

- The computer networks of multinational and domestic corporations can yield vital information concerning customers, products and anti-crime defence systems.

The potential for criminals to actually commit crime using technology has no boundaries. In January 1998, the German Verbraucherbank offered a 10,000 deutschmark reward for information leading to the arrest of a hacker who had been blackmailing the bank. The hacker was demanding a one million deutschmark payment from the bank: if he didn't receive it he would upload on to the Internet confidential customer data that he had obtained from the bank's systems. Stories and claims of similar blackmail threats – particularly against major banks – are commonplace.

The use of the World Wide Web as a medium to aid and facilitate money laundering has occurred and reoccurred during the course of this book: from the first chapter, with our summary of what can be obtained on the Internet to make yourself anonymous, to the many and varied services offered by offshore service providers via their Web sites. Certainly the Internet has been a major factor and facilitator in the growth of obscure and even obscurer offshore financial centres.

When Austrian banks offered Sparbuch accounts you originally had to travel to that country to open an account or hunt out a company that provided the service. Invariably this would involve you in trawling through classified ads and making numerous phone calls. However, by the end of the 1990s all this had changed: by then all you had to do was click on the button contained on a relevant Web site that said 'Order my Sparbuch now.' This particular anonymous account may now be a thing of the past, but there are still numerous other alternatives offered by thousands of providers on the Internet, all of whom claim to offer 'truly anonymous banking facilities'.

Even after 9/11 and its effects on AML regulation, the same principle applies to offshore banks – click your mouse and you can obtain full details of what is available, compare jurisdictions and order online.

More importantly, because we now live in a virtual digital world, a location that is so obscure that you have difficulty finding it in a world atlas suddenly becomes and feels more real, and far closer, because it has a Web site or is described and pictured on hundreds of others. In various books describing tax havens, details are given concerning how to get there, which hotels to stay at and where to eat. Such helpful details miss the point: to open an International Business Company or offshore bank the nearest that any prospective purchasers have to ever go to the actual location is by remaining seated in front of their computer screen.

Even more amazing is the fact that organized crime utilize the World Wide Web as an advertising and information medium for their activities. Whilst I haven't yet found a Web site that has a button marked 'Click here to join the Yakuza' (or any other organized crime group of your choice), there are a few that come perilously close. There used to be (until it was closed down by its owner) a www.gotti.com that was a spirited defence of John Gotti, the head of the New York Gambino crime family. There is a www.yakuza.com, which I presume is a joke site.

Various gangs in the United States have Web sites to promote their activities and simultaneously rubbish each other. However, it has also become apparent that organized crime groups are taking an active interest in associated areas of the Internet: traditional Mafia groups are known to be behind various online sports betting sites. Even more audaciously, it was disclosed in June 1998 that a New York based Italian mob family had set up a consultancy offering services to help businesses cope with the Year 2000 problem. The consultancy firm – boasting its own Web site and toll free 0800 number – had devised a remarkable solution to the Y2K bug. The firm's programmers came into the client company and re-jigged the financial software so that the company's funds were redirected to other offshore accounts operated by the mob.

The vast array of services, facilities and products now available to everyone are presenting wonderful new opportunities to criminals and simultaneously a new and even more difficult set of problems for regulators and investigators. Just on the Internet itself there is a dazzling choice of:

- free e-mail programs that mean you can assess your mail from any computer anywhere in the world;
- numerous free e-mail routing programs that send your e-mail to another e-mail address;
- state of the art encryption software;
- 'anonymizer' programs.

Bolt on to these facilities the other types of services available:

- If you use a free e-mail account then you can access it on the Internet from anywhere in the world – for example a public library, an Internet café, or even a friend's computer. Thus one could establish such an e-mail facility and only access it from public terminals – meaning that to track such communication access and usage would be almost impossible.

- The widespread availability of 'pay as you go' telephones, where you literally buy a phone off the shelf without your identity being known and top the phone up by credit card or, more suitably, cash, is an open invitation to anonymous communication. As such phones are so cheap – and can be used internationally – a criminal or money launderer could literally buy one, use it for a day or a week and then throw it away.
- Because of various cases where law enforcement officers have utilized bugging devices, criminals are routinely having their homes, offices and vehicles swept for electronic eavesdropping devices.
- The use of secure digital encryption on mobile phones by organized criminals has already frustrated attempts by law enforcement bodies to track and investigate such criminal activity. (Encryption is a critical tool for all concerned in technology. Legitimate providers need encryption to ensure the authenticity, integrity, privacy and security for legitimate transactions. Criminals on the other hand can communicate freely if all such communication is securely encrypted. The opposite side of this coin is that law enforcement's efforts to prevent, detect, investigate and ultimately prosecute criminals are severely diminished if they are unable to decrypt such messages.)

The irony of all of this is that the various public outcries about the new digital age totally removing the privacy of an individual have been turned inside out and on their head by money launderers and criminals carefully researching what is available and focusing in on the facilities that anonymize rather than publicize.

If you consider this to be scaremongering then reflect very carefully on a report that appeared in the Italian newspaper *Milano Finanza* in December 1999. According to that report, prosecutors and police in Palermo stumbled on a £330 million fraud that was part of a global money laundering operation masterminded by the Italian Mafia. Money was moved between a US company that was in fact registered in New Zealand, the Cayman Islands and had accounts in Israel and Spain. Subsequent to those movements the funds were deposited in Switzerland and physically transported to banks in Romania, China, Croatia, Russia and Liberia. Somewhere along the way the money disappeared into cyberspace and reappeared as stocks and shares purchased online. Palermo's prosecutor concluded that their 'Investigations have highlighted an unregulated and borderless financial market open to anyone with the capacity, for whatever reason, to exchange stocks and money.'

One should not, however, underestimate the potential of the Internet to be used either as a channel to facilitate money laundering or to generate the proceeds of crime that need to be washed. Moreover, as we have observed with traditional money laundering techniques, there are almost certainly various mechanisms that are a hybrid of both problems. Amongst the commercial sites available on the Internet the following types present significant opportunities to criminals:

- online gambling;
- pornography;
- online prostitution services;
- sexual exploitation of children;
- various other commercial sites offering illegal services or products (for example, drugs and body parts).

An analysis of the FATF's country blacklist (or to use its official title list of 'non-cooperative countries and territories') will show that one of the critical money laundering risk areas of the 21st century is absent. That place can be accessed by anyone: it has no formal entry requirements and is very cheap to travel in. The Internet has no geographical boundaries – and more importantly no regulation whatsoever. This new digital economy is one that has not been ignored by the criminal fraternity. Far from it: fraudsters and launderers have embraced the possibilities offered by it and turned them into certainties. There are endless opportunities offered in cyberspace – online betting being just one of them.

When I carried out some initial research into this aspect of cyber laundering in March 2000, a Web search using the exact phrase 'virtual casino' produced 36,000 matches. Today an identical search would produce over 45,000 results. By picking just one game (blackjack) a list of over 350 virtual casinos appeared – including one that managed to combine playing blackjack with the best in adult entertainment. The total number of virtual casinos must now be in the hundreds if not thousands. These sites seek to replicate the inside and experience of playing in a real casino – and just like the real world they aim to take as much money off you as possible. It has been estimated that during

2002 online gamblers would be losing $3 billion – but to lose that amount, the actual level of funds flowing through must be appreciably higher: estimates now put such revenue at $6 billion in 2002. However, in truth, no one knows just how many of these sites there are, how many players are involved or the level of financial transactions. The US House of Representatives has, in various documents, described Internet gambling as a haven for money laundering, and the United States has sought to forbid such gaming, originally seeking refuge in the Federal Wire Act of 1960. However, such attempts at prohibition bear an uncanny resemblance to King Canute's attempt to command the unstoppable waves of the sea to turn round.

The attempts by the United States to ban online gambling have forced legitimate gaming companies to move offshore. Thus legitimate operators become entwined with far more dubious entities in obscure offshore jurisdictions. A large number of such online casinos (it has been estimated up to 75 per cent of them) are said to have their physical presence in 'Caribbean locations'. Having said that, a couple of sites I went on either had no physical address shown or were almost impossible to locate. As with anything in the remoter offshore world, just because something has an address there doesn't mean that anything actually exists at that location. The governments of these countries profit handsomely from such registrations: roughly $75,000 fees per year for sports betting sites and $100,000 and over for virtual casinos. In 1999 it was reliably reported that the relevant jurisdictions that license these enterprises are raking in over $1.5 million per month thanks to annual fees.

Obviously anyone in the world can play on these virtual casinos – with no idea of what regulation (if any) exists in relation to their operation. There are additionally other risks such as credit card details being used fraudulently by the operators of such sites. Just as there is with terrestrial gambling there are wonderful opportunities for laundering funds. The FBI has in at least one previous investigation targeted such offshore Web sites and their connections with wire fraud and money laundering. The jurisdictions involved were Curacao, the Netherlands, Antilles, Antigua and the Dominican Republic. Additionally there are several pending FBI investigations that link Internet gambling to organized crime (as if to reinforce the dictum that cyberspace is in many ways simply a reflection of real life). The 'double whammy' of online casinos being dispersed across such offshore locations combined with the weak (or non-existent) background checks in these jurisdictions makes the Internet gaming market almost impossible to regulate.

Moreover, in all of this we are presuming that the relevant online casino does in fact 'trade' – ie take bets from genuine customers. It strikes me (and this is hardly an original idea) that one sure-fire method of successfully laundering funds is for launderers to claim that they operate a gambling Web site (but never to bother actually doing so), and thus establish a banking relationship on this basis. This gives a perfect cover for credits to come in from anywhere in the world, and payments to be made likewise. One additional complication – and advantage for the launderers – is that many online casinos use small offshore banks, which in turn have correspondent relationships with large US financial institutions (thus bringing us to the widely identified money laundering risks inherent in correspondent banking).

One is therefore not certain whether to laugh or cry when one finds something like the following on an online casino site (this is a paraphrase of an actual Web site entry, but its essential meaning has not been altered):

> *We are one of the most trusted casinos on the Internet… we operate under a licence granted by [offshore jurisdiction named]… To play for money you first must register credit with our casino. Any funds will be played and paid out in US dollars. You can pay by:*
>
> 1. *Valid credit card.*
> 2. *Wire transfer or bank wire.*
> 3. *Western Union money orders.*
> 4. *Banker's drafts, cashier's cheques or certified cheques.*
> 5. *Personal cheques.*
> 6. *You can send cash. However we do not recommend this method because it creates the wrong perception to government officials. We operate a legitimate business and do not wish to be involved in any money laundering activity. Sending cash should be the method of last resort. We will not accept more than $5,000 in cash* at any one time [my emphasis].
>
> *The method you use to establish your credit is the method we will send back your winnings or any unused credit… they will either be credited back to you by a credit on the credit card used, or sent by bank wire or company cheque.*

My advice then is send cash in sums of just less then $5,000 each time; play a few games (there are about 20 different ones to choose from) and then request online that your remaining credits are returned to you in the form of a cheque.

Quite what 'Know Your Customer' rules apply to online gambling sites is open to debate. In theory, each online gaming site should follow the KYC rules present in the jurisdiction in which it is registered. There are various obvious weaknesses in this framework (for want of a better word), as follows:

- Most, if not all, online gaming sites are registered in offshore jurisdictions where anti-money laundering regulation is consistently weak. Bear in mind that on the FATF's list of non-cooperative countries and territories are (amongst others) Nauru, Niue, St Kitts and Nevis, and St Vincent and the Grenadines.
- Even if the general anti-money laundering regime in a relevant location is adequate, it is highly unlikely that there are any relevant regulations regarding online casinos, particularly in respect of customer due diligence.
- Added to these factors is the lack of transparency that is a key element in such offshore havens.

Thus, in practice, based on a sample of offshore casinos we have visited (purely for research purposes, you understand), the general KYC procedures seem to be that casino operators will take whatever a customer says at face value and do very little – if anything – to validate such information.

As potential money launderers we particularly were drawn to a gaming site operating from a PO box in Antigua. This site accepts payments by bank cheque, bank draft, American Express money order – or good old cash. Cash payments are fine – as long as they are sent by registered mail. Then the site helpfully delivers your remaining account balance when requested by 'private courier anywhere in the world, free of charge', or alternatively will send 'any payment by registered mail completely free of charge'.

Combined with this anonymity are the attractions of remote access to place bets (and thus move funds) and the encrypted data being used. Thus whilst lawmakers, regulators and law enforcement bodies belatedly focus on closing down the money laundering loopholes that still exist in the 'physical' world, their opponents are making the optimum use of what is available in cyberspace. Anyone for a bet as to who is winning?

The proliferation of sex sites of every nature and description (and many that defy description) is obviously a fertile ground for organized crime to generate funds through their significant control of sex related industries. It has been stated that the annual growth rate for an Internet pornography site is approximately 400 per cent. Whilst adult pornography on the Internet is a very lucrative business the dissemination of pornography involving children is largely free. There is no widespread evidence of the involvement of organized criminal groups in such activities, but it can only be a matter of time before it happens – additionally raising the threat of the blackmail and extortion of the subscribers to such sites by the criminal operators.

The greatest boon to money launderers is the increasing utilization and promotion of online banking and electronic payment systems. Firstly it is important to distinguish between banks that have promotional Web sites and those that operate transactional services. Increasingly with the dot com explosion the banking industry is piling into sites that offer transactional services. More often than not, set up as subsidiaries with Web-friendly titles, the banking world sees the Internet bank as the logical extension of telephone banking. Recent research has shown that just as massive call centres were a cheaper alternative than branch networks, the back office staff needed to service a Web-based bank are even smaller and cheaper than call centres. Thus new legitimate banks are starting up on the Web offering account opening, direct payments, electronic funds transfers, issue of cheques, securities purchase and closing of accounts.

Additionally, customers of existing terrestrial banks are being encouraged, or perhaps cajoled is the more correct term, to bank via the Internet: rarely a month goes by without my main bank sending me a circular or computer program to encourage me to do this. The last such circular (with accompanying beautifully packaged CD ROM) informed me that this secure system meant that I could:

- view my account details including my balance and overdraft limit;
- view my current and last statement;
- print account information or save it on my PC;
- pay bills;
- move money between accounts;
- view, amend and cancel standing orders;
- view direct debits.

What more could I possibly need? I need never physically go into my branch again. And there's the rub... Like everything else in a virtual world it removes any need for physical contact. A bank has no way of knowing whether the person at the other end of the telephone line is their customer. Rather akin to the Sparbuch concept, that as long as you turn up in the bank with the passbook and the password the money is yours, the same it is with Internet banking: as long as you have the password the money is yours.

As with e-mail the bank's customer has the ability to access his or her account from anywhere in the world using a wide variety of Internet service providers, none of which can verify who it is that is accessing the account. By taking the provision online banking services to their logical conclusion, Know Your Customer procedures are thrown out of the window. This claim has been vehemently denied by online banking providers. In Japan it has been stated that online transactions can only be conducted on accounts that have been opened in a traditional face to face manner. In Belgium there is no distinction whatsoever between the medium by which any account is opened and thus money laundering KYC regulations are applicable to all of them. In the United States accounts can be opened online but the customer must supply official identification numbers that are verified by the bank. Yet all of this seems to miss the point by a long way: I have just been on the Internet, and many of the solely Internet based banks are promising prospective customers immediate decisions online. Moreover, even if KYC procedures are followed, if the account is Internet based there will be absolutely no physical contact whatsoever with the customer.

Let us imagine for a minute that a launderer can produce or have access either to genuine individuals' details and documents or counterfeit ID documents. He can then open up as many accounts as he wants, access them from anywhere in the world and wash money and spin it dry to his heart's content. Once again the question of jurisdictional control enters the equation: just which country is responsible for the regulation of such online service providers? The official response (I think) is that online financial service providers are subject to the same regulations in any particular jurisdiction as the terrestrial providers there. This sounds fine – until one compares it to the reality of the situation, which immediately renders such a view as being redundant. Take the European Union Bank in Antigua (well, registered there at least): the Bank of England warned potential customers of the risks of investing money in it, but in reality could do nothing about it. The whole point about the Internet is that wherever you are based you can tout for business from anyone anywhere.

The logical extrapolation of doing business on the Internet is the creation of some universally acceptable and negotiable form of cyber currency. For the past 15 years the financial environment has been leading us to a situation where the vast majority of money is virtual: your salary is paid into your bank account and all you see is the written representation of it on your bank statement or on the screen of an ATM; you pay for most goods by credit or debit card; when the credit card bill arrives you write out a cheque; you go on the Internet and pay for goods or services anywhere in the world with your universally acceptable piece of plastic. The next obvious step is the establishment of some mechanism that facilitates the transfer of financial value without the need for cash. Such a system has been termed a variety of things – Cyberpayments, digital currency, e-cash, e-money – but in essence is the same animal. There are a variety of different systems and techniques that are bracketed under the term Electronic Payment Technologies. According to FinCEN:

> *The common element is that these systems are designed to provide the transacting party with immediate, convenient, secure and potentially anonymous means by which to transfer financial value. When fully implemented this technology will impact users worldwide and provide readily apparent benefits to legitimate commerce, however, it may also have the potential to facilitate the international movement of illicit funds.*
>
> (FINCEN, *MONEY IN CYBERSPACE*, UNDATED WEB SITE DOCUMENT)

There are currently a range of different companies trying to sell their system as the one that will become the standard; additionally there are different types of systems being promoted. There are almost 100 forms of electronic cash already available to utilize the facilities of Web sites: if, for example, you go on to various news sites you set up an electronic purse or wallet through credit card payment and then the costs of your searches and article retrievals are deducted from this digital money storage facility. The concerns regarding the use of these systems by money launderers include:

- From a regulatory point of view banks and financial institutions have been increasingly relied upon both to report suspicious transactions and control money laundering attempts. If banks are no longer part of the loop this fundamental control point will be eradicated.
- Because at present the types of EPT systems are diverse it may be difficult to create and install common reporting principles.

- The KYC principle is once again running the risk of total erosion – there are few if any face-to-face transactions.
- The other old chestnut is the international jurisdictional issue, together with the mandatory need for extensive and enhanced international cooperation. As FinCEN puts it without pulling any punches:

> *The apparent and immediate erosion of international financial borders resulting from Cyberpayment transaction mandates enhanced cooperation and efforts among international entities to ensure that there are consistent policies and standards. It will not deter financial crime if one country has extensive links and regulations and another has none. The illicit money will merely move to the weakest link.*
>
> (FINCEN, *MONEY IN CYBERSPACE*, UNDATED WEB SITE DOCUMENT)

The United Kingdom's NCIS state the obvious fears in their 1999 *Project Trawler: Crime on the International Highways Report*:

> *It is conceivable that criminal organizations will take time to recognize and exploit new technology. Yet, historical precedent provides a contrary view. Following the introduction of various anti-money laundering obligations in the UK during 1993–95, criminal use of less regulated sectors (where risk of disclosure was less) accelerated sharply. It is reasonable to expect that new payment systems will be similarly exploited if the opportunities are sufficient.*

One fundamental point that has been simultaneously ignored and highlighted is this: to obtain electronic money the criminal has to convert real money; to cash in digital money he has to convert it back to real money. In fact whilst the first part of that argument is correct the second is not: whilst not suggesting that electronic money will completely replace and supersede real money, it will presumably be possible to buy high value items with electronic money (such as cars); in this way criminal funds will be laundered and there will be no need to convert electronic money back into real money. The risks inherent in electronic money is that it is incredibly mobile and can be anonymous. The situation at the moment with no predominant system or product is very attractive to money launderers: because a plurality of approaches and systems means no common controls or money laundering standards. Presently, many forms of electronic cash depend on funds being paid in from banks or credit cards. Presumably to achieve as much anonymity as possible and avoid any face to face contact, the best means to finance electronic money is to open a financial relationship with an Internet bank via the Internet. For example, the customer visits a virtual ATM and tops up his e-cash wallet or purse with real money credited from his bank account or credit card. Thus, at the moment, it could be argued that electronic money can be utilized as a tool in the layering phase of washing money, but not to achieve laundering per se.

A possible scenario of this type is: the proceeds of crime are placed with an offshore bank or even an onshore financial institution in a jurisdiction where money laundering controls are weak. From thereon in everything can be done via computer. Either the bank that has received the deposit operates an Internet banking system that can facilitate transfers to e-money, or e-money can be purchased using a credit card issued on the account. The criminal can then move the e-money around anywhere quickly and virtually anonymously. The money can then be used to buy a complete portfolio of stocks across the world. The only face to face contact was when the first deposit was made – and even that can be removed by opening the initial account with an Internet bank. Whilst the existence of electronic money makes this easier there is of course nothing to stop the adept criminal doing all of this now – and successfully.

Another form of electronic cash is smart cards. These have been trialled in various parts of the world, most commonly by Mondex (which is now part of Mastercard International), who to my knowledge have run experiments in the United Kingdom, Australia and New Zealand. At the time of writing there are a large number of franchise holders across the world waiting to launch this technology. Essentially these cards are similar to an electronic wallet in that you credit the card with funds and then use it like a credit/debit card to make purchases with the funds available on the card. Certainly in the trial in Swindon, in the United Kingdom, the impression gained was that it was not particularly successful as the Mondex card gave no great advantage over a credit/debit card and in fact was more troublesome because you had to make sure that it was loaded with funds.

However, in Australia and New Zealand it was possible to have a non-attributable card, where it could be charged by transfers from other cards but not by debiting and crediting bank accounts. Transfers to these type of cards could be made by telephone, online and by a special wallet that moves amounts from one card to the other. As

Stanley Morris, the director of FinCEN, observed in his 1995 speech to the Congress Banking sub-committee hearing on the Future of Money, such cards have deep, inherent money laundering risks:

> *Suppose an Internet user is a narcotics trafficker or an agent for a gang of sophisticated criminals of any other sort. Consider the invoices the trafficker might pay, the supplies he might order and the transactions he might accomplish if, for instance, he could download an unlimited amount of cash from a smart card to a computer and then transmit those funds to another smart card in locations around the world – all anonymously, all without an audit trail, and all without the need to resort to a traditional financial institution.*

Or as Mondex itself puts it in their promotional material and Web site in 2000:

> *Mondex electronic cash is unique amongst smartcards in that it has the security and the sophistication to permit 'person to person' movement of electronic cash – just as you give a member of your family or a friend some cash. Other smartcards act like a debit or credit card which need their transactions to be reported to a central computer system and so can only allow cash to move from customer to retailer to bank.*

And the Mondex card is also capable of holding various currencies simultaneously. Of course, just like every other mechanism utilized by money launderers, systems such as Mondex offer wonderful legitimate business opportunities and advances. Regrettably, such new developments can also be quickly subverted for criminal purposes.

The Internet and the onward progress of an electronic money system not only fundamentally changes the way we do business across the world, it will, if it has not already, provide considerable scope for the laundering of funds in cyberspace without the need for willing professional accomplices. In the current financial system there is a high degree of central bank control in each relevant country; in the electronic money arena the concept of individual countries and thus regulatory systems are rendered redundant. The new world of electronic commerce has at the moment no monitoring or controlling mechanisms in respect of money laundering, moreover banks are no longer needed to make funds transfers – you can do it from your personal computer using electronic cash on a peer to peer basis without the need to involve a traditional financial institution.

Electronic money is theoretically available anywhere in the world to be sent anywhere else in the world. At the beginning of the 21st century, criminals may have finally found the new technological detergent that washes whiter.

There is something sadly depressing about the fact that the terrestrial money laundering problem still rages unabated, one of the prime reasons being that a unified international effort cannot be established. The relevant authorities are now focusing on Offshore Financial Centres as *les bêtes noires* of the civilized world. However, launderers are already one step ahead of even that – moving money and washing it in cyberspace. If this arena remains unregulated there will be little need for criminals to make use of OFCs – why bother when the best washing machine is your personal computer?

Everything that the money launderer needs is now available online: they can open a bank account; order an International Business Company; enrol in a multitude of stock trading schemes; communicate by anonymous e-mail; trade using electronic cash systems that are already available; funnel money through online casinos and betting shops; buy houses online; funnel money through online auctions; open their own offshore or online bank; you name it, it can be done. And whatever the authorities say there are no country boundaries, no face to face meetings required, no professional advisors asking awkward questions, there is very little if anything at all at present that can halt or restrict washing in space.

THE LAUNDERING OF TERROR

Up until recently, most of us have viewed the problems of drug trafficking, organized crime, and terrorism as issues of obvious concern, really only of marginal nature, though. In other words, drugs were only a danger to a small percentage of our citizenry; that organized crime was a menace, but restricted to car theft, gambling scams, and racketeering in larger cities. And finally, the terrorist groups were dangerous but were usually operating in foreign countries and could only muster up an occasional suicide bomber.

We truly wish it was that simple. Regrettably, we are in something far worse. I will humbly suggest that what we are witnessing these days are three types of criminal activities – drugs, terrorism, and organized crime – which are like three huge geopolitical plates which are slowly starting to shift and grind together. They could ultimately produce an earthquake of unprecedented magnitude and destruction.

(BENJAMIN GILMAN, REPUBLICAN, NEW YORK, CHAIRMAN OF THE US HOUSE OF REPRESENTATIVES COMMITTEE ON INTERNATIONAL RELATIONS)

Benjamin Gilman grimly and eerily predicted future events – he made this statement not after 9/11 but on 1 October 1997. The awful events that happened on 11 September 2001 in New York, Washington and Pittsburgh still seem like a bad nightmare, from which one will eventually wake up. Sadly this is not to be the case – as Australia found out via the Bali bombing on 12 October 2002 and Israelis equally discovered in Kenya on 28 November 2002. This is not to mention various other smaller terrorist attacks that have occurred since 9/11 and are now widely presumed to be the work of Al-Qaida or associated cells. More worrying still, though, is what may still be to come. It has now become clear that one key strategy in any war on terrorism is to identify and close down routes of funding. In the end, 'follow the money' might be the most effective method to eradicate terrorism. Traditionally (although not exclusively) money laundering has been seen as relating to criminal activities, rather than terrorism. The events of 9/11 have permanently altered this focus.

The laundering of terrorist funds is nothing new; in fact in the United Kingdom much of the enforcement effort regarding money laundering originated in the late 1980s to prevent the washing of IRA funds. However, in recent years, whilst the anti-money laundering effort has intensified, the subject of terrorism in relation to it is being perceived as less important. I cannot help but think that the efforts, in full swing immediately prior to 9/11, to include tax evasion under the money laundering banner are now, in retrospect, misguided – as such energies could have been far better used fighting organized crime and terrorism. To confuse matters, some of the material that has surfaced in the media since 11 September is essentially old information repackaged – but that in itself raises serious issues as to why, if so much information was already available, no decisive official action was taken previously against Osama Bin Laden, his Al-Qaida group and its network of associates.

THE TRADITIONAL MONEY LAUNDERING MODEL

The traditional money laundering model of placement, layering and integration only partially explains money laundering by terrorists. I described money laundering earlier in this book as a 'robust, corrosive, all-consuming dynamic activity that has far reaching consequences and effects'. However, the basic premise of criminal money laundering is to wash large amounts of dirty money: terrorism can, and does, operate on a shoestring. It has been claimed that the Bali terrorist bombing cost £19,000: which, even assuming that AML controls were in place and effective, would take little effort to 'smurf' into the world's banking system. The US authorities believe that 9/11 itself cost a paltry $200,000. Two examples of the laundering of terrorist funds will demonstrate that there is no simple linear description of washing of funds in this respect.

First, the suicide hijackers of 9/11 were financed by those ultimately responsible for the atrocities. Whilst the amounts involved were not massive, living expenses for a considerable period of time would have to have been paid for 10 people (at the very least). Press reports have referred to investigations of withdrawals made by the hijackers at cash dispenser machines and the use of credit cards by them. However, to do this the hijackers would, as a minimum, have to have opened bank accounts. Thus whilst the ultimate aim of traditional money laundering is to totally disassociate the final cleaned cash from its criminal origin (achieving integration of the dirty funds), the perpetrators of the WTC outrage and their backers had to go through this traditional money laundering process, knowing that ultimately the cleaned funds would immediately be associated with terrorism in the investigations following the outrage. Simultaneously the funding of the suicide pilots, out of necessity, should have been separate to the more substantial funding stream of the Al-Qaida group. If no disassociation was made then the terrorists risked discovery and freezing of their main assets by investigations identifying them as a result of tracing backwards from the suicide pilots. Of course it is still fairly simple to open bank accounts in a false name particularly where only small amounts are being paid in. Moreover it is entirely possible to open a bank account in a Middle Eastern country (where banking secrecy is more prevalent), obtain a multi-purpose card (with credit, debit and cash dispenser facilities) and utilize that card anywhere across the world. However, the FBI has gathered evidence that confirms that the 19 hijackers were able to make extensive use of the US financial system. They legally opened bank accounts (opened using their legitimate US visas), used debit cards and benefited from wire transfers into these accounts (all of these transfers were under the suspicious reporting threshold of $10,000).

Second, the claims that Al-Qaida had been involved in short selling of stocks immediately prior to the WTC atrocity is an example of terrorists following the traditional money laundering process. Whilst we have no way of conclusively knowing whether the claims of short selling are true, what now appears to be certain is that Bin Laden has been involved in share dealing in the past. For this to be so, it must be presumed that various offshore entities or other kinds of front companies have been used. The ultimate aims of such corporate structures are totally to dissociate the companies dealing in the world's financial markets from the ultimate beneficial owner(s) of the funds used. Implicit in this process must be the utilization of not only financial institutions but also professional advisors such as lawyers, accountants and company formation/management providers.

The final morbid irony is that a key element of the funds laundered by the Al-Qaida group will almost certainly have been funnelled through firms in the World Trade Center or surrounding area that were decimated on 11 September 2001. A further, more philosophical irony is that such an attack on the symbols of capitalism is almost rendered meaningless in any fundamental religious sense when one appreciates that the terrorists themselves receive direct (and substantial) financial benefits from their investments in the capitalist system that they seek to destroy.

SOURCES OF TERRORIST FUNDING

To starve terrorists of money can be achieved in a variety of ways – one key way is to try to identify and eradicate the original sources of funding. In the case of Bin Laden, much intelligence has been available for the last few years about how his operations are funded. Immediately after 9/11, I was asked to comment and provide information to various newspapers and TV stations across the world on the funding of terrorism. Even I was shocked when my research showed that since the mid-1990s extensive detail had been known (and was in the public domain) about Bin Laden's finances. Consider, as an example, the US State Department fact sheet on Bin Laden issued on 14 August 1996. It contained the following comments:

- 'By 1985 Bin Laden had drawn on his family's wealth, plus donations received from sympathetic merchant families in the Gulf region… to organize… Al-Qaida.'
- 'He embarked on several business ventures in Sudan in 1990… [his] company Al-Hijrah for Construction and Development Ltd. built the Tahaddi road… as well as the modern international airport near Port Sudan.'

- 'Bin Laden and wealthy National Islamic Front members capitalized Al-Shamal Islamic Bank in Khartoum. Bin Laden invested $50 million in the bank.'
- 'A joint Egyptian–Saudi investigation revealed in May 1993 that Bin Laden's business interests helped to funnel money to Egyptian extremists.'

In addition the fact sheet named various other Bin Laden companies in Sudan such as Wadi al-Aqiq Company Ltd, Taba Investment Company Ltd and Al-Themar al-Mubarak-ah Agriculture Company Ltd. This document was one of many that already provided a detailed insight into Osama Bin Laden's business interests and financial dealings. Even more damning is the fact that this intelligence was not of a general nature – but extremely specific. How much more specific can you be than naming the bank in which Bin Laden kept his funds – which is exactly what Wadih el-Hage did in the Southern District Court of New York on 20 February 2001 in the *United States of America* v *Usama Bin Laden et al* case? Just one short exchange detailed in 139 pages of transcripts relating to just that date reads as follows:

> *Question*: What banks did he [Bin Laden] keep his money at?
> *El-Hage*: Bank el Shamar.
> *Question*: Any other banks?
> *El-Hage*: I think he had accounts in different banks, but I only recall Bank Shamar.

Thus, our knowledge of Bin Laden's dirty dealings is not based on what has happened since 11 September 2001, but dates from at least the mid-1990s. The following areas are viewed as critical in this consideration.

Charities

The *Philippine Daily Inquirer* (in August 2000) reported that the Islamic Relief Organization (IIRO) was set up in 1992 by Bin Laden as a front for funding terrorist activities. The IIRO worked under the Muslim World League, an organization supported by the Saudi Arabian Government. This relief organization is alleged to have provided Bin Laden with funds for acquiring weapons under the guise of giving charitable donations to Muslim communities. Various other so-called charities are now suspected of being fronts for Bin Laden's operations.

Donations by Saudi business executives

It is now certain that business executives in Saudi Arabia have made substantial donations for at least five years to Bin Laden. Estimates of the amount involved go up to $50 million. Allegations have surfaced that such donations were made by bank transfer to New York and London banks into the accounts of the Islamic Relief Organization and Blessed Relief Organization. It is hotly debated as to whether such payments were voluntary donations or 'protection' money. Moreover such donations raise an ethical quandary. This is because the origins of such financial support from Saudi Arabia began when Bin Laden was fighting the Russians in Afghanistan (with US assistance). At that time he raised millions from Saudi Arabia – and continued to utilize those contacts and supporters in his later exploits. A report issued on 10 July 2002 written by Laurent Murawiec of the Rand Organization and presented to the US Pentagon's Defense Policy Board was damning in its evaluation of the involvement of Saudi Arabia. The report did not shy away from strong opinions, stating that Saudi Arabia was 'the kernel of evil, the prime mover, the most dangerous opponent' in the Middle East. It went on to observe that 'The Saudis are active at every level of the terror chain from planners to financiers, from cadre to foot soldier from ideologist to cheerleader.'

Opium earnings

Allegations abound that Bin Laden handled the multibillion dollar opium earnings of the Taliban. In addition to this are various accusations of groups close to Bin Laden being involved in narcotics trading. The UK Government document containing evidence of Bin Laden's responsibility for the 9/11 attacks (issued before the fall of the Taliban) concluded that 'Osama Bin Laden's Al-Qaida and the Taliban have a close and mutually dependent alliance. Osama Bin Laden and Al-Qaida provide the Taliban regime with material, financial and military support. They jointly exploit the drugs trade.'

State sponsorship

The position of Saudi Arabia is one of the many interesting and controversial aspects of the funding question. Yossef Bodansky, Chief of Staff for a key congressional committee on counter-terrorism, commented in the weeks after 9/11 that 'There's government money being laundered in the interest of keeping Bin Laden away from Saudi Arabia', thus implicitly stating that the government of Saudi Arabia had been funding Bin Laden, to keep him away from the country. Other allegations have been made that suggest that disgruntled members of the Saudi Royal Family are amongst Bin Laden's financial sponsors. There are also many rumours and accusations concerning the possible involvement of other rogue states.

The role of Saudi Arabia in respect of Al-Qaida is a topic that keeps returning to haunt the kingdom. Leaving aside the fact that 11 of the 19 hijackers on 9/11 were Saudi nationals, there are repeated claims of Saudi support for Al-Qaida. This is not surprising, taking into consideration that there is an unknown proportion of Saudis who consider Osama Bin Laden to be a freedom fighter and are convinced that it was Mossad, not Bin Laden, that was responsible for 9/11. A lawsuit filed by the families of 900 of the victims accuses Saudi nationals, including senior princes, of funding Bin Laden.

'Genuine companies'

Bin Laden and his associates have operated various 'legitimate' businesses, such as:

- Wadi al-Aqiq, a fertilizer wholesaler;
- a Sudanese road contracting firm;
- road construction companies;
- agricultural companies;
- currency exchange companies.

When Bin Laden was based in Sudan in the early 1990s, to all intents and purposes he operated his empire like a 'normal' business. Testimony by Jamal Ahmed al-Fadl, a former key Bin Laden associate, stated that Al-Qaida used 80 front companies on a global basis to manage, transact and (most importantly) conceal its activities.

Links with organized crime

Just as it is now accepted that separate organized crime groups work together with one another (for example, the Russian 'mafia' and Colombian drug cartels) it is obvious that terrorists and organized crime groups have mutual interests and also cooperate. Terrorist groups have always been implicated in the international narcotics trade. Robust and well-substantiated claims have been made for a number of years concerning the involvement of the PLO, IRA, KLF and ETA in such activities. Criminal groups also have a key role to play in the terrorist acquisition and transport of arms and weapons. Other areas of cooperation between terrorists and organized crime gangs are in the spiralling problem of human trafficking and the actual money laundering process itself. The possibilities offered by a global economy have been embraced by both criminals and terrorists. The UK Northern Ireland Select Committee in a report issued in July 2002 confirmed such theories. It concluded that Irish paramilitary groups were involved in tobacco and fuel smuggling, social security fraud and counterfeiting. The Organized Crime Task Force for Northern Ireland came to a similar conclusion in its 2002 threat assessment. This document portrayed an increasingly blurred line between paramilitary activity and organized criminals – of 76 criminal groups in the province, 'nearly half' have links to paramilitary operations. Sadly the equivalent synthesis of effort has not happened, until now, by individual countries and their cooperation with one another. The level and extent of international cooperation on money laundering issues at an investigative and enforcement level has been woeful – if not non-existent. A senior official at an international law enforcement agency commented after 9/11 that 'The problem is that this is a phenomenon that respects no borders. The organized crime groups and the terrorist organizations are far more attuned to the realities of the globalist century than Western governments are.' Remember also that in 1998, shortly after Bin Laden's attacks on two US embassies, President Clinton signed an order to block his business interests in the United States. The aim then – as now – was to make him so 'radioactive' that all of his business activities would be shunned by banks. History has proved that this attempt, however well intentioned, failed miserably.

Inheritance

There have been various claims made about the scale of Osama Bin Laden's inherited fortune: up to $300 million has been quoted in total, which started with an $80 million inheritance. This figure has also been utilized as the total figure available to him (from all sources). The scale of Bin Laden's wealth enabled him to pursue the course that he has because of his independent means; simultaneously, because no one knows how much money he has, it will be almost impossible to know if any funds identified and frozen comprise the majority of his assets or just a small part. Previous trials of alleged accomplices have presented conflicting evidence – some witnesses talk of bank accounts with multimillion dollar balances at various financial institutions in the Middle East, the United States, Europe and Asia; other witnesses give copious examples of operations being run on a shoestring.

Use of the world's banking system by terrorists

Al-Qaida, and all international terrorist groups, must make extensive use of the world's financial systems – this is notwithstanding the stories of Bin Laden's associates travelling round the globe with suitcases full of cash. Such tales are almost certainly true – to operate as Al-Qaida does, without being discovered, requires an approach that embraces diversity and multiplicity when it comes to managing and moving money. The *Guardian* in the UK commented that 'City sources suggest that few financial jurisdictions will be untouched by Bin Laden's operations and that many banks have inadvertently allowed his money, or that of his associates, to pass through their operations' (17 September 2001). Even before recent events, various pieces of intelligence had surfaced that show the extent of Al-Qaida's financial network:

- Allegations surfaced in April 2001 that Bin Laden holds bank accounts in Nicosia, Cyprus, and also uses the island as a transit point for exports.
- Claims have been made in the past that Bin Laden operates a substantial amount of business through companies registered in Luxembourg and Amsterdam with unconnected people paid to act as fronts.
- Over the years, information has surfaced concerning alleged large transfers of funds to Bin Laden from the National Commercial Bank, Saudi Arabia.
- The US State Department has in the past confirmed reports that Bin Laden funnelled funds through the Dubai Islamic Banks but these claims have been denied by the Bank itself.

- Immediately after the attacks, the *Sunday Times* (UK) claimed that an account at Barclays in London operated by Khalid al-Fawwaz under the title of 'The Advice and Reformation Committee' was a front for part of Bin Laden's operations.
- Rumours have abounded regarding accounts and facilities in London, Switzerland, Sudan, Hong Kong, Monaco, Pakistan, Malaysia, the Cayman Islands and Panama (to name but a selection).
- It is now believed that terrorists, like traditional launderers, made extensive use of bureaux de change.

To operate such worldwide facilities, Bin Laden must have effective and secret communication facilities. It is known that he had a satellite phone (telephone number 00873 682505331) and this has been used extensively in the past. Somewhat unsurprisingly this phone is now switched off. The hi-tech aspect of his communications (which include other encrypted mobile phones and faxes) is supplemented by his personal emissaries who travel the world to conduct his business in person.

Hawala and hundi banking

Media coverage of money laundering by Al-Qaida has made copious mention of the hawala or hundi banking systems. In India, Pakistan and the Middle East these systems create significant money laundering problems. One difficulty is being able to distinguish between legitimate transactions and those involving money laundering. Such systems are not designed to deal with 'official transactions': they provide complete confidentiality and no paper trail. They are essentially based on trust, and involve no physical transfer of funds. For example, a hawala broker in one country instructed by his client arranges for a broker in another country to make a payment to the intended beneficiary. Increasingly the funds to be 'transferred' are paid in gold to the brokers, who have later to rationalize their own 'interbanking' levels and fund flows. The 'transfers' are between the brokers and so will consist of both legitimate transactions and money laundering. The money laundering risks inherent in such systems have long been identified: the only new twist is the awful realization as to just how effective such systems are, and what the end product can be used for.

Official action against terrorist money laundering

In the aftermath of 9/11, the US media were highly critical of the US efforts in the past to halt and identify domestic money laundering. The executive order signed on 24 September by President Bush was not primarily aimed at the United States, but at banks in other countries that are involved in the funding of terrorist organizations. The message was clear. Bush commented:

> *If you do business with terrorists, if you support or sponsor them, you will not do business with the United States. We're putting banks and financial institutions around the world on notice: we will work with their governments and ask them to freeze or block terrorist ability to access funds in foreign accounts. If they fail to help us by sharing information or freezing accounts, the Department of the Treasury now has the authority to freeze their banks' assets and transactions in the United States.*

Simultaneously the US administration immediately examined their long term response to tax havens – some official sources referred to offshore banking secrecy being 'history'. This in turn raised serious issues about the privacy of the individual and civil liberties.

In the United Kingdom the Government confirmed immediately after 9/11 that British laws against money laundering and underground banking would be strengthened. The UK Government also called on the international community to close loopholes that allow terrorists access to legitimate channels to finance their activities. However, one underlying thread that consistently appeared is that even in Western countries the official bodies that deal with money laundering enforcement are underfunded and under-resourced and, as mentioned earlier, have difficulties with international cooperation.

And in the cold light of the continuing war on terrorism, are we any further forward than we were after Clinton's freezing order in 1998? If one believes various eloquent, but ultimately self-congratulatory, reports issued by national governments, then the answer is that we have come a very long way indeed. My view is somewhat less positive – and I am not the only one who has doubts about what has been achieved. In September 2002 a UN Security Council report commented that, 'Despite initial successes in locating and freezing Al-Qaida assets, the network continues to have access to considerable financial and other economic resources.' The report then says that 'Al-Qaida is by all accounts "fit and well" and poised to strike again at its leisure', which of course it (or those associated to it) did in Bali and Kenya within weeks. The UN report highlighted various key elements that still existed:

- Backers in North Africa, the Middle East and Asia manage as much as $300 million in investments.
- There are bank accounts under the name of (unidentified) intermediaries in Dubai, Hong Kong, London, Malaysia and Vienna.
- Private donations, totalling an estimated $16 million per annum, 'continue, largely unabated'.

The report also highlighted the trend for Al-Qaida to move their assets outside of the traditional banking system into precious metals and gems. The report goes on to highlight a key deficiency that is hampering international efforts – that of different terrorist warning lists by the United States, United Nations, European Union and other countries, which are creating confusion and hampering efforts to freeze Al-Qaida of funds.

In October 2002 the UK Government in its 'Combating the financing of terrorism report' commented that 'since September 11 over 175 countries have taken concrete action to freeze terrorist assets and some US $112 million has been frozen worldwide'. The response to this statement was actually made a month earlier by Swiss Attorney-General Valentin Roschacher, when he commented that 'If you compare the number of millions blocked all over the world and the estimate of Bin Laden's worth and that of his group, you come to the conclusion there is a lot of money not yet found.' Roschacher also returned to a now common theme: that Al-Qaida's wealth had been converted into gold and diamonds. This theme becomes louder and more sustained as the months pass:

- In September 2002 it was alleged that Al-Qaida and Taliban officials sent several shipments of gold from Pakistan to either Iran or the United Arab Emirates, and then by chartered aircraft to Sudan. It was denied by both Sudan and Iran.
- At the end of 2002 various allegations surfaced concerning the presence of Al-Qaida operatives in Western Africa both prior to, and after, 11 September. Media reports quoting a joint investigation by European intelligence agencies stated that the governments of Liberia and Burkina Faso facilitated a terrorist plot to

transfer diamonds and weapons through both countries. It was alleged that Charles Taylor, the Liberian president, received $1 million to give safe haven to senior Al-Qaida personnel after 9/11. These terrorists were also supposed to have bought $20 million worth of diamonds (which effectively meant that they controlled the precious stones market in West Africa) together with attempting to buy various types of sophisticated weaponry, including anti-aircraft missiles.

- Earlier in this chapter we referred to the testimony of Wadih el-Hage, who is now serving a life sentence in the United States after he was convicted for his part in the conspiracy to bomb the US embassies in Kenya and Tanzania in 1998. However, in early 2003 further information emerged as to his activities prior to his detention. Court documents reveal that he planned to visit jewellers in Bond Street and Hatton Garden (both in London) to sell gems there. Western intelligence agencies now suspect that prior to 9/11 Al-Qaida sold more than $20 million worth of precious stones.

UK authorities themselves had previously expressed frustration at the progress made in the chasing of terrorist assets. Annoyance was particularly directed at lawyers and accountants. Jon McNally, the head of the economic crime unit at NCIS, was reported in the *Guardian* as being 'frustrated' that the two professions had done relatively little to help the police since 11 September. The rise in suspicious activity reports filed in the UK in 2001 had risen to 31,251 (from 13,000 in 2000) but only 1 per cent of the total were from lawyers and a pitiful 0.35 per cent from accountants. Just to ram the point home it was reported that in recent years UK motoring organizations such as the AA and RAC had submitted more reports than accountants. I think that we may have been at this point before – specifically in Chapters 2 and 4 of this book, which were originally written the year before 9/11.

In the aftermath of 11 September the FATF issued a two-page document giving 'Special recommendations on terrorist funding', outlining eight key recommendations. On 27 March 2002 an additional set of guidance notes was issued to give further advice on how to implement the recommendations. These documents contain the following important observations:

1. Each country should ratify and implement relevant UN instruments. The guidance notes provide full details of the six elements of the UN convention and Security Council resolutions.

2. Each country should criminalize the financing of terrorism, terrorist acts and terrorist organizations. The guidance notes give additional information on exactly what this involves, including the key observation that 'jurisdictions should ensure that terrorist financing offences are predicate offences even if they are committed in a jurisdiction different from the one in which the money laundering offence is being applied'.
3. Freezing and confiscating terrorist assets: the three key elements of freezing, seizing and confiscating are further explained and defined.
4. Reporting suspicious transactions relating to terrorism: the two key elements of suspecting and having 'reasonable grounds to suspect' are further explained. Additionally the types of entities that should report such suspicions are stressed: not only banks but also non-bank financial institutions (which, as a minimum, should include bureaux de change, stockbrokers, insurance companies and money remittance/transfer services).
5. International cooperation: further information is given regarding the five elements of this recommendation as they apply to each jurisdiction, which are: exchange of information through mutual legal assistance mechanisms; exchange of information other than through mutual legal assistance mechanisms; having specific measures to permit the denial of 'safe haven' to those involved in terrorist financing; having procedures to permit extradition; jurisdictions should have provisions or procedures to ensure that 'claims of political motivation are not recognized as a ground for refusing requests to extradite persons alleged to be involved in terrorist financing'.
6. Alternative remittance: this recommendation attempts to tackle the difficult area of value transfer systems such as the Black Market Peso Exchange, hawala or hundi systems and other methods prevalent in China and East Asia. The notes give clarification of the three major elements of this recommendation:
   - Jurisdictions should require licensing or registration of those providing such services;
   - Such systems should be subject to FATF recommendations;
   - Jurisdictions should be able to apply sanctions on such systems if providers fail to obtain a licence or register and fail to comply with relevant FATF recommendations.
7. Wire transfers: the three elements of this recommendation have a direct impact on the operations of financial institutions, and in

our opinion should be viewed as, at the very least, best practice guidelines. The three aspects are that jurisdictions should require financial institutions to:
- include originator information on funds transfers sent within or from the jurisdiction;
- retain information on the originators of funds transfers, including at each stage of the process;
- examine more closely or monitor funds transfers when originator information is not available.

8. Non-profit organizations: this recommendation consists of two key elements:
   - Jurisdictions should review the legal regime of entities, in particular non-profit organizations, to prevent their misuse for terrorist financing purposes;
   - Non-profit organizations should not be used to disguise or facilitate terrorist funding and thus escape asset freezing measures.

In the weeks that followed 9/11, I received numerous requests as to what individual organizations should do to identify and prevent money laundering by terrorist organizations. Believing strongly that the best and more effective approach to this problem is a 'holistic' one rather than strictly following a set of regulations without deviating from them, I prepared a basic checklist of what to do. My contention has always been that the prevention of money laundering can never solely depend on the legislation and it is far more likely to be successful if there is a suitable mindset and culture within each relevant organization. The suggestions I made were:

1. Know your customer – due diligence procedures. There will be very little defence for an organization if due diligence procedures are not followed when an account or relationship is established. However, even rigid adherence to set procedures will not ensure that suspect accounts are avoided. If fundamental groups can persuade people to make martyrs of themselves, it is totally logical that individuals (who have no discernible terrorist connections) will be willing to operate as fronts to open and operate accounts, companies or other key relationships. Thus the ultimate beneficial owner is completely obscured. Moreover there is substantial evidence that terrorists are utilizing false identities – of either living or dead persons who have no

connection with terrorism. Even with all of these caveats, the importance of due diligence at the beginning of a relationship (or during it, if suspicions are aroused) cannot be underestimated – if only to give some protection to the organization by showing that it took all reasonable steps possible.

2. Monitor suspicious transactions. Again, this is an essential element of any money laundering control strategy. But once again the monitoring of transactions does have drawbacks – based on initial information, the bank accounts of the suicide pilots do not appear to have exhibited any characteristics that would lead to suspicions being raised.
3. Report suspicions to relevant authorities. This becomes a very important requirement, both to frustrate terrorism and to ensure that the reporting organization has fulfilled its legal requirements. Additionally it is worth remembering that, however horrendous the WTC outrage was, at some stage in the future some kind of normality may return. At this time, the spotlight will also turn to traditional money laundering and launderers – so any reports to the relevant authorities must not only include suspected terrorist launderers but also 'mainstream' washers of dirty money.
4. Obtain and analyse available information. The executive order issued by President Bush immediately after 9/11 is by no means the sole listing of suspected terrorist organizations and individuals. There are various other US Government listings and information supplied by other national administrations. It is not particularly easy to keep up with such information – particularly when some media reports linking organizations and individuals to terrorism are not necessarily correct. However, based on our previous experience, we think that organizations or professional advisors would have severe difficulties defending their position if it involved a relationship with an individual or entity that had been linked to terrorism. The obvious way to ensure that this does not happen is to monitor events and intelligence, and if it is discovered that you may have a possible link to anyone named then report your suspicions to the relevant authorities.
5. Train staff. The necessity of training staff to identify suspicious accounts and transactions (and equally what is not suspicious) is now paramount. Moreover the need to circulate relevant information, guidance and listings of suspect organizations and individuals is crucial.

6. Don't underestimate the problem – but simultaneously don't overreact. Now is not the time to panic – one of the great difficulties of reporting suspicious transactions or customers to the authorities is that there now exists a strong possibility that such reports, if they refer to innocent individuals, could result in legal action against you by those individuals. Moreover a 'Know Your Customer'/due diligence policy too rigorously applied could result in no customers whatsoever. A sensible, robust policy applied in a systematic and logical way is what is now required – not a set of knee-jerk reactions.

Importantly the shockwaves generated by 9/11 combined with the work of the FATF have meant that the majority of countries have revisited, amended and strengthened their AML legislation. Probably the most important advance was in the United States itself, with the Patriot Act, which is considered in the next chapter. However, the inescapable conclusion that keeps returning to haunt all such efforts is that it is almost an impossibility to stop terrorist funding. At its roots, terrorism is a social and cultural problem, in that, in very simple terms, in much of the Islamic world Al-Qaida is seen not as the world's number one enemy but as freedom fighters righting perceived wrongs. If this view prevails then no legislation can prevent the funding of terrorism and/or the transmission of funds through the global financial system via sympathetic nations and compliant bankers. However, the problem is actually worse than even that, for two key reasons. The first one is that a terrorist attack that can claim hundreds (or thousands) of lives can be, has been, and is being mounted on a shoestring. Secondly, it is now accepted that since the mid-1990s (at the latest) Al-Qaida has utilized numerous methods to gather funding, move such assets around the globe and ultimately frustrate attempts to freeze and confiscate its war chest. Many of the techniques employed are beyond those that can be regulated by traditional AML legislation/regulation: informal money transmission services (such as hawala and hundi) and trading in precious gems and metals are but two key elements of this strategy. Perversely this situation has been further worsened by the successful military campaign in Afghanistan. The scattering of Al-Qaida, which operated as a cell-like structure anyway, from Afghanistan means that it is now active in virtually every country of the world, supplemented by numerous other sympathetic terrorist groups that operate using similar methods. All of this leads me to conclude depressingly that the war on terrorism will be a very long one indeed.

WHITER THAN WHITE: THE OFFICIAL RESPONSE

International financial transactions are carried out in a realm that is close to anarchy. Numerous committees and organizations attempt to coordinate domestic, regulatory policies and negotiate international standards but they have no enforcement powers.

(RANDALL KROSZNER, ASSOCIATE PROFESSOR OF BUSINESS ECONOMICS AT THE UNIVERSITY OF CHICAGO GRADUATE SCHOOL OF BUSINESS)

At the beginning of the 21st century it is obvious that organized criminal groups across the globe have adapted and thrived on the new world order. More than that they have realized the importance of strategic alliances between each other to advance their united cause. They have identified the weak points in the international financial infrastructure and exploited them. They have embraced and developed new technologies and delivery channels. They have diversified. They thrive and grow. And what have the nations of the world and their respective legal and regulatory authorities done? In some cases a tremendous amount; in others, as we have already seen, very little. The following examples show the guile, agility and international extent of organized criminal money laundering. One could also suggest that these illustrations demonstrate how the battle against dirty dealing is being successfully waged. One could advance that argument, were it not totally incorrect.

Bank Leu is a legitimate bank in Europe: it has no representation in the United States of any kind, or at least did not in 1993. Thus it may be somewhat surprising to discover that in that year it was convicted of laundering Colombia drugs money in a California district court. The sequence of events that led to this conclusion began in Luxembourg, and also in the main took place there. Bank Leu in Luxembourg opened an account for a customer who presented negotiable instruments for the credit of his account. The instruments were drawn on a legitimate Californian bank and were accepted by Bank Leu. In total the credits to this account totalled more than $2 million – however, the instruments were all slightly less than the magical suspicious reporting figure of $10,000. This reporting figure is, of course, applicable in the United States not Luxembourg. The US authorities took a different view as they claimed jurisdiction on this matter as the financial instruments were drawn on a bank in California: hence Bank Leu was convicted in that state. Ultimately the bank returned $2 million to the US authorities and approximately $1 million to the Luxembourg authorities.

In February 2000, the US Federal Bureau of Investigation announced that it was opening its first office abroad (at least the first official one) – in Budapest. The Hungarian Government requested help from the United States to counteract the growth of Russian organized crime groups there. Budapest is an ideal portal to the West and this office of five US agents and ten Hungarian ones is being set up to deal with this threat. The US agents will carry weapons and have the right to make arrests. The United States Ambassador to Hungary, Peter Tufo, commented that 'Our objective is to strangle the Russian mafia that operates here. This is not a mom-and-pop operation. It's a multibillion dollar global enterprise.'

In Israel, in the closing months of the last century and the opening ones of this, there were numerous high level investigations into money laundering:

- The now infamous Bank of New York case.
- Cash transfers linked to a Russian telecommunications company and insider trading to the extent of $340 million.
- A Chechen subject who opened an account with $50 million worth of cheques drawn on a bank in Venezuela from the account of a Gibraltar Investment firm, that was probably just a shell company.

- The conviction in 1999 of an Israeli organized crime leader in Miami who was running a money laundering business for the Colombian Cali cartel.

But there is a major problem: as we have already discussed money laundering was not a crime in Israel at that time. Even if criminals are successfully prosecuted for different criminal offences then it is very difficult to confiscate the proceeds of crime. In 1998 a Russian immigrant entrepreneur, Gregory Lerner, was convicted in Israel of bribery, blackmail and fraud in local dealings. But that was merely making use of existing laws to cover a money laundering offence: what he had actually done was defrauded Russian banks of $48 million and used that money in an attempt to establish a bank in Israel. He was sentenced to six years' imprisonment – but the proceeds of crime were not confiscated as there was no legal provision to do so and he got away with a fine of $5 million.

In March 1998 it was reported that Italian paramilitary police had successfully stopped an attempt by the Italian Mafia to sell uranium that could be used to manufacture nuclear weapons. This report is one of many that has surfaced over the last few years, all telling essentially the same story: that organized criminal groups have achieved access to nuclear material and are selling to the highest bidder, whether that is a country, corporation, terrorist group or individual. This particular incident revolved around a 27-inch uranium rod that was offered for sale for £7.7 million by Mafia groups – the buyer, claiming to be from a Middle East country, was, in fact, an undercover Italian police officer. He was also offered first refusal on eight other radioactive bars.

In 1997 a confidential United Kingdom Government briefing paper entitled 'An Outline Assessment of the Threat and Impact by Organized/Enterprise Crime upon United Kingdom Interests' confirmed some worst nightmares:

- The report highlighted the threats posed to security, the banking system and businesses by Serbian gangs, the Russian mafia, Hell's Angels, Chinese Triads, Jamaican Yardies, Lebanese hashish dealers, Indian and Pakistani groups.
- It highlighted links that had been forged between the various gangs: the Hell's Angels had linked with organized criminals in Scandinavia and North America; South American cocaine dealers had moved their operations to the United Kingdom because of pressure from US law enforcement agencies, and on

the way they had acquired passports from Belize; Serbian groups have associates in Germany and the Benelux countries.

- The document outlines the infiltration of business by these groups through the establishment of 'legitimate' companies staffed by innocent men and women. And of course they had enrolled the services of suitable professional advisors such as lawyers, bankers and accountants. The report comments that 'Many of these criminal directors have gained the skills of international class financiers.'

In May 2001 Mario Villanueva was arrested in Mexico. The United States requested his extradition in 2002. Villanueva is a former Governor of the Mexican state of Quintana Roo and is accused of drug trafficking and money laundering both in Mexico and internationally. Villanueva holds the dubious distinction of being the only Mexican governor to be investigated for drug trafficking whilst still in office. Not surprisingly the connection is with Colombia – more specifically the Juarez drug cartel. One of the allegations levelled against Villanueva is that he allowed cocaine shipments to be moved along the Caribbean coast in return for bribes.

Canadian authorities are becoming increasingly concerned that their country is being perceived as a soft touch by organized criminals. Hence the importance of the successful prosecutions that came in early 2000 as a result of Project Omerta. This three and a half year operation had been conducted against a criminal organization that had operated for more than 30 years in Canada, Venezuela, Aruba, the United States, Mexico, the United Kingdom, Switzerland, Italy, France, Spain, Germany, India and Thailand.

Because of the national and global spread of this criminal network not only were the Canadian Special Enforcement Unit involved but a dazzling array of other law enforcement bodies: Ontario and Quebec Royal Canadian Mounted Police Units; Surete du Quebec; Montreal Urban Community Police; the FBI; the US Drugs Enforcement Administration; the US Customs service; the Texas Department of Public Safety; Raggrupamento Operativo Speciale – Carabinieri and Servizio Centrale Operative of the State Police in Italy; the Swiss Federal Office for Police Matters; and the Federal Anti Drug Task Force in Mexico. Four members of the same family ultimately pleaded guilty to smuggling massive amounts of Colombian cocaine into Canada and Europe, together with laundering its own profits and providing money laundering services to other criminal organizations. The

Cuntera–Caruana family was said to be one of the largest crime families in the world based in Venezuela and Sicily with links into North America, Western Europe and Asia. Four members of the Caruana family were finally sentenced to a total of 50 years' imprisonment.

And at almost the same time as these successful convictions in Canada, Spanish police arrested 24 individuals in relation to laundering money relating to drugs originating in Colombia. The funds involved came from Colombian cocaine sold in Britain and in Spain and was laundered through banks in Portugal, France and Andorra. The money was then transferred to the United States where it was converted to dollars and ultimately went back to the drug kings in Colombia. Amongst the 28 people arrested in Madrid and Barcelona were five Spaniards, two Colombians and one American. Not only were people arrested but Spanish police grabbed false documents, luxury cars and very sizeable sums of pesetas and sterling held in Spain and Portugal.

It is not as if there is no documentation available to provide model laws for money laundering control. Not only are there the FATF's 40 recommendations, there are also:

- The Organization of American States – CICAD Model regulations concerning laundering offences connected to illicit drug trafficking and related offences;
- The United Nations Model Bill on Money Laundering and Proceeds of Crime formulated in 1998;
- The United Nations Model Mutual Assistance in Criminal Matters Bill (1998);
- The United Nations Model Foreign Exchange Bill (1998);
- The United Nations Model Extradition (Amendment) Bill (1998);
- The United Nations Model Law on Money Laundering, Confiscation and International Cooperation in relation to drugs issued in 1995.

Probably the most relevant of these is the Inter-American Drug Abuse Control Commission Model Regulations concerning laundering offences connected to illicit drug trafficking and other serious offences. Notwithstanding the catchy title, this document provides 21 articles together with an introduction and annex outlining everything any country needs to do to combat money laundering. At the heart of these model laws – which are as up to date as June 1999 – is the equally catchily titled United Nations Convention Against Illicit Traffic in Narcotic Drugs and Psychotropic Substances (1988). Once again, at the risk of stating the obvious, 11 years separate these documents – and the money laundering predicament is still there, still unresolved.

The first obvious difference – or progression – over the intervening 11 years is that the definition of the offences that give rise to money laundering have been broadened:

> *Serious offences... including, for example, drug trafficking, illegal activities that relate to organized crime, terrorism, illicit trafficking of firearms, persons or body arms, corruption, fraud, extortion and kidnapping.*

The remaining 20 articles spell out what is needed (and still needed) to defeat organized crime and money laundering. Laundering criminal offences are defined as those committed by:

- any person who acquires, possesses, uses, administers, converts, transfers, transports property and knows or should have known or is intentionally ignorant that such property is proceeds from serious offences;
- any person who conceals, disguises or impedes the true nature, source, location, movement, rights concerning the ownership of property and knows, or should have known, that such property is proceeds from serious offences;
- any person who participates in, associates with, conspires to commit, aids and abets, facilitates and counsels, incites publicly or privately the commission of any of the offences.

Article Three addresses the issue of Jurisdiction and recommends that a competent authority can try such offences – even if the offences took place in another jurisdiction. Articles Four and Five establish crucial recommendations regarding freezing and seizure of property:

- Relevant property can be frozen and/or seized.
- When an individual is convicted the court should order that relevant property or assets obtained by such offences should be seized; if such assets no longer exist or cannot be seized then other assets of an identical value should be forfeited or a fine paid of the same amount.

Various articles make clear what both governments and businesses must do to combat money laundering:

- Each state must establish a central agency to receive, request, analyse and disseminate disclosures of information – that is, suspicious transaction reports.
- Financial institutions covered by these regulations include not only banks, trust companies, savings/loan/building/credit/thrift institutions, but also offshore service providers, securities brokers, futures dealers and currency dealers.
- Each of these bodies must take identification, record this process and maintain and make available relevant records.
- Each of these bodies must record details of cash transactions exceeding a specified amount.
- Each of these bodies shall report suspicious transactions (completed or not) without tipping off the relevant customer.

The model regulations then elaborate on the mandatory nature of these regulations and the critical need for training programmes and compliance audit evaluations. Then the stick is produced:

- Financial institutions shall be liable for the actions of all their staff.
- Severe sanctions should be applied to Financial Institutions and/or their staff who participate in such serious offences or don't comply with the regulations.

But it does not only stop with 'Financial Institutions'; the following other types of business are identified as also being at risk and thus should be regulated:

- sale and transfer of real estate;
- weapons sale;
- precious metals dealing;
- art dealers;
- jewellery sales;
- automobiles;
- boats and planes;
- other consumer durables;
- provision of travel or entertainment related services;
- casino and other gambling related enterprises;

- professional service providers such as notaries and accountants;
- insurance companies and brokers;
- investment funds and companies;
- any activity related to the international movement of goods and services;
- any activity related to the transfer of technology and movement of cash and other instruments;
- and the real cruncher: **any other commercial activity that, due to the nature of its operations, could be used for money laundering**.

The model regulations then go on to address the international context of the problem, stating that: if funds are sent across borders such transfers or movements should be reported to the relevant authorities; and international cooperation is paramount including freezing orders, seizure, assistance and sharing of information. And just to stress the point the final Article states that:

> *The legal provisions referring to bank secrecy or confidentiality shall not be an impediment to compliance with these Regulations, when the information is requested by or shared with the court or other competent authority in accordance with the law.*

Criminals buy International Business Corporations off the shelf, but nations cannot do the simple thing and implement such model laws as these, which spell out everything you ever need to implement to control money laundering in words of one syllable. Why not? One rather cynical view is that those who make such laws are prone to the same excesses as those that they are trying to regulate against.

There must exist, somewhere subliminal, a link between the three words 'politician', 'money' and 'laundering'. Consider the following evidence for this theory:

- Asif Ali Zardari, husband of Benazir Bhutto, the former Prime Minister of Pakistan, was imprisoned there for kickbacks and indicted for money laundering in Switzerland. Benazir Bhutto herself was also alleged to have benefited from corrupt payments and laundered money.
- When the pendulum swung back in Pakistan, Nawaz Sharif, after being overthrown by a military coup, was also accused of extensive money laundering.
- Roland Dumas, the former French foreign minister, and a cast of many other French politicians, up to and including the late

President Mitterand, have all been alleged to have benefited from the laundering of illegal payments made by the French oil giant Elf.

- Former German Chancellor Helmut Kohl has admitted to receiving up to £670,000 secret donations to the Christian Democratic Union Party whilst in power. It is claimed that sizeable proportions of this money were laundered through Liechtenstein.

  Kohl, architect of a reunited Germany, is also alleged to have been involved in the laundering of secret donations to his party, and is now being implicated in the Elf scandal.
- Various politicians in Hungary, Romania and Slovakia have been accused (either formally or through the press) of receiving illegal payments and corruption.
- Raul Salinas, brother of the former President of Mexico, was imprisoned for murder and investigated for illicit enrichment.
- Allegations against everybody and anybody up to Boris Yeltsin in the Kremlin, for laundering funds offshore.
- Jaime Lusinchi, former President of Venezuela and a client of Citibank, charged with misappropriating government funds.
- Nigerian claims that the former Head of State, Sani Abacha, and 14 other persons (including various family members and official representatives) 'systematically plundered' the Nigerian Central Bank for many years together with committing a series of property crimes (including fraud, forgery, embezzlement and money laundering). As at 21 January 2000, Swiss authorities had frozen funds totalling $645 million.
- Two daughters of the former President of Indonesia, Radon Suharto, have been accused of looting billions of dollars from the country.
- Former political leaders of Kazakhstan have been accused of large scale money laundering through Geneva, other parts of Switzerland and Liechtenstein.
- Pavlo Lazarenko, the former Prime Minister of Ukraine, was charged by Switzerland in 1998 with money laundering whilst he was head of the government.

Whilst this catalogue of allegations against the formerly perceived great and good may prove beyond any doubt the dictum that absolute power corrupts absolutely, it also, without wishing to appear flippant about such cans of worms, suggests that the chances of getting away with money laundering if you are a politician are substantially less than if you are a criminal. The criminalization of politics reaches its zenith in the narco-state, where it is hard to tell the difference between organized criminals and the ruling power. It has long been held, for example, that the Burmese military junta is actively involved in drug trafficking.

The final days of the Clinton administration produced not only a large number of questionable presidential pardons but also a new set of guidance notes to assist US financial institutions to avoid transactions that may involve the proceeds of foreign official corruption.

The guidance, which is voluntary, is specifically aimed at private banks and similar institutions 'where accounts may involve the proceeds of corruption by senior foreign political figures, their immediate family or close associates'.

The basic guidelines that the report promotes revolve around defining a 'Covered Person'. This is where an individual is a 'senior foreign political figure', 'any member of a senior foreign political figure's immediate family' and any 'close associate' of a senior foreign political figure. In respect of these 'Covered Persons' the following enhanced guidelines are recommended:

- Ascertain the identity of the account holder and the account's beneficial owner.
- Obtain adequate documentation regarding the Covered Person – including assessing his or her business reputation.
- Understand the Covered Person's anticipated account activity – the report suggests that 'reasonable steps should be taken to determine whether the Covered Person has any legitimate business or investment activity in the United States that would make having an account in the United States a natural occurrence'.
- Determine the Covered Person's source of wealth and funds – the report suggests that financial institutions should take reasonable steps to determine the official salary and compensation of the Covered Person as well as the individual's known legitimate sources of wealth apart from his or her official position.
- Apply additional oversight to the Covered Person's account – recommendations include that the decision to accept (or reject) an account application from a Covered Person should be taken by a more senior level of management than is typically involved in account opening, and that annual reviews should be undertaken.

The report also identifies questionable or suspicious activities that may warrant enhanced scrutiny of transactions involving Covered Persons. Such activities include:

- a request to do business with a financial institution that is unused to doing business with foreign persons;
- a request by the Covered Person to associate any form of secrecy with a transaction (such as booking the transaction in the name of another person);
- the use by a Covered Person of accounts at a nation's central bank or other government owned bank, or of government accounts, as the source of funds in a transaction;
- unexplained rapid increases (or decreases) in funds or asset value in the Covered Person's account;
- large currency or bearer instrument transactions either in or out of the account;
- multiple simultaneous transactions that are each below the relevant suspicious transaction reporting thresholds.

In 2002 the FATF recommended that banks should have policy and procedures for handling banking relationships with politically exposed persons (PEPs). It also states that 'Banks should not accept or maintain a business relationship if the bank knows or must assume that the funds derive from corruption or misuse of public assets.' Recommended policies and procedures are:

- identification of a politically exposed person among new or existing customers;
- identification of persons or companies related to them;
- verification of the source of funds prior to account opening;
- senior management approval for establishing banking relationships with PEPs.

As we have seen in Chapter 3, early in 2000 the FATF published a report on non-cooperative jurisdictions, in which they outlined the key factors that facilitate non-compliance to the FATF's 40 money laundering regulations. The naming and shaming of non-cooperative jurisdictions began in June 2000 and has continued apace since that date (see Appendix I). However, the members of the FATF themselves – never mind offshore financial centres – have difficulty in achieving full compliance with the recommendations; and even if the member states do comply then their approaches can be different. All of this is not to criticize the work of the FATF, which is laudable, but to demonstrate how difficult it can be to establish a common framework of laws and preventative measures over a group of countries who agree with the fundamental requirements.

Australia is widely perceived as having one of the most effective anti-money laundering regimes in the world and has done important work in trying to establish the volume of funds that are being washed through the Australian economy. It has implemented legislation that covers customer identification procedures, cash transaction reporting, mandatory suspicious transaction reporting, reporting of international wire transfers, asset seizure and forfeiture, together with criminalizing money laundering in respect of serious crimes. The suspicious reporting procedure relates to cash transactions or international wire transfers of 10,000 Australian dollars or more – which is roughly equivalent to $6,500. In at least two respects Australia is even more advanced than many other nations: firstly it requires members of the public to report cash transfers in and out of the country of 5,000 Australian dollars or more. Secondly, it has already (and for a number of years) bracketed tax evasion with money laundering. These comprehensive procedures do not just apply to banks. The following businesses are covered:

- banks, building societies, credit unions and financial corporations;
- cash carriers;
- insurance companies and intermediaries;
- securities dealers and futures brokers;
- trustees and managers of unit trusts;
- traveller's cheque and money order dealers;
- currency and bullion dealers;
- casinos and gaming houses;
- bookmakers and similar entities.

Australia have also achieved something else – domestic sharing of information. The Australian Transaction Reports and Analysis Centre (AUSTRAC), which has been in existence since 1989, receives and collates all the relevant data, but then can be accessed by a wide range of official law enforcement and related agencies. The country has also encouraged and actively engaged in international mutual assistance.

Austria, on the other hand, appears to be straddling between two stools and continually runs the risk of disappearing down the large black hole in the middle of them. Yes, money laundering is a criminal offence covering the assets of all serious crimes. Yes, freezing and seizure of such assets are possible under Austrian law. Beyond that there seems to be a certain reluctance to implement all of the FATF's 40 recommendations, and Austria has not in fact implemented all of the EU Money Laundering Directive. We have already covered the Sparbuch issue in depth but another area of concern is that suspicious transaction reporting applies to banks, insurers, bureaux de change and mutual savings bodies, but not under normal circumstances to casinos, lawyers and real estate brokers.

Belgium, which, in particular through Brussels, is an important financial centre, takes money laundering seriously and defines it legally as the proceeds of all crimes. The anti-money laundering legislation covers: banks and other financial institutions; estate agents; notaries; bailiffs; accountants; auditors; casinos; and very interestingly (an area that is often overlooked) security firms that transport money. There are KYC regulations, training requirements, suspicious transaction reporting requirements and retention of records requirements.

We have already discussed the infiltration of organized criminal activities into Canada's economy and business infrastructure in various other sections of this book: particularly how Canadian authorities are now quickly coming to the view that the country is being perceived as an 'easy touch' for such nefarious pursuits. A very large part of this problem is due to Canada's lack of mandatory requirements for reporting suspicious transactions. Moreover, although Canada is attempting to rectify these omissions, there has not existed in the past any central agency to collate and investigate suspicious transactions, neither has there been any system for identifying suspicious cross border transactions. As we have already seen these weaknesses have enabled organized crime groups from across the world (not just across the border in the United States) to move money through Canada and also base themselves in the country.

Denmark, as can be seen from the country evaluation section later in this book, is probably one of the very few countries in the world that is perceived as having a minimal money laundering problem. One of the major reasons for this could be that the Money Laundering Act of 1993 defined money laundering to all crimes and established suspicious reporting procedures, KYC requirements, retention of records and applied these procedures to: banks and other similar financial institutions; life assurance companies; investment firms; mortgage credit institutions; securities brokers; bureaux de change; and all branches of foreign financial and credit institutions. Danish law also allows the confiscation of assets.

Finland is in a similar position as a low risk international money laundering centre, although there are continued and ongoing risks posed by Russian organized criminals, bearing in mind the relatively close proximity of Helsinki to St Petersburg. It has been estimated that money laundering in Finland is 90 per cent non-drug related and there domestic legislation is fairly comprehensive including the reporting of suspicious transactions, mutual assistance and a central money laundering reporting unit.

France has legally defined money laundering as relating to the proceeds of all crime, has customer identification procedures and suspicious transaction reporting regulations covering: banks; other financial institutions; insurance brokers; post offices; bureaux de change; notaries; and property agents. All of these reports are dealt with by a central agency, TRACFIN.

In Germany, money laundering is a criminal offence that extends to all serious crimes. The general regulatory and control framework in the country is very good, but somewhat strangely there is no centralized money laundering reporting/financial intelligence unit. However, Germany has made money laundering prevention a requirement in: banks; credit institutions; financial service institutions; financial enterprises; insurance companies; auctioneers; casinos; and bullion dealers.

Greece is suffering from its close proximity to Cyprus and also fears have been expressed concerning the proceeds of crime being invested in casinos. However, Greece, since 1995, has had comprehensive laws criminalizing money laundering.

Hong Kong is an obvious target for money launderers, particularly the washing of proceeds from the sale of illegal drugs. A variety of factors contribute towards the importance of Hong Kong as a money laundering target:

- the strength and high level of infiltration of Chinese organized crime groups;
- a low tax system;
- acting for China as its offshore banking centre;
- sophisticated financial environment and infrastructure;
- the absence of any currency and exchange controls;

- the presence of various offshore company structures that can be used by non-residents.

Money laundering in Hong Kong extends to all serious crime, and all banking and financial institutions must take customer identification and report suspicious transactions to a central unit. However, because of the size and complexity of Hong Kong's financial world there still remain problems:

- the relatively low level of suspicious reports – the vast majority of which come from banks with very few coming from insurers or professional advisors like solicitors and accountants;
- the opening of accounts with forged documents;
- the utilization of cash through bureaux de change and money remitters.

Iceland is one of those countries that is in the fortunate position regarding money laundering, in that it has an isolated financial sector and thus any problems with the washing of criminal proceeds is a domestic not an international problem. The problems within the country itself that could give rise to money laundering are fraud, smuggling and customs/VAT offences. The Icelandic legislation ensures that money laundering covers all types of serious crime and covers customer identification, keeping of records and reporting suspicious transactions.

Ireland on the other hand has a growing money laundering problem focused on the domestic drug trafficking problem. Although it is contradicted by the figures – that only 4 per cent of suspicious transactions reported in 1998 came from its growing offshore services centre in Dublin – my experience is that sizeable risks exist in that centre. In the mainstream world of money laundering there has been increased usage of established high cash turnover businesses such as pubs, restaurants, garages and bookmakers. Because of the high priority that the Irish Government place on preventing money laundering the legislation present is robust and accords with the recommendations of the FATF. Covering banks, other financial institutions, futures and options brokers, credit unions, post offices, stockbrokers and bureaux de change, solicitors, accountants, estate agents and auctioneers, any suspicious transactions over a specified limit have to be reported to the Money Laundering Investigation Unit; KYC and record keeping procedures are mandatory.

Italy has its own problems concerning money laundering – most of which originate from the south of the country. The good news is that Italy is not a major centre for the laundering of international criminal proceeds by groups of non-Italian origin. The bad news is the Mafia. Showing particularly Italian flair, the authorities operate a system that requires the identification of clients together with the recording and reporting of significant transactions above approximately $11,000, including the transfer of sums above this limit across borders. These laws apply to banks, other financial institutions, stock brokers, insurance companies and exchange houses. The one amazing statistic that all this produces is a reporting level of over 30 million 'suspicious' transactions... per month! The response by the Italian authorities towards money laundering has been described as exemplary. Which is just as well because the traditional Italian Mafia exerts a residual stranglehold over Southern Italy, which is exhibited in the financial spheres as property investments, control of front companies, investments in hotels and the gold market. And of course there is the issue of tax avoidance in the country, which is probably best left alone within the confines of this summary. Another key factor is the propensity of Italians to take their money abroad: Lugano and other financial centres of Switzerland remain popular destinations.

Japan, as is to be expected, has substantial money laundering problems as a result of the many and varied trades that domestic organized criminals are involved in: from illegal drugs, through extortion, to the high level of property/finance crime. Unfortunately until the aftermath of the Japanese financial crash the influence of organized crime groups in banking and property companies and transactions was substantial. The focus in Japan has, in the main, been on drug proceeds and its success has at best been very limited. Although a suspicious transaction reporting scheme has been in place since 1991, the levels of such reports are very low, as have been successful prosecutions and asset seizures. As if all of this was not bad enough there is obviously the inherent problem of Japan's economy being intensively cash based.

Luxembourg is something of a dark horse. On the one hand since 1998 it has had comprehensive anti-money laundering regulations extending to banks, other financial institutions, insurance employees, accountants, notaries and casino employees. All of these institutions must report suspicious transactions. This legislation includes, under the definition of money laundering, the proceeds of prostitution, kidnapping, arms trafficking, organized crime and child exploitation.

But, on the other hand, Luxembourg is a sizeable and influential offshore centre: so much so that it is rumoured that Saddam Hussein, Gaddafi and President Mobutu have all availed themselves of the financial services offered. In guestimate figures the Grand Duchy has a population of approximately 360,000 and 215 banks, 1,500 offshore trusts, 95 insurance companies and 255 reinsurance companies. Somewhat worryingly in this context is the low level of suspicious transaction reporting – and it is usually the same banks who make the reports. This means that there is a very high percentage of banks and financial institutions who never report any suspicious transactions, combined with an equally low (or almost non-existent) level of suspicious transaction reports from professionals. It is also my understanding that if an institution closes an account, refuses to open one, or rejects a transaction there is no obligation on them to report it.

The Netherlands has two problems: drugs and Aruba. The country operates a fairly robust money laundering prevention system: suspicious reporting mechanisms; customer identification procedures; keeping of records. This applies to banks, stockbrokers, casinos and credit card companies. Even the Central Bank of the Netherlands is included in the suspicious reporting programme. Both civil and criminal seizure of assets is possible. Somewhat strangely then, lawyers, notaries and accountants report on a voluntary basis. Because of its offshore location and its promotion of such facilities on the Internet, Aruba is perceived as being a high risk target of money launderers.

New Zealand and Norway are similar countries regarding money laundering as in both nations the problem is a domestic one with little evidence of large-scale infiltration of international organized crime groups. Both countries have fairly comprehensive money laundering prevention legislation.

Money laundering in Portugal does not appear to be taking place on any significant scale although the washing of proceeds of drug trafficking is a particular problem. The scope of the country's anti-money laundering law is impressive: customer identification is mandatory; records have to be retained for 10 years; suspicious transaction reporting is mandatory; and if the transaction is unusually large a customer statement must be obtained concerning their origins.

Singapore is simultaneously a major financial centre with many shops trading in high value goods, and a country that has a strong anti-drug culture. Additionally, there exists a persistent underground banking system, which when allied to the various shops selling high value goods provide a strong conduit for the washing of Asian heroin dealers' cash. To make this situation worse there are no controls on currency being brought in or taken out of Singapore. The anti-money laundering laws apply to banks, insurance companies, bureaux de change and money remittance companies but are currently only drugs related. The regulations mean that suspicious transactions must be reported and customers engaged in significant currency transactions should be identified.

Spain defines money laundering as the proceeds of all serious crimes and the country's regulations apply to banks, casinos, property developers, jewellers and antique dealers. However, the stock market remains outside the anti-money laundering regulations. The general perception is that Spain is taking positive and vigorous steps to combat money laundering.

Sweden is not perceived as having major money laundering problems; the Financial Supervisory Authority has issued guidelines that require financial institutions, insurance companies and currency exchange houses to verify customer identification and report suspicious transactions.

The positive steps taken by Switzerland are referred to in various other sections of this book. Certainly the new anti-money laundering law that came into effect on 1 April 1998 has improved systems concerning record keeping, customer identification and the reporting of suspicious transactions. These regulations apply not only to banks but also accountants, lawyers, independent financial advisors and insurance companies.

Turkey only passed an anti-money laundering bill in late 1996, with regulations following in the middle of the next year. These included the reporting of suspicious transactions above 2 billion Turkish lira and the taking of customer identification. Interestingly these regulations apply not only to banks but also many other relevant businesses such as insurance firms and jewellery dealers. However, there is a very low level of suspicious reporting and there are no regulations relating to training. Bearing in mind the highly cash intensive nature of Turkey's economy, problems still remain.

The United Kingdom is a major financial centre and as such is a target for money launderers. Whilst there is extensive legislation and regulation regarding money laundering there remain accusations that money laundering is taking place on a fairly large scale. Amongst the relevant legislation is: The Drug Trafficking Act 1994; The Criminal Justice Act 1993; and The Money Laundering Regulations 1993. Additionally there have been guidance notes issued to relevant financial sectors. Various criminal offences have been established for non-adherence to procedures. Those procedures, which apply to banks, lawyers, accountants and other professionals, detail requirements in respect of: identification procedures; record keeping; internal reporting systems; and staff training. The National Criminal Intelligence Service (NCIS) has the role of a central money laundering reporting unit.

The United States has been the prime mover in most, if not all, of the key international moves on money laundering and has internally imposed various legislative and regulatory standards to control the problem. These include:

- The Bank Secrecy Act of 1970;
- The Money Laundering Control Act of 1986;
- The Anti-Drug Abuse Act of 1988;
- Section 2532 of the Crime Control Act of 1990;
- Section 206 of the Federal Deposit Insurance Corporation Improvement Act of 1991;
- Title XV of the Housing and Community Development Act of 1992, referred to as the Annunzio-Wylie-Anti-Money Laundering Act.

The net effect of all of this legislation is that it requires banks and other financial institutions to retain records and report suspicious transactions in excess of $10,000 in currency (with various exceptions to cut down on unnecessary documentation), and to demand customer identification. The legislation has been frequently amended and improved with a pivotal development being the requirement for businesses to make a suspicious transaction report when customers spend over $10,000 in cash, bank drafts, traveller's cheques or money orders. The relevant businesses are airlines, finance companies, hotels, pawn brokers, restaurants and wholesalers and/or retailers of certain commodities.

The United States' *National Money Laundering Strategy for 2000*, released in March 2000, provides yet more tangible proof of the high importance placed by the US administration on tackling money laundering. This document is essentially a blueprint for what domestic action is be to be taken to stem the dramatic rise of washing dirty money. The laundering process is described as 'a global phenomenon of enormous reach'. The 127-page report comments that it is crucial to fight money laundering for three fundamental reasons:

- By fighting money laundering the criminals who are committing the underlying offences can be pursued.
- Money laundering facilitates foreign corruption, thus undermining US efforts to promote democracy and stable economies overseas.
- By fighting money laundering the integrity of the financial system is being defended against the corruptive influence of dirty money.

US authorities are to take further steps to identify and control domestic money laundering. Federal authorities have increased scrutiny in four geographical areas that have been designated 'high risk money laundering and financial crime areas'. The four are:

1. New York and New Jersey: obviously in the spotlight because of the recent and ongoing Russian money laundering case involving the washing of billions of dollars through banks such as the Bank of New York. In 1998 and 1999, financial institutions in this major financial centre reported $33 billion worth of suspicious transactions to the authorities.
2. Los Angeles: a fairly obvious target because of its importance as a drug manufacturing centre and port.
3. San Juan, Puerto Rico: a gateway to the USA for drugs.
4. The country's south-west border of Arizona and Texas: convenient for smugglers from South America, particularly relevant nowadays due to the high level of activity from drug cartels in Mexico as well as Colombia. However, its inclusion is because of cash being smuggled out of the country using this route.

The new strategy also calls for casinos, brokerage firms and other firms involved in money transactions to notify authorities of suspicious transactions. Additionally, one element of the strategy is to put more resources into stopping the smuggling of currency out of the United States. In 1999, US Customs seized $60 million in cash that was being taken out of the country – including $16.5 million on the south-west border.

On the international front the strategy document shows how the US government are particularly focusing on offshore financial centres – as various recommendations relate to taking punitive action against non-cooperative jurisdictions. Once again the United States clearly states that it will give training and technical assistance to nations that are making efforts to control money laundering. Even more interesting is the proposal to develop initiatives to address the problem of foreign government officials who systematically divert public funds and assets to their personal use.

The horror that was 11 September 2001 forced the United States to address the money laundering problem as never before. Barely six weeks later, on 26 October 2001, George Bush signed into law the Money Laundering Abatement and Anti-Terrorist Financing Act of 2001. This formed Title III of the United and Strengthening America by Providing Appropriate Tools Required to Intercept and Obstruct Terrorism ('USA Patriot') Act of 2001. This has been called by the US administration 'the most significant legislation of its kind since 1970' and targets known laundering risks and the future ability to identify and eliminate specific problems as they occur. Key AML provisions are:

- The definition of 'financial institutions' is very broad and includes (amongst others): a currency exchange; an issuer, redeemer or cashier of traveller's cheques, cheques, money orders or similar instruments; an insurance company; a pawnbroker; a loan finance company; a dealer in precious metals, stones or jewels; a travel agency; a licensed sender of money; a business engaged in vehicle sales; persons involved in real estate closings and settlements; casinos; and not forgetting banks.
- Requires financial institutions to establish AML programmes that must include:
  - development of internal policies;
  - designation of a compliance officer;
  - on-going employee training programmes;
  - an independent audit function.
- Allows the United States to apply graduated, proportionate measures against a foreign jurisdiction, foreign financial institution, type of transaction or account that is considered by the Secretary of the Treasury to be 'a primary money laundering concern'.
- Requires special due diligence for correspondent accounts and private banking accounts involving foreign persons or financial institutions.
- Prohibits US financial institutions from establishing correspondent accounts with foreign shell banks that have no physical

presence. The Act also generally requires financial institutions to take reasonable steps to ensure that foreign banks with correspondent accounts do not use those accounts indirectly to provide banking services to a foreign shell bank.

- Requires the Treasury to adopt regulations to encourage cooperation among financial institutions, their regulatory authorities and law enforcement authorities to share information regarding individuals, entities and organizations engaged in terrorist acts or money laundering activities.
- Money laundering crimes are broadened to include foreign corruption offences.
- The Secretary of the Treasury or the Attorney-General may issue a summons or subpoena to any foreign bank that maintains a correspondent account in the United States and request records related to the account (including records held outside the United States). A financial institution covered by the Patriot Act must terminate the correspondent relationship with the foreign bank if the latter does not comply with the request for information.
- The maximum criminal and monetary penalties for money laundering are increased from $100,000 to $1,000,000.
- Requires brokers and dealers to file suspicious activity reports consistent with the requirements applicable to financial institutions.
- Adds to the definition of 'money transmitter' informal value banking systems – such as hawala and hundi.
- Makes the smuggling of bulk cash (above $10,000) into or out of the United States a criminal offence and authorizes the forfeiture of any cash or instruments of the smuggling offence.
- Requires the Secretary of State to establish a watch list identifying persons worldwide who are known to be involved in or suspected of money laundering.

So, now it may become clear just why this piece of legislation was the most significant of its kind since 1970 – not just for the United States, but also on a worldwide basis.

However, the pen of the lawmaker can never overwrite the problems of the real world: the 40 recommendations of the FATF to combat money laundering are probably the best guidelines we have (or are ever likely to have) to restrict the spread of money laundering and thus reduce the influence and power of organized crime gangs. But, and it is a big but, the nation members of the FATF have had difficulty implementing those recommendations on anything approaching a global and consistent basis. The fundamental areas that still do not benefit from anything approaching uniformity and conformity are:

- There is no uniform definition of what money laundering comprises.
- The need for customer identification is different from country to country.
- Some nations do not have any central national office dealing with suspicious reporting.
- Technology is being used to varying degrees – to great effect in Australia and in Italy (to sort out those 30 million suspicious transactions every month). In other member states I have doubts as to whether it is being used at all.
- There are no accepted definitions as to which businesses money laundering regulations apply – thus the differing groups covered in various countries.
- The emphasis and importance attached by governments to the money laundering problem varies widely.

Money launderers seek out and exploit weak points and control gaps. I am certain, for example, that it is known which banks in Luxembourg have never made a suspicious report to the authorities. If washing of criminal funds can be achieved in respectable and mainstream financial centres then the better it is for the washers – and the more they are likely to pay those who assist them for the privilege.

Simultaneously, as we have already noted, launderers are already washing in cyber space: there are various working groups that have been set up by relevant bodies to examine this issue – but hasn't the horse already bolted out of the stable by now whilst we are still trying to build the door, never mind shut it?

COMING CLEAN: PREVENTATIVE STRATEGIES FOR BUSINESS

Omne malum nascens facile opprimitur; inveteratum fit plerumque robustious. ('Every evil in the bud is easily crushed; as it grows older it becomes stronger.')

(CICERO)

It is not possible within this book to describe and comment in depth on the fine detail of anti-money laundering legislation on a country by country basis. Neither is it feasible to outline the various regulations relating to specific professions or industry sectors. However, as money laundering is a global problem there are many principles and guidelines that have universal applicability. In fact, as has been argued, one of the key problems with trying to fight global crime is the lack of coherent worldwide standards. This section highlights:

1. Red Flag warning signs that indicate possible signs of money laundering activity – these are what 'suspicions' are based on.
2. Best practice guidelines that should ensure that your business (and you personally) is doing all that it is possible to do to identify and prevent money laundering.

KYC: WHY YOU MUST KNOW YOUR CUSTOMER

The basic tenet of all anti-money laundering legislation and regulations over the world is the need for customer identification. In essence this means that at the beginning of any financial relationship the accepting business must satisfy themselves that the new customer/client/business partner is who he/she says he/she is and there are no grounds for suspecting any involvement in money laundering and/or criminal activities. Usually this system of control involves taking identification in some prescribed form. Typically documents such as National Identity Cards, passports and driving licences are suggested to be taken and the details contained on them recorded.

KYC red flags

- Beware of new business customers who are reluctant to provide information on their business activities, location and directors.
- Beware of new personal customers who supply incomplete, conflicting or incongruous information when establishing a relationship.
- Be suspicious of customers who do not provide phone or fax numbers or the numbers provided relate to serviced office/ accommodation addresses (see below).
- Beware of camouflage passports (see Chapter 1).
- Beware of diplomatic passports from obscure countries – particularly ones in Africa where such passports can easily be obtained by paying for them (see Chapter 1). Whilst the passport may be genuine (ie genuinely issued after payment), this does not mean that the holder is genuine or the name shown on the passport is the real one. Obviously another aid in this type of scenario is to try and evaluate whether the other details given, together with the appearance/attitude of the person, match whatever diplomatic post he/she is claiming to hold.
- Beware residential addresses provided by applicants that, in reality, are merely mail drop addresses (beware 'Suite' numbers, home addresses in downtown business areas, incomplete addresses). Two quick ways of double-checking are to see if there is a telephone listing for the person at the given address and carry out a credit reference check on that address.

- Do not accept photocopies. You must see the original and copy it yourself. Although obvious it is surprising how many businesses are happy to do business on the strength of photocopies (or faxes). Just because someone has a copy of a passport it does not mean it is theirs – photocopying technology is such that it is easy to put another ID photograph on a document and for it not to be obvious on the resulting copy.
- It is doubtful whether one organization can rely on the due diligence/KYC checking done by another organization. This is very relevant when clients are referred from one party to another. Check what the exact situation is in relation to your business operations. My advice is simple: it is you that will carry the can if and when it all goes wrong and thus relying on what others may or may not have done is foolish.
- The use of International Business Companies, shell companies and the like pose problems for KYC procedures. You may be in the situation where you are presented with a business entity with nominee directors who produce ID that is valid and acceptable. However, if you are aware that these individuals are front men you are not establishing the identity and probity of the beneficial owner(s).
- Be suspicious of businesses that present financial reporting that is at odds with similar sized businesses in the same industry sector.
- Be suspicious if a group of accounts or relationships are opened by foreign nationals who visit your organization together on the same day. A situation that is far more difficult to identify is where multiple accounts or relationships are opened on the same day by a group of foreign nationals at different banks/companies in the same city.
- Suspicions should be aroused if multiple business relationships are opened by an individual using the same address, or different individuals using the same address. Additionally, definite suspicion should result if numerous accounts or relationships are established using variations of the same name.

One of the important trends of the last two or three years is the willingness of some organizations to carry out advanced due diligence enquiries on their prospective customers. Such companies are not necessarily taking what they are told by their customer at face value – because they know that if they do, and what they have been told is patently untrue or incorrect, then severe problems could result. Moreover, such detailed enquiries should be able to validate documents and information provided by the customer together with substantiating claims regarding source of funds. Increasingly it is being viewed by regulatory authorities in sophisticated financial centres that it is not merely enough to know your customer through identification documents but by going behind the information provided to test its validity.

And at the risk of stating the obvious the fundamental precondition of any KYC regime is that if you cannot obtain sufficient detail to establish the customer's identity or you have any suspicions about the background and/or probity of the customer you should not establish a relationship with him or her.

Record it and keep it

Applicable legislation always specifies what period of time internal documents and records must be kept for so that an audit trail of your dealings and involvement with any particular customer can be established. The FATF, for example, recommend that records on customer identification, account files and correspondence should be kept for a minimum of five years after the account is closed or relationship ended.

The importance of record keeping is twofold: not only can transactions and relationships be reconstructed by official investigators, more importantly for you it can (hopefully) be shown that you acted in a legitimate fashion and there was no reason for you to be suspicious. Conversely, if you report your suspicions and they are founded it is vital that you are able to pass on to the relevant body any documentation in your possession.

When should I be suspicious?

One of the most common questions asked is how one defines 'suspicious'. What is suspicious behaviour? What are suspicious transactions? How suspicious do I have to be before I do anything about it? Because each customer relationship and account pattern is different there can never be a definitive listing of 'red flags' of suspicion: you cannot compare the transactional history, to take an extreme example, of an older person's savings account with a day to day office account of a large multinational corporation. Because money laundering moves with technology there may be a new red flag event or trend appearing tomorrow, or even in a nanosecond's time. The only sensible piece of advice is that events must be viewed in the context of the customer and in comparison with similar customers for an effective evaluation to be made as to whether they are suspicious or not.

With those caveats in mind the following list can only be an attempt to suggest the type of events or behaviour that, when judged in their context, can be indicators of money laundering:

Red flags of suspicion

- Of crucial relevance is where the activities of the customer are not consistent with his/her apparent business; for example, a business that claims to trade only on a regional or national basis having a large number of international transfers in and out.
- Be wary of the customer who either issues unusual instructions or comes from outside the normal client catchment area of the business.
- The obvious red flag: large sums in a case. Yes I am still told of mysterious men with large suitcases full of notes turning up unannounced at the offices of banks and lawyers.
- Suspect jurisdictions: the list contained in Appendix I highlights countries and/or areas where organized crime, drug production and lax banking are prevalent. Customers from these areas, or transfers to and from these high risk territories, should raise suspicions.
- Changes in business requirements, or changes in transactions, for a customer should be investigated.
- In many countries there are reporting requirements relating to large sums paid into banks and/or transfers made. The old chestnut – which is still attempted – of numerous transactions made just under the reporting limit remains as relevant as ever.
- A variation on the above is where one customer operates numerous accounts that each continually receive 'small' payments. Then the balances on each of these accounts are transferred to one master account(s).
- There exist a large number of transfers (in and/or out) involving offshore banks, offshore companies or high risk areas. This

advice does not only apply to banks – it can relate to a customer of any business.

- Customers make loans to, or receive loans from, offshore banks.
- Be very wary of any customer, deal or financial transaction that is somehow guaranteed, underwritten or supported by an offshore bank.
- A high volume of cash receipts or payments from a business or individual where such activities are not normally cash intensive.

CREATE EFFECTIVE WRITTEN POLICIES FOR ALL STAFF

There is nothing particularly difficult in this: many business sectors now have a legal or regulatory requirement for written policies to be in place regarding money laundering. Obviously such documents are largely dependent on specific country or industry regimes but common in any written policy should be:

- The overall stance of the organization/firm in respect of money laundering.
- What the organization/firm has to do legally to comply with relevant laws and regulations.
- What money laundering is.
- What you are going to tell your customers in respect of money laundering. (This is actually very important as, in my experience, the vast majority of honest customers have no problems with identification and similar procedures – as long as someone takes the time to explain to them why the organization is doing it.)
- KYC procedures.
- When staff should be suspicious.
- The details of a senior person within the organization who is responsible for all matters relating to money laundering – including being the internal person to whom any suspicions of money laundering are to be reported.
- What legal obligations individual staff members have – and what the penalties are for non-compliance.
- What training the firm/organization is providing to prevent, identify and control money laundering.

Train staff – and keep on training them

In all of the many and, it must be said, varied legislation, regulation and best practice documents issued across the world on money laundering, all of them agree on one thing: the importance of training you and your staff to identify and combat money laundering. You cannot want, expect and need people to be suspicious if you do not explain to them what they must be suspicious about. Simultaneously bad or ineffective training can cause havoc – it has been known for well-meaning but badly trained staff to report a large percentage of both new and existing customers as being suspicious.

Many government bodies issue suitable training material; normally industry regulatory bodies also provide training and educational material. There is a substantial amount of useful and usable material available on the Internet. For example, I would argue that the Royal Canadian Mounted Police booklet entitled *Money Laundering: A preventive guide for small business and currency exchanges in Canada* can be used as basic training material for any business anywhere in the world (see Web Directory for details). There are many videos available from both official and commercial bodies that provide viewer friendly guides to money laundering problems and their prevention. Computer based training and CD ROM packages are also available.

Even if anybody wanted to, training cannot be delivered as tablets of stone. Because if they were, as soon as we had started carving they would be out of date. The money laundering world – which regrettably all commerce is part of – is an ever changing environment. Criminals move very quickly with both the times and the technology. To ensure an effective regime to combat money laundering, and achieve regulatory compliance, you must do likewise by delivering both new and current training material delivered through relevant channels and mechanisms. So what are you waiting for?

Achieving Patriot Act compliance

The US Patriot Act has substantially increased the pressure on all relevant organizations to ensure AML compliance and supervisory procedures. Just as important are two knock-on effects. Firstly, the implications of the Patriot Act are that each regulated organization must implement an AML plan that fits its own situation, and not merely adopt a 'one size fits all' solution. Secondly, it would be foolish for an organization to ignore the Patriot Act because it is based outside the United States. The US authorities have made it clear, on repeated occasions and in numerous different ways, that they will attempt to take action against those institutions and professionals involved in money laundering wherever they are located.

This section provides basic guidelines from which to develop an AML plan both to ensure compliance with the Patriot Act and to ensure best practice in this area. The key elements to consider are:

- Your organization must have a written policy regarding money laundering and compliance with relevant AML rules.
- This written policy must be given to all employees.
- A senior employee must be given the role of AML compliance officer and his/her duties must be described.
- Your organization must state its rules regarding official requests for information on money laundering activity and what it will do concerning sharing of information with other financial institutions.
- Your organization must have (and follow) reasonable procedures to verify the identity of your customers (KYC procedures). In essence you must create an environment where your organization has, in every case, a reasonable belief that it knows the true identity of each customer.
- Based on risk assessment principles you should outline the information you will gather for different types of accounts. This should include consideration of such topics as PEPs (politically exposed persons), high risk jurisdictions and non-cooperative jurisdictions.
- You should describe and follow your organization's policy regarding customers who do not provide the requested information (or have provided misleading or incorrect information). In essence this is simple: you will not open any new account under these circumstances and will close any existing one.
- You must describe the steps you will take to verify the accuracy of information provided to you by customers.
- Your organization should outline the steps it will take to check national and international warning lists of terrorists, money launderers and other criminals.
- You must notify your customers that you intend to verify their identities.

- The Patriot Act (with limited exceptions) prohibits the maintenance of correspondent accounts for unregulated foreign shell banks. The key issue is to make sure that you detect such possible or actual relationships.
- You need to describe – and follow – procedures regarding your organization's stance regarding foreign correspondent accounts.
- You must outline your organization's procedures for 'private banking' accounts particularly regarding proof of identity, source of funds and ascertaining whether such relationships involve PEPs.
- You must have supervisory procedures at the account opening stage.
- You must monitor accounts for suspicious activity. Red flags to be monitored (and acted upon) include but are not limited to:
  - Account patterns of unusual size, volume and type of transactions.
  - Transactions involving 'non-cooperative' jurisdictions.
  - Transactions that lack financial sense, or are out of character for the customer.
  - When the customer has unusual concerns or objections to your AML procedures.
  - The information provided by your customer is false, misleading or downright incorrect.
  - Your customer has a questionable background, or you are made aware (through media reports, for example) of possible or actual criminal, money laundering or terrorist activities.
  - Your customer seems unconcerned about your charges.
  - Your customer appears to be acting for an undisclosed principal but will not disclose information relating to this.
  - Your customer appears to know very little (or absolutely nothing) about the business he/she claims to be active in.
  - Your customer seeks to carry out a large number of transactions in cash and/or currency.
  - Your customer is involved in cash (or equivalent) transactions that appear to be structured to avoid reaching the monetary level at which such transactions must be reported to the relevant authorities.
  - Your customer has multiple accounts in the same name (or different names) and has a high level of inter-account transfers or third party transfers.

  - Your customer is from, has accounts in, or has substantial links to, a FATF non-cooperative country or territory.
  - Your customer's account has a large number of wire transfers to unconnected third parties that appear to bear no relationship to the customer's stated business or personal activities.
  - Your customer has large or frequent (or both) wire transfers to high risk countries or known tax havens.
  - Your customer deposits funds and then requests a wire transfer for the same amount to a third party where there appears to be no business logic for this transaction.
  - Your customer has an account turnover that is vastly in excess of his/her known income and savings/fortune.
- You must outline and then follow your organization's procedures for the internal identification of suspicious transactions and then the process whereby they are reported to the relevant authorities.
- You must describe the procedures for keeping of records.
- You must describe, develop and implement an AML on-going employee training programme or programmes.
- You must describe how you are testing the effectiveness of your AML programme.
- You must monitor the conduct of employees and their accounts.

CARRY OUT COMPLIANCE AND ASSURANCE REVIEWS

The critical test of the success or failure of any organization's response to money laundering rests in its procedures. Compliance and assurance reviews are vital, both as a first step, and then on a regular basis, to review present procedures against such factors as:

- Do staff know what the policies and procedures for preventing and identifying money laundering are?
- Does the firm/organization actually know what is classified as money laundering and what is not?
- What training exists?
- Are there any procedures at all?

'Know your customer' identification procedures

As has been constantly stressed the essence of all money laundering regulations relates to robust procedures and controls to identify the customer (or beneficial owner) and validate the source of funds. The types of checks to be performed are:

- Is there a recognized procedure for obtaining satisfactory evidence of identity for those with whom you do business?
- Is the information provided by potential customers taken at face value or is it validated in any way?
- Are there any 'loopholes' that unscrupulous staff could exploit to introduce business and customers that are involved in money laundering?
- Are you relying (falsely) on money laundering checks or due diligence enquiries carried out by third parties – when you do not even know the depth of such enquiries, or when they were carried out (if at all!)?

Record keeping

Both to preserve possible evidence for any official investigation – and also to ensure that you are covering yourself against any eventuality – it is critical to maintain documents and records for the stipulated time period. This normally applies to both client and transaction records. You need to perform a full health check on this issue – including how easy it is to retrieve records from where they are stored!

Internal reporting mechanisms

For both regulatory compliance and logistical reasons it is imperative that a senior person within the firm or organization has responsibility for money laundering reporting and control. However, it is also essential that this person has the necessary authority and responsibility to discharge his or her duties. Moreover, it must be clearly set out in procedures the reporting line present. Once again you must completely review all relevant matters to guarantee a workable and strong internal reporting mechanism. This can include advanced training and assistance for the senior person given the ultimate responsibility for money laundering matters.

Identifying suspicious transactions

The success of all money laundering legislation hinges on the reporting of suspicious transactions. However, what may be suspicious to one organization is run of the mill to another. The Global Market Place has made the transmission of funds across and around the globe in seconds commonplace. We firmly believe that the only useful intelligence on how to identify suspicious transactions, activities and suchlike is that which is tailored to your specific business operations and operating environment. Reliance on some sort of general list of suspicions will inevitably lead, and has led, to disaster. We look at your business, understand what is commonplace and what is rare, and then provide detailed information on what you and your staff should be looking for to identify possible money laundering.

Reporting suspicions of laundering

Without wishing to be flippant the reporting of suspicions is probably the easiest part: the difficult steps are getting to that stage and if you do report what is your stance with your relevant client. Dependent on the relevant jurisdiction/regulations there are a variety of issues we address including:

- whether to freeze accounts internally;
- whether you can continue to act for the client;
- the danger of 'tipping off' (informing) the client of your suspicions.

Training

At the heart of all money laundering legislation is the total need for training. Not just on a one-off basis – but on an ongoing basis for existing staff, to keep them up to date with new issues, and also of course induction training for newly recruited staff. It needs to be ensured that not only are your staff fully trained, but you also have the necessary records and documents to show that they have been trained and that the training is on-going.

THE FINAL SPIN

He who passively accepts evil is as much involved in it as he who helps to perpetrate it.

(MARTIN LUTHER KING)

Do not drive the tiger from the front door, whilst letting the wolf get in the back.

(HU ZHIDANG, CIRCA 210 BC)

If you sit by the river bank long enough you will be able to watch the bodies of your enemies float past.

(ANCIENT CHINESE PROVERB)

The original edition of this book ended on a grimly pessimistic note. The arguments that I offered in 2000 ran as follows: Global Organized Crime Inc was the ultimate business success story of the 20th century. It had overcome every problem it faced, reinvested its funds and grown to a supremely influential position. It had diversified and embraced new technologies, formed key strategic alliances and kept on identifying new market opportunities. Money laundering by such organized criminals is a corrosive social and business problem that ultimately is a threat to national (and international) security. I also suggested that 'there are certain multinational companies and business sectors that do not give a damn about where their turnover and profits originate'. The proliferation of the money laundering process has been facilitated by a borderless business environment, instant facilities to transfer funds, the extensive utilization of non-financial businesses to launder money, the willingness of professional advisors to be part of the loop and the growth of numerous offshore centres. At that stage I bemoaned the lack of facilities and human resources to tackle the problem within law enforcement combined with the lack of terrestrial uniformity in legislation, regulation and enforcement. All in all I feared a business and financial apocalypse.

Unfortunately my views have not radically altered. The terrorist threat may have supplanted the one posed by organized crime as the most serious risk to both the world and individuals, yet the inherent problems remain. By its very nature the financing of terrorism may not involve the washing of the proceeds of criminal activity – in fact the funds may be completely clean and the laundering is to conceal their ultimate use rather than initial origins. Thus we have both criminal money laundering and terrorist financing, which in at least one of its forms is the complete reversal of the traditional laundering model. Added to this are terrorist financing that involves the proceeds of crime; organized crime groups cooperating with terrorists; and – the most dangerous trend of all – laundering of criminal and terrorist funds outside the banking system (including the use of alternative remittance systems, the Internet, precious metals, gems and anything else that is suitable to be used in this way).

The governments of the world (or rather those that want to tackle these problems) have, quite correctly, introduced new measures or amended their existing AML regulations but still, in the main, they are focusing on the banking and financial arena whereas the launderers (of all persuasions) have moved on to less regulated business sectors.

Yet even within the banking sector it is entirely possible to launder funds successfully: the 9/11 hijackers proved this to be the case (and my view is that they could still do the same today without raising any alarms). However, there is also clear evidence that even in this now highly regulated banking world things are not all they should be (or are presumed to be). In November 2002 the US District Authorities fined Broadway National Bank $4 million for not alerting the US Government to a two-year series of transactions that involved the laundering of $123 million of drug money. The bank (which has assets of only $89 million) was the first US financial institution to be charged with failing to maintain an effective AML programme. Thus, there are various positive points to note about this incident: that the US authorities are becoming very serious about pursuing banks that do not comply with relevant AML regulation; that the transactions in question occurred before the introduction of the Patriot Act; and – the most fundamental point of all – that the dirty dealings at this bank were identified and prosecuted. All of that being said, this case exhibits some factors of great concern. US prosecutors commented that Broadway National Bank 'became a bank of choice for narcotics money launderers and other individuals who wished to shield their financial activities from the government'. One such customer was Alfred Dauber who subsequently pleaded guilty to laundering money for a Colombian drug cartel. His accounts were operated by the bank between 1996 and 1998: on a typical day his employees went to the bank with more than $150,000 in cash (in duffel bags, which make a nice change from a suitcase!). On one day they arrived with more than $660,000 in cash. The funds were then wired immediately to Colombia, Panama and Miami. Bear in mind that Dauber had told the bank that he ran an electronics business. Ultimately he laundered $46 million through the bank and used it because its personnel 'did not ask any questions'. In fact Broadway National Bank was so cash rich that it never sought cash from the Federal Reserve Bank of New York – it actually delivered cash to the Fed (which raises another interesting point: why didn't this sound any alarm bells?).

All of this was before 9/11 though, and things are so different since then. Perhaps no one bothered to tell that to the Royal Bank of Scotland. On 17 December 2002 the Royal Bank of Scotland plc was fined £750,000 by the UK Financial Services Authority for money laundering control failings. And what were these failings? According to the FSA press release, the bank 'failed to obtain sufficient "know your customer" documentation adequately to establish customer identity, or to retain such documentation, in an unacceptable number of new accounts across its retail network in early 2002'. Although the bank discovered these problems itself, it had previously managed to retain insufficient evidence to show that some of its customers were who they claimed to be, and was unable (in some cases) to supply copies or details of documents used to verify identity of customers. Examples quoted were where the bank verified a customer's name but not his or her address, or took documents that were not valid for verifying identity. Remember, also, that all of this happened in the immediate aftermath of 9/11 when the attention of the media was firmly focused on the money laundering aspects of terrorist financing. If a major bank finds it difficult to implement a basic 'Know Your Customer' system, what hope is there?

To paraphrase Tom Peters, how can this problem be made simple enough so that all of you clever people will understand it? Terrorists and organized criminals have no respect whatsoever for laws, regulations, decency or – ultimately – human life. They will do whatever they need to do to wash the proceeds of their criminal acts or, in the case of terrorists, ensure that their funds are available when and where they need them to mount their latest outrage. If they can find a compliant government, head of state, bank, banker, lawyer or accountant to help then their task is made all the easier. If they cannot, then they will make use of whatever is available – whether that is a primitive (but still perfectly legal) alternative remittance system or cutting edge facilities via the Internet or similar electronic means. The history of money laundering by organized criminals (some of which is presented in this book) is that such groups always surmount any obstacles that are erected in their path. Terrorists – with strong unwavering ideologies powering them – must be expected to do the same.

Even after 9/11, as the UK Home Secretary said in 2002, organized criminals are far more organized than national or international authorities and official bodies. My own experience since 9/11 in dealing with various important money laundering related cases proves to me that cooperation between national law enforcement agencies remains woefully inadequate (due to various factors, primary amongst them being turf guardianship and mutual distrust). At a governmental level, particularly in relation to terrorism, some governments (led by the United States) are willing to issue warnings to identify and freeze terrorist funds based on 'suspicions' whilst others want hard proof of the link. Where organized criminals and terrorists act, governments waver and delay. At the time of writing, various parts and aspects of the Patriot Act have yet to be implemented – and more importantly severe reservations have been expressed in the United States and elsewhere as to the general negative economic effects that robust AML regulations might cause. It is argued that AML controls will drive foreign investment out of the US economy, with severe consequences for US citizens.

I have always praised the United States' actions against money laundering. In the final paragraphs of the original edition of *Dirty Dealing*, I observed that 'What is obvious, though, is that if any sensible effective action is taken it will be originated and promoted by the United States Government who are without equal in continuing the fight against money laundering and organized crime.' The Patriot Act (and corresponding legislation in other countries) is a massive step forward. However, at best all of this is at least five years too late; at worst it is just too late. The FATF have been at the forefront of waging the regulatory war against money laundering for a number of years – on occasions being a solitary credible voice in this respect. Nevertheless, I have increasing concerns about their policy concerning non-cooperative countries and territories. My reservations centre not on which jurisdictions are blacklisted, but perhaps more crucially on which are not blacklisted. Why is Egypt listed but no 'rogue states'? Why have Liberia and North Korea never been blacklisted? What about severe organized crime problems combined with corruption and inherent money laundering in various parts of the former Soviet Union?

The inexorable truth is that, for every 9/11 outrage, for each Bali bombing, for any woman or child trafficked for sexual exploitation and for all organized crime activities, somewhere in the process money is laundered in the dirty washing cycle. My fears of an incipient business and financial apocalypse were incorrect. We are already in the eye of that storm: the apocalypse is now.

APPENDIX I: COUNTRY INDEX

Whilst there is a tremendous amount of information about money laundering, organized crime and terrorism, it is obviously very difficult to produce definitive statistics as to the true scale of the problem. However, what becomes clear both when this section was compiled and, hopefully, when you read it is that very few countries or geographical regions remain untouched by the problem. What also becomes noticeable is that although offshore financial centres obviously provide loopholes for launderers to exploit there still exist many onshore and more mainstream locations that can be, and are being, used for the washing of criminally obtained funds.

The purpose of this section is not merely to prove the universal and corrosive influence and infiltration of criminal activity but more importantly to provide information on countries:

- that you may be intending to do business with;
- that you are doing business with already;
- where you are considering setting up an office/facility;
- where you are establishing customer relationships with individuals who live there, have no previous experience of dealing with those countries – and don't know the inherent problems that exist there.

The moral of the story is not however to adopt a Howard Hughes stance and become a recluse, not doing business with anybody from anywhere; rather forewarned is forearmed – by being cognizant of the risks that you run you should be able to manage, control and mitigate them. All of the information here, whilst country specific, is of a generalized nature: to control your money laundering risks you need to carry out specific and focused background research/due diligence enquiries on the individual(s) and/or companies you are contemplating getting into bed with.

In compiling this section attention has been paid to the various interlinked factors that can give rise to money laundering problems. These include:

- major drug producers, either as producing countries or as transit points;
- major problems with organized crime, of either a domestic or transnational nature;
- loosely regulated offshore centres;
- countries where corruption is a significant problem;
- countries and/or areas where human trafficking is prevalent.

Also highlighted are countries where information is hard to come by and countries where there are no significant money laundering problems. Additionally, at the end of this appendix are complete listings, together with analysis, of the blacklists of non-cooperative countries and territories issued by the FATF since June 2000.

The risks outlined regarding money laundering in major financial centres are, by their very nature, something of a tautology – it is almost impossible to have a domestic or regional financial centre without the scourge of money laundering being present. Equally evident is the fact that the most attractive centres for money launderers to aim for, usually in the integration stage of the process, are the major respected financial centres of the world.

Afghanistan

Major drug producer

Prior to the removal of the Taliban, Afghanistan was one of the largest producers of opium in the world (major production regions are Helmand, Kandahor, Uruzgan and Nangarhar provinces). This provided a substantial source of revenue and influence to the producers. However, because the banking system had effectively been destroyed by political upheaval the country was not used by domestic (or international) money launderers. Regrettably the situation in the post-Taliban era remains very much unchanged: the opium harvest in 2002 is estimated as being between 3,500 and 4,000 tons, which is close to the record crop of 4,500 tons in 1999. This production then causes substantial problems in neighbouring countries that are used as transit routes to Western markets. The military action to remove Al-Qaida has obviously been a success in Afganistan itself, but as a result has scattered the terrorists and forced them to revert to their cell-like structure in numerous other countries across the world.

Albania

Major organized crime problems
Money laundering is a widespread problem as anti-money laundering measures are not enforced by banks. Remember also that this is the country that was nearly destroyed by a series of fraudulent pyramid schemes. Apart from ruthless domestic organized crime groups that specialize in human trafficking between Albania and Italy, the country also plays hosts to criminals from Macedonia, Italy, Greece and Turkey. Governmental enforcement is weak in relevant areas. Albania is also a major exporter of organized crime problems to Western Europe (see Chapter 1). The 2002 US Department of State report on human trafficking rates Albania at Tier 2 (a country not in compliance with minimum standards for elimination of trafficking but making significant efforts). The report states that Albania is both a source and transit country for women and girls trafficked for sexual exploitation to Italy, Greece, Belgium, France and the Netherlands. Young boys are also apparently trafficked from Albania to work as beggars in Italy and Greece. Ranked 81st equal out of 102 (where 102 is the worst) of countries where corruption is perceived as a key problem in a survey by Transparency International in 2002.

Andorra

As at April 2002 Andorra was classified as being an 'uncooperative tax haven' by the OECD because of its lack of commitment to the specified concepts of transparency and effective exchange of information.

Anguilla

Possible up-and-coming money laundering centre
The money laundering risks appear to be small at present but because of development of offshore facilities this location has the potential to pose major problems in the future. This prediction, however, must be balanced against the island's position as a United Kingdom overseas territory. This status carries with it increasing pressure from the British Government for such territories to clean up their acts. International Business Companies are available that can be incorporated within minutes: all you need is a minimum of one director (can be a nominee); no taxes; bearer shares; no exchange control; beneficial owners not disclosed to the authorities.

Antigua

Is possibly one of the most enticing Caribbean locations for money launderers – subject to various official warnings, particularly as a result of the failure of the European Union Bank in 1997. IBCs are available and there is no disclosure of beneficial ownership. Until fairly recently there was no anti-money laundering legislation, but because of international pressure the situation appears to be improving. A US financial advisory warning on doing business with Antigua was lifted in 2001.

Argentina

As it is an important financial centre with a mature banking system, Argentina increasingly risks becoming involved in the flow of funds from Colombia and other similar South American countries. Estimates put the figure laundered each year at $6 billion. The situation has been exacerbated by the financial crisis of 2002. Ranked 70th out of 102 (where 102 is the worst) of countries where corruption is perceived as a key problem in a survey by Transparency International in 2002. Member of the FATF.

Armenia

Major organized crime problems
Armed organized crime has a heavy presence; the grey economy is massive; public corruption is widespread. The situation is made worse

by high unemployment, low salaries and a large underground economy. However, as Armenia is not a major international financial centre, the problems are predominantly domestic ones. Ranked 80th equal out of 99 (where 99 is the worst) of countries where corruption is perceived as a key problem in a survey by Transparency International in 1999 but not surveyed in the 2002 report.

Aruba

The US Government position is that Aruba is a major drug producing and/or transit country but it has either cooperated fully with the United States or taken its own steps to comply with the 1988 UN Drug Convention. Aruba has a major drug transit problem from South America to Europe due to its good transport links by air and its proximity to Colombia and Venezuela. A free trade zone and offshore industry facilitates money laundering. The offshore industry has up to 20 financial institutions. There are no problems with organized crime internally as such, but obvious risks of outside infiltration by organized crime groups because of offshore status and aspirations. Aruba is part of the Kingdom of the Netherlands and thus a member of the FATF. Although it has a substantial offshore industry Aruba is perceived as being a location where anti-money laundering regulations are being taken and applied seriously.

Australia

One of the countries that has done most work both to control and to measure money laundering activity. Nevertheless because of the country's strong regional presence it has obvious attractions to money launderers. The Bali terrorist outrage in 2002 would suggest that Australia will be particularly vigilant in identifying terrorist funds in the country; however, in November 2002 an Australian bank warned that identity frauds at Sydney banks pointed to the use of those banks as channels for financing terrorism. Member of the FATF. See also Appendix II: Web directory for relevant Web sites.

Austria

Member of the FATF and has significantly reduced the risks of money laundering by the removal of Sparbuch accounts (see Chapter 1).

However, the Austrian banking system has been utilized in the past by such groups as the Italian Mafia, the Stasi of East Germany and more recently Eastern European criminals. Certainly there has been a problem with joint venture companies and Eastern European money: so much so that I was told that after the initial flood of funds following the fall of communism many banks would no longer open accounts for Russian clients. Recent cases dealt with by Proximal Consulting suggest that Vienna is still a popular location for fraudsters to use when opening a bank account or incorporating a company, thus laundering the proceeds of crime through the city. Member of the FATF.

Azerbaijan

Major organized crime problems
A strong organized crime presence, weak legal system and endemic corruption are present in Azerbaijan. The country does not have any anti-money laundering legislation but the problems are mostly domestic and specifically related to tax evasion. Ranked 95th out of 102 (where 102 is the worst) of countries where corruption is perceived as a key problem in a survey by Transparency International in 2002.

Bahamas

Named by FATF as 'non-cooperative' in June 2000; removed in June 2001
The US Government considers the Bahamas to be a major drug producing and/or transit country but it has either cooperated fully with the United States or taken its own steps to comply with the 1988 UN Drug Convention. Because of its strategic location between Colombia and the United States it is an important drugs transit point. Moreover the Bahamas is the fifth largest offshore centre in the world and thus a target for money launderers. There are very few domestic organized crime problems *per se* but the obvious danger is external organized crime groups making use of the offshore financial centre. There are strong anti-money laundering regulations, which means that although financial institutions are strictly regulated the loophole is International Business Corporations, of which there may be 100,000.

Belarus

A country that already exhibits major factors that give rise to concern. The country has a vast stockpile of former USSR arms and is engaged in illegal arms trading to rogue nations and groups (Tajikistan and then on to Afghanistan, Angola, Algeria and Sudan). Belarus is also a conduit for arms produced by other CIS countries to Iraq. The country is ruled as a virtual dictatorship by Alyaksandr Lukashenka: transparency in politics and business is virtually non-existent partly because of the Soviet legacy of secrecy that still prevails. The 2002 US Department of State report on human trafficking rates Belarus at Tier 3 (a country not in compliance with minimum standards for elimination of trafficking and not making significant efforts). The report states that Belarus is a country of origin and transit for women and girls trafficked for sexual exploitation to a wide variety of end destinations (Russia, Ukraine, Lithuania, Germany, Israel, Poland, Czech Republic, Turkey, Cyprus, Greece, Hungary and former Yugoslavia).

Belgium

Belgium, and more specifically Brussels, is an attractive centre for criminals because of a variety of factors: the city is a strong financial centre; there is an abnormally high number of wealthy individuals because of the strong diplomatic presence; in some areas of financial operations regulations need to be strengthened (reinsurance for instance). There is reliable evidence of penetration by Russian and other Eastern European organized crime groups particularly in systematic theft and illegal exportation of high value automobiles. Every stolen BMW, Mercedes or other prestigious car marque ends up being converted into the cash that pays for drug shipments from Uzbekistan, Afghanistan and Tajikistan. Additional information suggests that Hong Kong/Chinese Triads are active in fraud, drugs and prostitution (including human trafficking). The country is a member of the FATF.

Belize

The US Government's position is that Belize is a major drug producing and/or transit country but it has either cooperated fully with the United States or taken its own steps to comply with the 1988 UN Drug Convention. It is a major transit point for drugs entering the United States from Colombia. Whilst a small player in the offshore scene, Belize does offer offshore banking licences. Of great concern is the possible infiltration by global organized crime groups through the offshore sector. The Government have implemented anti-money laundering laws but the obvious high risk area is the offshore sector where International Business Companies are available – approximately 11,000 in existence: can be incorporated within 24 hours; only one director is required who can be a nominee; bearer shares available; no exchange control; no disclosure of beneficial owners. Belize has escaped being termed a FATF non-cooperative territory because the Government took action as a result of the OECD labelling the country a 'tax haven'.

Bermuda

Bermuda is a substantial offshore centre: after London and New York, it has the highest level of insurance premium inflow. Exempt companies are available but these do not have bearer shares, and effectively beneficial owners are known but not in the public domain.

Bolivia

Major drug producer
The US Government position is that Bolivia is a major drug producing and/or transit country but it has either cooperated fully with the United States or taken its own steps to comply with the 1988 UN Drug Convention. The country is the world's third largest producer of coca leaves. Drugs are reckoned to generate $1 billion – which is critical as the country's GDP is only $8 billion. Fears are now surfacing about the involvement of the Italian Mafia in Bolivia. Bolivia was ranked 89th equal out of 102 (where 102 is the worst) of countries where corruption is perceived as a key problem in a survey by Transparency International in 2002. As the country was rated at 80th in 1999, the situation regarding corruption in the country is perceived as worsening.

Brazil

Drugs and money laundering problems are exacerbated by poverty in the country and proximity to Colombia and other 'problem' South American countries. Money laundering is becoming a larger problem due to inroads made into the banking and business environments by drug gangs from other South American countries. It is also alleged that important transnational crime groups have established footholds in Rio because of the general chaotic state of the country. Amongst those cited as being present are Italian Mafias, Colombians, Russians, Nigerians and Japanese. The Brazilian Government is showing a strong commitment to the problem – presumably as they have the rather dubious model of Colombia to observe as to what happens when there is no resistance to organized crime. In 2000, a 1,600-page report by a congressional commission recommended that charges be brought against 827 people. These include judges, mayors, federal congressmen and state legislators. Between 1992 and 1998, $60 billion worth of drugs money passed through Brazil from Bolivia, Colombia and Paraguay. The commission discovered not only drugs related money laundering but also arms smuggling, cargo theft and tax evasion. Member of the FATF.

Bulgaria

Major organized crime problems
High level of national organized crime activity – credited with almost bankrupting the economy; money laundering flows from that activity. Corruption is widespread; tax evasion, protection rackets, prostitution, software and CD counterfeiting, VAT related offences, murder and racketeering are almost endemic. Probably the only good thing is that whilst some Bulgarian gangs have ventured outside the country the warfare between gangs is so intense that they probably have more than enough to occupy themselves with inside the country. Conversely of course if softer targets can be found in other countries expect migration of the problems particularly as lax security (and corruption) at Bulgarian airports provides drug groups a gateway into Europe, particularly for cocaine. A report released in November 2001 by the Bulgarian National Service for the Fight against Organized Crime stated that more than 100 armed gangs operate in the country, each with approximately 500 members. The chilling footnote to this estimation is that these figures do not include criminal activity in Sofia. These groups are in contact with other criminals in Europe and South America. Ninety-four per cent of the members of these groups are Bulgarian, but also included are Russians, Turks, Albanians and Arabs.

Burma (Myanmar)

Named by FATF as 'non-cooperative' in June 2001; remained blacklisted as at February 2003
Major drug producer

The country is the world's second largest producer of opium. Money laundering problems are exacerbated by a cash-based economy, and whilst anti-money laundering legislation exists it is not enforced. Details are sketchy but because of the major drug producing levels it must be suspected that domestic money laundering is substantial. Commentary suggests that casinos on the country's borders are used for money laundering, as these establishments are entry points to the international financial system. The Government actively encourages drug groups to invest their profits in legitimate enterprises, and it is rumoured that the Government itself is involved in drug trafficking. There is no problem with international organized crime as such, but domestic groups are obviously present as part of the drug production and distribution culture.

The Burmese Government cease-fire agreements with drug groups in various areas (particularly the Shan State) have in effect legitimized the production of narcotics and the resultant money laundering – in fact the Government have encouraged such groups to launder funds through investments in hotels and construction enterprises. Thus the laundering of drugs cash is a significant factor in the Burmese economy – appearing in major infrastructure projects, banks, airlines and property. In fact some drugs money has been used to supplement government funding of development projects. This environment is further worsened by rumours that government and/or army officials are heavily involved in drug production, or are corruptible to allow others to engage in such businesses without constraint.

Cambodia

Cambodia's law enforcement bodies are chronically under-resourced and lack even basic relevant training. The long history of internal disputes means that the country has endemic corruption problems, which are further exacerbated by low levels of pay for civil servants, a weak judicial system and a perception that justice can be 'bought'. However, such corruption and money laundering are merely two difficulties in a country that is poor, fragile and developing. One of the most difficult issues is that this state of affairs makes the country particularly vulnerable to organized crime groups, especially bearing in mind the country's position as a transit country for heroin from the Golden Triangle.

Canada

Canada has had weak anti-money laundering laws that have led to the country being perceived as a 'soft touch' for organized criminals. Research has suggested that citizens of Canada are exposed to criminal acts each year totalling up to $30 billion. The Royal Canadian Mounted Police estimate that at least C $17 million is laundered per annum. Certainly evidence (and court cases) confirms that probably every organized criminal group is active in the country: Russians, Colombians, Chinese, the Italian Mafia, to name but a few. Additionally and most prevalent in Canada are the criminal activities of motorcycle gangs. The good news is that (albeit slightly late) the Canadian authorities are moving against such operations with a vengeance. Member of the FATF.

Cayman Islands

Named by FATF as 'non-cooperative' in June 2000; removed in June 2001
Exempt companies allowed that can be formed within three to five days; minimum of one director; bearer shares available; no exchange control; no disclosure of beneficial owners. Featured heavily in the Enron debacle because of the use of offshore corporations registered here.

Chile

Possible up-and-coming money laundering centre
Another potential South American flashpoint – the country's inadequate laws have facilitated attempts by Mexican drug cartels to utilize the country as a new laundering base through the banking system or construction projects. The Government appears to be taking the problem seriously.

China

China has a complete range of organized crime groups and escalating crime rates together with increasing domestic drug problems. Official corruption is widespread, but greater effort is being focused on money laundering, one reason being that the Government views such activities as one way of simultaneously tackling corruption.

Colombia

Major drug producer/major organized crime problems

One of the key countries – if not still the key one – that is responsible for the dirty money generated by narco-crime that needs to be washed elsewhere in the world, preferably into clean dollars. Major producer of cocaine, now trying to muscle in on the US heroin market. As with any other successful global business, the drug cartels are attempting dramatically to increase their market share by selling a good product (high purity) and simultaneously undercutting the competition on price. What else can be said about Colombia – apart from that things may be getting ever so slightly better? The governmental position is to introduce strong anti-drug initiatives but the drug cartels are very strong, heavily armed and supremely organized. The United States is pouring money and resources into the country (it gave Colombia more than $2 billion over the three years prior to 2002 and was intending to pay about another $500 million in 2002): this position led to fears before 9/11 that the United States was being sucked into a situation it would find difficult to get out of. Somewhat ironically, in late September 2002 almost 80 Colombian police officers including a former high level anti-drug official were arrested and accused of stealing more than US $2 million of aid provided by the United States to combat the narcotics trade. The aid money was intended to pay for counter-drug operations but was spent on personal expenses. One unfortunate consequence of the sustained action against drug producers in Colombia is that the problems have migrated to nearby countries where enforcement action is currently weaker. Colombia is now also regarded as the source of the world's finest counterfeit currency. This has developed as an offshoot of the cocaine trade, as the demand for fake dollars to buy coca base from easily duped farmers has encouraged the growth of counterfeit workshops. These are particularly prevalent in the agricultural region that surrounds the city of Cali. Colombia was ranked 72nd equal out of 99 (where 99 is the worst) of countries where corruption is perceived as a key problem in a survey by Transparency International in 1999, but is not included in the 2002 survey.

Cook Islands

Named by FATF as 'non-cooperative' in June 2000; remained on blacklist at February 2003

These South Pacific islands are causing concern because of their offshore industry, which provides banks, insurance companies, trusts and IBCs. Information has surfaced that suggests penetration of the sector by Russian organized crime groups. Additionally services are promoted via the Internet. In June 2000 the FATF concluded that the Government had no relevant information on approximately 1,200 international companies it had registered. More worryingly seven offshore banks were registered that could take deposits from the public but did not identify customers or keep their records. Whilst the Cook Islands have made progress on AML matters, deficiencies still exist.

Costa Rica

A major transit point for drugs entering the United States from Colombia. Money laundering is ever present.

Côte d'Ivoire

Possible up-and-coming money laundering centre
Whilst not an offshore financial centre Côte d'Ivoire is an important regional financial centre with money laundering problems. Ranked 75th equal out of 99 (where 99 is the worst) of countries where corruption is perceived as a key problem in a survey by Transparency International in 1999 (was not included in the 2002 survey).

Cyberspace

The location that simultaneously brings together all of the terrestrial restrictions detailed here and unequivocally does away with them. Every service and facility imaginable (and some that probably aren't) to facilitate money laundering is available – from anonymous accounts and false identification documents to online gambling. Cuts across all jurisdictions with little (if any) regulation present. All services and facilities can be accessed from any PC anywhere in the world. Funds can be transferred anywhere at the click of a mouse. Know Your Customer guidelines go out the window – even if they are enforced, financial relationships set up in cyberspace never have to be inconvenienced by face to face meetings. You can be anybody you want to be and set up a dazzling portfolio of anonymous vehicles to disguise the source of funds in virtually any way you want. Integrate the awesome possibilities of technology with the anonymity offered by some of the more 'liberal' offshore locations listed here and I doubt you will ever be found out. Invest in stock, gamble, make purchases – you name it, it's all here.

Cyprus

Because of its location and business environment, Cyprus is an ideal location for meetings of drug cartels to discuss business. No International Business Companies; no bearer shares; nominee directors are permitted; but beneficial owners are disclosed.

Czech Republic

The country is a narcotics trans-shipment route from the Balkans, Middle East, South America and South Asia. The freedoms created by the dismantling of communism have unfortunately created a climate where organized crime (and not solely that from other former Eastern Bloc countries) can flourish. Crime groups include Russians, Ukrainians, Chechens and Vietnamese. The Vietnamese criminals were the first to flood in after the fall of communism and are involved in smuggling, human trafficking, money laundering, cigarette smuggling, drugs and extortion. The number of Russians in the country is unofficially estimated as being 20,000. They are centred on Prague and Karlovy Vary (Spa Centre). Rumours abound that hotels and prime property in Karlovy Vary are owned and operated by Russian criminals. Illegal arms dealing by Czech citizens is a further problem, as is corruption of MPs. In October 2002 an EU report expressed serious concerns about corruption and economic crime.

Denmark

No significant money laundering problems
In the 1999 Transparency International Survey, Denmark holds the honour of being perceived as the least corrupt country in the world. In the 2002 survey it was named the second least corrupt country. Almost certainly one of the very few major countries in the world that seems to be free of money laundering difficulties caused by international crime groups whilst simultaneously taking such a threat seriously and implementing sensible precautionary controls. Member of the FATF.

Dominica

Named by FATF as 'non-cooperative' in June 2000; removed in October 2002
CIA information confirms that Dominica is a trans-shipment point for narcotics destined for the United States and Europe. Various AML regulations have been introduced since 2000 but doubts still remain in relation to international mutual legal assistance requests.

Dominican Republic

The Dominican Republic is a major trans-shipment point for drugs from Colombia on their way to the United States with a high level of money laundering present. The country does not have a coordinated policy to tackle money laundering. This situation is exacerbated by the fact that over 1 million Dominicans live in the United States: it is suspected that money is sent back to their homeland to be laundered. Figures of $100 million per month cleaned in this way have been quoted.

Ecuador

The US Government's position in 1999 was that Ecuador is a major drug producing and/or transit country but it has either cooperated fully with the United States or taken its own steps to comply with the 1988 UN Drug Convention. As for money laundering, with an economy that has been teetering on the brink of collapse the most logical route for money is out of the country rather than in; but that of course provides opportunities for drug gangs from Peru and Colombia. Scored 82nd equal out of 99 (where 99 is the worst) of countries where corruption is perceived as a key problem in a survey by Transparency International in 1999 (was not included in the 2002 survey).

Egypt

Named by FATF as 'non-cooperative' in June 2001; remained blacklisted as at February 2003
In the original edition of *Dirty Dealing* I commented that 'Egypt is actually in a slightly strange situation in that the country's authorities seem to be continually drawing attention to its money laundering problems.' In June 2001 Egypt was blacklisted by the FATF but has now made significant progress in combating money laundering. The

situation is exacerbated by suspected links within the country to Islamic terrorists. The country has big opium and marijuana plantations in remote areas. Egypt is also a transit point for heroin from Asia on its way to the United States and Europe.

El Salvador

A major transit point for drugs entering the United States from Colombia. Money laundering threats grow because of a vibrant banking system that is outward facing.

Ethiopia

No significant money laundering problems
Whilst not wishing to commit heresy, this is a country so desperate that money from any source would be welcome, as long as it was solely utilized to alleviate the human suffering that appears to be ever present.

Fiji

Possible up-and-coming money laundering centre
Risks are present from Nigerian organized crime groups and Russian gangs.

Finland

No significant money laundering problems
In the 2002 Transparency International Survey, Finland holds the honour of first prize: being perceived as the least corrupt country in the world. Nevertheless the country (or more specifically Helsinki) faces some problems from Russian organized crime groups. Finland's historical ties with Russia through St Petersburg, and the country's recent self-promotion as the portal to the former Eastern Bloc, may yet cause problems. Member of the FATF.

Former Yugoslavia

Major organized crime problems

Internal strife and warfare have created an ideal environment for the former Yugoslavia to be exploited by, amongst others, Russian organized criminal groups. Problems include human trafficking of women into prostitution in the West; arms; fuel; drugs; and the black market. Scored 90th equal out of 99 (where 99 is the worst) of countries where corruption is perceived as a key problem in a survey by Transparency International in 1999 (not included in 2002 survey).

France

The French Government has taken a very strong line on what action should be taken against non-compliant offshore financial centres. This is admirable, but slightly ironic, considering the never ending Elf scandal. The ramifications from the 'fees' paid by the oil giant continue to reverberate, and if press reporting is believed implicate French Government ministers, African heads of state and a supporting cast of thousands. In France itself, Russian and other Eastern European crime groups (Georgians, Chechens and Kazaks) favour property in the South of France. Whilst there they engage in kidnapping, fraud, money laundering, contract killing, drugs and extortion. The French financial system is very strong, but links with former African colonies should not be dismissed. Member of the FATF.

Germany

Because of its geographical position and the former control of East Germany by the Soviet Bloc, Germany has considerable problems with Russian and other Eastern European crime gangs. They are involved in large scale car thefts and subsequent illegal exportation; drugs; the sex trade (including human trafficking); illegal arms trading; and money laundering. Because of its border with Poland, Germany has found itself with a popular route for the transportation of arms, drugs and nuclear material. German TV documentaries delight in running programmes giving graphic details of the sex business that has developed under the auspices of organized crime on the borders with the former Eastern Bloc. Germany also has a strong internationally focused financial centre and thus is a money laundering target. The country is a member of the FATF.

Gibraltar

Gibraltar is both a major entry point for drugs into mainland Europe and an offshore centre. As a Dependent Territory of the United Kingdom it could be expected that money laundering control is a priority. However, various Spanish claims persist that Gibraltar is a haven for money laundering.

Greece

Whilst Greece is not a major international financial centre, it has domestic problems because of Russian and Albanian criminal groups based in the country. These groups are involved in drug trafficking, trafficking in women and children, arms smuggling, blackmailing and illegal gambling activity. Key problem areas are casinos and cross-border movement of illicit currency. Greece was rated 44th out of 102 (where 102 is the worst) of countries where corruption is perceived as a key problem in a survey by Transparency International in 2002. Member of the FATF.

Grenada

Possible up-and-coming money laundering centre
Named by FATF as 'non-cooperative' in September 2001; removed from the blacklist in February 2003
In the original edition of this book, written in early 2000, I wrote of Grenada: 'Possibly top of the list of up-and-coming locations: Grenada has ventured into the offshore world since 1996. The services and products offered are comprehensive: Grenada has International Business Companies (almost 1,000); offshore banking licences (over 30); and Internet gaming licences. Even more attractive may be that for $40,000 a family of five can purchase economic citizenship and at the same time change their names. Remember where you read it first.'

The FATF blacklisted Grenada in June 2001 because Grenadian supervisory authorities had inadequate access to customer account information and inadequate authority to cooperate with foreign counterparts. Additionally Grenadian financial institutions did not have adequate qualification requirements for owners of financial institutions. As at the end of 2002, whilst significant progress has been made, the FATF still had concerns about whether adequate resources are devoted to Grenada's new anti-money laundering bodies and about the limitations on cooperation with foreign regulators. Grenada was taken off the blacklist in February 2003 as it had implemented significant reforms to its AML system.

Guatemala

Named by FATF as 'non-cooperative' in June 2001; remained blacklisted as at February 2003

The country is a major transit point for drugs from Colombia, which in turn generates money laundering. The problem isn't helped by corrupt public officials. Organized crime is also an import from Colombia. The Government's position was willing but weak and confused, with laws containing secrecy provisions and money laundering as a criminal offence only relating to narcotics violations. Whilst these legal deficiencies have been resolved, the FATF (as at the end of 2002) still have doubts about adequate licensing procedures for offshore banks.

Guernsey

A pre-eminent respectable offshore centre, which by its very nature experiences problems with money laundering.

Haiti

Possible up-and-coming money laundering centre

Widespread corruption, economic and social decline, and lack of governmental action have all contributed to both drug trafficking and money laundering.

Honduras

A major transit point for drugs entering the United States from Colombia. Rated 94th out of 99 (where 99 is the worst) of countries where corruption is perceived as a key problem in a survey by Transparency International in 1999 (was not included in 2002 survey).

Hong Kong

Hong Kong is an obvious target for money launderers, particularly for the washing of proceeds from the sale of illegal drugs. A variety of factors contributes towards the importance of Hong Kong as a money laundering target:

- the strength and high level of infiltration of Chinese organized crime groups;
- a low tax system;
- acting for China as its offshore banking centre;
- sophisticated financial environment and infrastructure;
- the absence of any currency and exchange controls;
- the presence of various offshore company structures that can be used by non-residents.

Money laundering in Hong Kong extends to all serious crime. All banking and financial institutions must take customer identifications, and report suspicious transactions to a central unit. However, because of the size and complexity of Hong Kong's financial world there still remain problems – exhibited by:

- the relatively low level of suspicious reports – the vast majority of which come from banks, with very few coming from insurers or professional advisors like solicitors and accountants;
- the opening of accounts with forged documents;
- the operation of cash cleansing through bureaux de change and money remitters.

Member of the FATF – which in turn raises interesting questions about the position of China.

Hungary

Major organized crime problems
Named by FATF as 'non-cooperative' in June 2001; removed in June 2002
Budapest is a magnet for many transnational organized criminal groups, and there is also the influence of domestic groups. Various criminal activities are prevalent: for example, in December 2002 a CD piracy ring was smashed that had produced counterfeit product worth US $0.28 million. The country has however made significant progress in AML matters, including the abolition of the Hungarian version of Sparbuch accounts.

Iceland

No significant money laundering problems

Iceland was rated 3rd out of 102 (where 102 is the worst) of countries where corruption is perceived as a key problem in a survey by Transparency International in 2002. Member of the FATF.

India

Money laundering is a growing problem in India but is mainly confined to domestic activities that are far from being only drugs related: fraud, corruption and smuggling are obvious additional ones. The laundering dynamic is exacerbated and facilitated by the hawala alternative remittance systems. In 1998 (the latest available reliable figures) the amount of money thought to be in India's hawala system was estimated at $680 billion. The legal position in India in relation to money laundering is also confused. India scored 71st out of 102 (where 102 is the worst) of countries where corruption is perceived as a key problem in a survey by Transparency International in 2002.

Indonesia

Named by FATF as 'non-cooperative' in June 2001; remained blacklisted as at February 2003
Indonesia previously lacked comprehensive anti-money laundering legislation, which was a critical defect because the country's economy is particularly vulnerable to money laundering. The reasons for this are:

- the geographical location of Indonesia;
- strict banking secrecy;
- high levels of corruption;
- various banking scandals including fraudulent schemes.

Historically, most money laundering in Indonesia has related to domestic narcotics trafficking and the proceeds of corruption. The country was rated 96th out of 102 (where 102 is the worst) of countries where corruption is perceived as a key problem in a survey by Transparency International in 2002. This is actually a minor improvement on the 1999 rating, where the country came 96th out of 99.

Iran

Hard information difficult to obtain
Whilst the death penalty exists in relation to drugs and over 1,000 people have been executed for this reason since 1989, the country remains a significant route for getting drugs to Europe from Afghanistan. The country's economy is predominantly cash based but it would require a large stretch of the imagination to see the country becoming attractive to international money launderers. The primary reason has been because of the breakdown in relationships between the country and the United States. Proclaimed a key part of the 'axis of evil' by the United States in 2002, with Iraq and North Korea.

Iraq

Hard information difficult to obtain
With the world breathing down its neck, a chronically weak currency, a thriving black market in dollars and severe problems with the United States and its Western allies, although little information is available, Iraq is another one of those places that you can't see cropping up on a list of favourite places to launder money. This situation seems unlikely to change, owing to sanctions against Iraq, and thus there is the difficulty (but not impossibility) of integrating funds that originate from the country into the world's banking system.

Ireland

The country has domestic money laundering problems; but the offshore financial centre appears to have few official reported problems with money laundering. However, my professional experiences over the last few years suggest that an Irish registered company (with nominee directors) is a popular method used by both launderers and fraudsters as part of a global *modus operandi*. Member of the FATF.

Isle of Man

The island has a vibrant offshore industry and is obviously a target for money launderers. Particularly attractive is the Exempt Company where the ultimate beneficial owner need not be disclosed. Whilst the Isle of Man is extremely vigilant in its attempts to counter money laundering and maintain its reputation, gaps that can be exploited (and are being) still exist.

Israel

Named by FATF as 'non-cooperative' in June 2000; removed in June 2002
Israel's entry in the first edition of this book read: 'There is key penetration of criminal structures by Russian organized crime groups. The biggest problem is that there still exist no anti-money laundering laws. Thus it is almost impossible to estimate the level of money laundering: the best guess is that it is substantial.' Under pressure from the FATF, Israel enacted the Prohibition on Money Laundering law on 2 August 2000, which criminalized money laundering together with addressing customer identification, record keeping and reporting requirements. Further regulations have followed for stock exchanges, portfolio managers, insurance companies and the postal bank.

Italy

Major organized crime problems
The old alliances remain: if there is any saving grace on an international basis it is that the majority of money laundering problems in the country are domestic ones. That said, there is increasing evidence that the Italian Mafia are creating strategic alliances with other international organized crime groups together with successfully exploiting new channels such as Internet stock trading. The dangers posed by Italy are concerned with the exportation of problems rather than the country necessarily being utilized as a money laundering centre by outsiders. Ironically (or perhaps not, on reflection), Italy has one of the most sophisticated computer systems to identify suspicious transactions. Italy was rated 31st out of 102 (where 102 is the worst) of countries where corruption is perceived as a key problem in a survey by Transparency International in 2002. Member of the FATF.

Japan

Japan has significant domestic problems with the Yakuza who are alleged to have in excess of 100,000 members. They were key factors in the collapse of various major Japanese banks due to the somewhat irregular loan arrangements that were set up with them. First-hand evidence from my own research confirms that until fairly recently Japanese banks accepted all kinds of funds without questioning their provenance. Because Japan is a major financial centre, any weaknesses in the country's banking systems mean that the proceeds of domestic crime have an easy entry point into the world's banking system – particularly that of the United States. The country is a member of the FATF.

Jersey

Jersey is a major offshore financial centre offering sophisticated financial products, and thus must be a target for money launderers in later stages of the process. However, the desire to maintain a good reputation combined with effective laws will, hopefully, ensure that the problems are controlled.

Jordan

No significant money laundering problems
Whilst intelligence is sketchy, what there is suggests there is no relevant problem with international money laundering.

Kazakhstan

Major organized crime problems
The country is on the transit route of drugs from Afghanistan and Pakistan together with being an opium producer itself. Widespread and endemic corruption doesn't help matters, and neither does the country's fairly advanced financial services environment. The country has, however, criminalized money laundering in relation to drugs and other serious crimes. Unfortunately the enforcement of the relevant laws is weak. Rated 88th out of 102 (where 102 is the worst) of countries where corruption is perceived as a key problem in a survey by Transparency International in 2002.

Laos

Laos is the third largest producer of opium in the world, although much of it is consumed domestically. The country has no anti-money laundering legislation, even though it is a regional financial centre. Because Laos has strict laws on the exporting of currency it is suspected that laundering out of the country is achieved through alternative remittance systems. In 2001 the Government of Laos agreed to freeze terrorist financial assets and to establish a financial intelligence unit to search for terrorist transactions.

Latvia

Major organized crime problems
Possible up-and-coming money laundering centre
The country has attracted organized crime groups from Russia, the Balkans and Asia. Whilst Latvia is taking the money laundering problem seriously it is already at risk from Russian organized crime infiltration of the banking system as a conduit for laundering. This is both helped and hindered by the reputation the country has acquired of being stable and progressive. Banking regulation was previously poor but has improved. The country is perceived as having two other key problem areas in this context: drugs and corruption. The country is being used as a transit route for drugs from Russia and Central Asia to Europe, through Riga. Corruption is viewed as a problem – for example, there is alleged to be large scale corruption of members of parliament.

Lebanon

Named by FATF as 'non-cooperative' in June 2000; removed in June 2002
My original view of Lebanon was that 'As the country's financial structures are now recovering, Lebanon, with a liberal financial regime, is an attractive target for money launderers. It has a cash intensive economy combined with banking secrecy (anonymous accounts exist); thus it is somewhat surprising to learn that there have been no money laundering prosecutions (even though relevant – but weak – laws exist) and there are apparently no current money laundering investigations.' In June 2000 the FATF named the country as non-cooperative because of the country's banking secrecy regime, lack of a financial intelligence unit and the fact that, although banks were allowed to terminate account relationships, such account terminations did not have to be reported. In July 2000 the US Treasury issued an advisory notice to US financial institutions, warning them to give enhanced scrutiny to any transaction originating in or routed through Lebanon. Various policies and regulations have since been put in

place, which led to the country's removal from the FATF blacklist in June 2002.

Liberia

As at April 2002 Liberia was classified as being an 'uncooperative tax haven' by the OECD because of the country's lack of commitment to the specified concepts of transparency and effective exchange of information. The most polite way of describing this verdict is a vast understatement. Under its president, Charles Taylor, Liberia has been the subject of UN sanctions because of Taylor's role in regional conflicts (particularly Sierra Leone) and human suffering (Amnesty International allege serious human rights abuses). The sanctions attempt to prevent Taylor and his cronies from travelling, buying weapons and selling diamonds. However, in late 2002 it was claimed that Al-Qaida operatives have been at work in the country since 1998 and oversaw a $20 million diamond buying spree that effectively cornered the region's market in precious stones (as well as laundering funds away from the banking system). It is alleged that Taylor was paid $1 million to harbour the operatives for two months after 9/11. The terrorist diamond buyers also appear to have been attempting to procure sophisticated weapons.

Liechtenstein

Named by FATF as 'non-cooperative' in June 2000; removed in June 2001
Liechtenstein is a major offshore financial centre with a very sophisticated banking sector. Key facilitators of the money laundering process are available: anonymous accounts, bearer shares and various other suitable vehicles. Whilst money laundering is a criminal offence, suspicions continue to linger that money laundering is an on-going problem, which resulted in the FATF blacklisting in June 2000. This event caused severe embarrassment in Liechtenstein and a flurry of legal and regulatory improvement. Whilst now removed from the FATF blacklist, unconfirmed rumours circulate concerning Al-Qaida's previous use of Liechtenstein's financial centre. Additionally as at April 2002 Liechtenstein was classified as being an 'uncooperative tax haven' by the OECD because of the principality's lack of commitment to the specified concepts of transparency and effective exchange of information.

Lithuania

The country has severe problems with drug trafficking, which has doubled since 1995. Heroin is entering the country in increasing quantities from Kazakhstan, Tajikistan, Afghanistan and Ukraine. Lithuania is also a transit point to Scandinavian countries. Lithuanian domestic organized crime groups operate at both a national and an international level. Laundering in the country is known to have been successfully achieved by both domestic groups and international ones.

Luxembourg

One of the great dark horses – a secure banking system that is of ongoing interest to the German tax authorities, because it is estimated that $7.5 billion is lost every year in unpaid taxes by German nationals who place money in the grand duchy. If tax avoidance is a key concept of the new money laundering order, then Luxembourg is a location of major importance. Moreover, confidential reports suggest that Gaddafi, Mobutu and Saddam Hussein have all placed funds in Luxembourg. Whilst money laundering has been a crime since September 1992, for a country with over 200 banks the reporting of suspicious transactions is extremely low. Member of the FATF.

Madagascar

Possible up-and-coming money laundering centre
Whilst little information is available, what there is suggests that organized crime groups already operate here and thus money laundering is a risk (particularly because the economy is conducted on an informal basis). Madagascar has been implicated in laundering by Al-Qaida using Pakistani rice. Came very near the bottom of the survey by Transparency International in 2002: rated 98th out of 102 (where 102 is the worst) of countries where corruption is perceived as a key problem.

Maldives

No significant money laundering problems
Possibly an offshore financial centre of the future, but no problems at present.

Malta

No significant money laundering problems
Currently an offshore centre but, somewhat bucking the trend, the island's Government has announced that it intends to phase out all offshore operations by 2004.

Marshall Islands

Named by FATF as 'non-cooperative' in June 2000; removed in October 2002
In June 2000 the FATF blacklisted the Marshall Islands as they had no basic anti-money laundering regulations. The situation was exacerbated by the registration of approximately 3,000 IBCs – which had grown to 5,200 by early 2002. Additionally it has been suspected that such anonymous vehicles have been utilized by Russian criminals. On 31 October 2000, the Banking (Amendment) Act of 2000 was passed, which criminalized money laundering and established customer identification procedures for accounts and the reporting of suspicious transactions. Removed from the FATF blacklist in October 2002 due to progress made but as at April 2002 was classified as being an 'uncooperative tax haven' by the OECD because of a lack of commitment to the specified concepts of transparency and effective exchange of information.

Mexico

After Colombia, probably the most important country in the South American drug world, particularly bearing in mind its borders with the United States. The drug trade is dominated by three cartels: the Tijuana cartel, which mainly smuggles heroin and marijuana; the Gulf cartel; the Juarez cartel. Not only is Mexico producing and supplying drugs to the United States but there is also a growing domestic market. Drug related violence and almost open warfare are rising dramatically. Corruption is a key issue and concerns have been raised about the links that exist between the drug cartels and politicians to the extent that it has been suggested that one may control the other – and it may just be, contrary perhaps to expectation, that politicians control the drug cartels and not vice versa. Member of the FATF.

Moldova

Major organized crime problems
Moldova has severe organized crime problems caused by domestic groups that also launder funds through the primitive banking system. At the moment there is very little international money laundering taking place. However, the situation is exacerbated by a high level of official corruption. Moldova was rated 75th equal out of 99 (where 99 is the worst) of countries where corruption is perceived as a key problem in a survey by Transparency International in 1999 (no entry in 2002 survey).

Monaco

An attractive tax haven, described famously by Somerset Maugham as 'a sunny place for shady people', which has been traditionally used by the Italian Mafias. The Russian mafia also came here, laundering through the purchase of property and the casinos. However, the common perception is that the Russians have now moved on as things are tighter than they were. In June 2000, a French parliamentary report once more drew attention to Monaco's role in money laundering. The report concluded that the principality lacked the will and means to cooperate in global efforts to fight money laundering. The report also commented that Monaco 'risks destabilizing markets through a lack of surveillance of its banking and financial sectors'. This French view has been supported by tales such as that of an Israeli gentleman arriving at a bank with $5 million dollars in cash (although admittedly, if one believes the tale, he was arrested). Additionally, as at April 2002 Monaco was classified as being an 'uncooperative tax haven' by the OECD because of the principality's lack of commitment to the specified concepts of transparency and effective exchange of information.

Mongolia

Major organized crime problems
Whilst details are sketchy there is some intelligence that suggests Russian organized crime groups are making use of the country's banking system.

Nauru

Named by FATF as 'non-cooperative' in June 2000; remained blacklisted as at February 2003 and subject to counter-measures

No anti-money laundering legislation existed before August 2001, and there were some highly attractive offshore and anonymous services available. The US Treasury has stated that 'significant opportunities over time for the laundering of the proceeds of crime' have existed here. Unfortunately for Nauru, it now has something of a stigma attached to it – see Chapter 5 for full details. It is almost certain that substantial money laundering has taken place here by Russians, Asians and South Americans. In early 2001, 11 of the country's 18 MPs signed a petition demanding the recall of parliament and threatened to overthrow the president, Bernard Dowiyogo. The protesters accused the Government of involvement in corruption such as the diversion of US $970,000 into US bank accounts for the sale of Nauruan passports – claimed to have been sold to Thai and Chinese nationals to create new false identities for criminals. Another key complaint was the licensing of 'banks' by the Government that have subsequently been used for money laundering activities. Remained on the FATF blacklist as at February 2003 and, as at April 2002, Nauru was classified as being an 'uncooperative tax haven' by the OECD because of its lack of commitment to the specified concepts of transparency and effective exchange of information.

Nepal

Nepal has no anti-money laundering legislation. It has, however, problems with drugs, currency smuggling and the trafficking of human beings. A high level of corruption is suspected, and commented on by internal governmental reports. The Government also has plans to establish an offshore financial centre in Kathmandu.

Netherlands

The Netherlands has had problems in the past with money laundering, particularly through bureaux de change. It has long been realized that it is inconceivable that organized criminal elements cannot be heavily involved in the drugs and sex industry, particularly taking into account the Dutch liberal attitudes to both. Russian and other

Eastern European organized crime groups have colonized various parts of the sex trade in Amsterdam and elsewhere (using human trafficking to ensure an on-going supply of 'willing' girls). Hong Kong/Chinese Triads are active in fraud, drugs and prostitution (including human trafficking). Member of the FATF.

Netherlands Antilles

A growing offshore and gaming sector make this set of islands vulnerable to money laundering.

Nigeria

Major organized crime problems
Named by FATF as 'non-cooperative' in June 2001; remained blacklisted as at February 2003
In drugs the prime importance is that of Nigerians acting as drug couriers – taking Asian produced heroin to the United States, and South American generated cocaine to Europe. Official estimates put Nigeria as the third largest heroin smuggling area in the world. Corruption is alleged to be widespread in customs staff, facilitating trafficking. There are substantial internal problems in the country, and the endemic spread of Nigerian organized fraud to all other parts of the world has established Nigeria as the No 2 nation in Transparency International's index of countries perceived as being corrupt (1999). This unenviable accolade was repeated in the 2002 survey, when it was perceived that only Bangladesh was worse in this respect. In other comparable surveys Nigeria has gained a similar position, quite frequently topping the list. The country is the centre of major fraud and money laundering activity. The funds generated by the now infamous 419 letters are still (amazingly) substantial: and that is merely one facet of a global, highly organized fraud effort. All funds achieved by these widespread criminal activities need to be laundered. Particular reference should be made to Nigerian groups operating centres of fraud/money laundering from diverse locations such as the United States, Canada and South Africa. Blacklisted by the FATF but not subject to more severe countermeasures because of progress made (December 2002).

Niue

Named by FATF as 'non-cooperative' in June 2000; removed in October 2002
Everything was readily available in this offshore location to facilitate money laundering (also see Chapter 5). When blacklisted in June 2000 the FATF highlighted lapses in customer identification requirements together with having serious concerns about the regulatory regime that oversaw around 5,000 IBCs and five offshore banks. Significant reforms have followed, which deal with reporting suspicious transactions, the establishment of an FIU, eliminating offshore banks and providing better information on IBCs registered there. Because of this progress, Niue was removed from the blacklist in October 2002.

North Korea

Hard information difficult to obtain
One of the most closed countries in the world – another one to cross off the list for the would-be launderer. One of the three countries named by President Bush as being in the 'axis of evil'.

Norway

No significant money laundering problems
Member of FATF, some domestic problems with money laundering but no international ones – another safe Scandinavian location. Norway came 12th in the 2002 Transparency International survey of perceived corruption.

Oman

No significant money laundering problems
No known problems but country does have a predominantly cash based economy.

Pakistan

The country is a major distribution and refining area of opium (mainly in the Khyber region and Northwest Frontier province). With its formal economy in tatters, various political scandals that contain allegations of money laundering by various former leaders, a costly nuclear programme and a government that has placed the rooting out of corruption at the top of its agenda, Pakistan has more than enough domestic problems to contend with. However, the aftermath of 9/11 brought two other key problems in the country to the surface: moral and financial support for Al-Qaida combined with the use of the country's hawala alternative remittance system for money laundering by both criminals and terrorists. Rated 77th out of 102 (where 102 is the worst) of countries where corruption is perceived as a key problem in a survey by Transparency International in 2002 (previously 87th out of 99 in 1999, so things are perceived as improving slightly).

Palau

Possible up-and-coming money laundering centre
In the previous edition, I commented: 'Will it or won't it become an offshore centre – or is it already? See also Chapter 5.' Offshore banking licences in Palau now are available via the Internet for as little as $7,500.

Panama

Named by FATF as 'non-cooperative' in June 2000; removed in June 2001
Colombian cartels cultivate coca in the Darien region of the country. Panama has a strong financial sector and a dollar based economy – it is an attractive target for money launderers. The FATF blacklisted Panama in June 2000 because of the country's previous refusal to criminalize money laundering apart from drug trafficking related offences. Panama was removed in June 2001, when the FATF commended the country for the progress it had made over the previous 12 months in tackling the problem and introducing significant new legislation/ regulation to control it.

Paraguay

A transit country for cocaine trafficking with widespread official corruption present. Scored 98th out of 102 (where 102 is the worst) of countries where corruption is perceived as a key problem in a survey by Transparency International in 2002 (a worse outcome than in 1999 when it was 90th out of 99).

Peru

Peru is the world's largest producer of cocaine; coca is the country's second largest crop – about 60 per cent of the world's coca crop. Domestic money laundering does obviously occur; international laundering probably does not to any significant degree.

Philippines

Named by FATF as 'non-cooperative' in June 2000; remained blacklisted as at February 2003

Prior to the FATF blacklisting in June 2000 there existed no effective AML legislation, much political uncertainty and public corruption. The country is also a key trans-shipment route of opium and other drugs from China. Organized crime groups from China, Taiwan and Hong Kong are all active here. There is strict banking secrecy. The US Treasury had already issued an advisory notice recommending enhanced scrutiny for transactions involving the Philippines. Local media coverage has described Manila as 'Asia's money laundering capital', drawing attention to anonymous safe boxes, tight bank secrecy laws and the irony that being awarded such a dubious accolade actually attracts a substantial inflow of funds. On 10 September 2001 the FATF reviewed its list of non-cooperative countries and territories and, in simple terms, concluded that the Philippines had done nothing to implement AML regulations or legislation and thus recommended countermeasures against the country unless it enacted significant legislation by 30 September 2001. With one day to spare, on 29 September 2001 the Philippines enacted the Anti-Money Laundering Act of 2001, which criminalized money laundering, introduced the mandatory reporting of certain transactions, required customer identification and created a legal basis for an FIU. However, problems still exist, such as a conflict in the reporting of suspicious transactions and banking secrecy remaining in respect of deposits made prior to 17 October 2001.

Poland

Major organized crime problems

Poland produces about a fifth of the amphetamines sold in Europe. Drugs and drug related crimes are a serious national problem. The country is an important base for Chinese and Colombian drug/organized crime groups together with Turkish gangs, Albanian mafia groups, Nigerians and domestic criminal groups. There are more than 400 domestic crime groups – but internal feuding between them has allowed foreign groups to muscle in with a vengeance. Polish police estimate that more than 15,000 women (in the 16–20 age group) are illegally imported into Poland for prostitution annually. This racket is now increasingly controlled by criminals from Ukraine or Belarus. There is a substantial black market in cigarettes, particularly from the country into Germany. The local Pruszkow mafia is well versed in car and art theft, money laundering, extortion, prostitution, drug trafficking and illegal arms dealing. The Polish finance ministry has estimated that around $3 billion is laundered through the country on an annual basis, although in November 2002 the ministry speculated that the actual total could be up to $8 billion. Although Polish laws are now compliant with FATF standards, enforcement is weak. One key problem is lack of police resources, which is exacerbated by lack of cooperation between financial institutions and investigators.

Romania

Major organized crime problems
A cash based economy, a major trans-shipment point for arms, drugs and humans together with a corrupt police force make this a disturbing location. Apart from domestic criminal gangs, Turkish, Kurdish and French groups are also operating here. In November 2001 the Romanian media reported that Arab businessmen living in the country had donated 'hundreds of millions' of dollars to Islamic terrorist organizations. The money, it is claimed, was laundered through legitimately registered Romanian companies. An Egyptian businessman in the country transferred $150 million to Egyptian based associates with close terrorist links. The transfer was classified as an 'advance payment' for non-existent goods.

Russia

Named by FATF as 'non-cooperative' in June 2000; removed in October 2002
Russia was blacklisted because:

- It had a lack of comprehensive money laundering laws and regulations.

- The country had no customer identification procedures.
- There were no suspicious transaction reporting procedures.
- There was no central FIU.

After dragging its feet Russia finally introduced significant reforms to its anti-money laundering system, which led to its removal from the FATF blacklist in October 2002. There are various problems that still exist in the country, which are made more confusing by various misconceptions: the country's ever recurring business scandals (which invariably are simultaneously linked with politics) are virtually inexplicable to an outsider; Russian organized criminals are still highly active – for example, in November 2002, 250,000 pirate CDs, DVDs and videos were confiscated at three military bases, which had rented out space to the infringers!; human trafficking of women and girls for sexual exploitation remains a serious unresolved problem. However, there still exists a key confusion between capital flight (still estimated at $20 billion a year) and 'true' money laundering (even in the Bank of New York money laundering scandal it was never established which was which); moreover, the country has suffered because there has been a tendency in the West mistakenly to refer to all former Eastern Bloc criminals as the 'Russian mafia'. In this respect, there are far worse countries – Ukraine being the prime example. All in all, the situation is improving, particularly as Western facing Russian companies now realize that the only way that they can compete on the global stage is by adopting Western standards and transparency. Rated 71st out of 102 (where 102 is the worst) of countries where corruption is perceived as a key problem in a survey by Transparency International in 2002 (previously rated 82nd out of 99 in 1999). See also 'The international groupings of organized criminals' in Chapter 1.

Saudi Arabia

Hard information difficult to obtain

Criminal money laundering possibly is a problem but public information is hard to come by. The highly publicized laws of the kingdom regarding drugs (public execution), the extreme and laborious process of obtaining a visa, and a traditional Islamic banking system are just a few good reasons why, if any problems do exist, they will be localized rather than international. However, the key problem, which in my opinion will be almost impossible to resolve, is the moral and financial support given to Al-Qaida (see also Chapter 7).

Senegal

No significant money laundering problems
There are some domestic money laundering problems that may be exacerbated by lack of anti-money laundering laws, but no international dimensions.

Singapore

Singapore is simultaneously a major financial centre with many shops trading in high value goods and a country that has a strong anti-drug culture. Additionally there exists a persistent underground banking system, which, when allied to the various shops selling high value goods, provides a strong conduit for the washing of Asian heroin dealers' cash. To make this situation worse, there are no controls on currency being brought into or taken out of Singapore. The anti-money laundering laws apply to banks, insurance companies, and bureaux de change and money remittance companies, but are currently only drugs related. The regulations mean that suspicious transactions must be reported and that customers engaged in significant currency transactions should be identified. Member of the FATF.

Slovakia

Major organized crime problems
The country has a predominantly cash based economy and is a drug transit country. Not only are domestic organized crime groups active and laundering here but also Russian, Italian, Chechen and Ukrainian gangs. According to the Slovakian Government in 2000, 29 organized crime groups operated in Slovakia: five in the Bratislava region, 12 in the western Slovak regions, four in central Slovakia and eight in eastern Slovakia. These groups are engaged in extortion, drug dealing, illegal smuggling of immigrants, prostitution, car theft, tax evasion and black market trading. It has now been accepted that between 1994 and 1998 the Government of the country actively discouraged police investigations into organized crime activity. The long term effects of this were not only the proliferation of such gangs but also a lack of police human resources, equipment and properly trained officers.

Slovenia

Major organized crime problems

The country's Office for Money Laundering Prevention comments that Slovenia is 'confronted by serious problems of organized and economic crime… combined with the fact that Slovenia borders on Italy, Austria, Hungary and Croatia, which has had an impact on crime phenomena. In the last few years we have witnessed a trend towards rising serious crime, and money laundering in particular.' A 2002 opinion poll found that more than half of all people questioned acknowledged the probability of corruption by doctors, lawyers and public notaries. There are also large gaps perceived in the ability of law enforcement agencies to fight corruption.

South Africa

South Africa is another of those countries that has a strong national/regional financial industry but it currently suffers a predominantly domestic rather than international money laundering problem. Organized (and petty) crime is prevalent in the country – with hijacking of cars being just one symptom of the malaise. Added to this is widespread corruption, which doesn't encourage a transparent environment. One frightening problem concerns Nigerian drug trafficking and associated criminal activity. Whilst the South African authorities record about 2,000 Nigerians living in the country, it has been estimated that the true figure is anywhere between 45,000 and 100,000.

Spain

Spain is sometimes overlooked, apart from previously being a safe haven for criminals on the run. These coastal areas are now popular with Russian criminals. However, much more important are Spain's historical links with Latin America, which have left a lasting influence in a robust trading relationship between Spain and Latin America together with an efficient air timetable between the two areas. This has all meant that although Spain's anti-money laundering controls are rigorous the country's banking and business systems are an appealing target for groups such as the Colombians. The Observatoire Geopolitique des Drogues in its 1998/99 Annual Report (published in

April 2000) is damning about the role of Spain in drugs and money laundering. The country is described as 'a narcotics clearing house' together with claims that Spain is the largest drug money laundering centre in Europe for the Colombians with up to $12 billion per annum being washed. Member of the FATF.

St Kitts and Nevis

Named by FATF as 'non-cooperative' in June 2000; removed in June 2002
These are actually two competing offshore centres that have posed key money laundering risks. Economic citizenship has been available (in other words, the buying of a new passport) together with International Business Corporations and non-disclosure of beneficial owners. The US Department of State reported in 2000 that there is a sizeable level of drug trafficking on and around the islands. Known traffickers are present on the islands, and some Russian organized crime figures live in St Kitts. The blacklisting by the FATF was due to the following:

- Money laundering was only a criminal offence in relation to narcotics trafficking.
- There was no reporting of suspicious transactions.
- There was little supervision of the offshore sector.

The enactment of significant legislation ensured that these islands were removed from the FATF blacklist in 2002.

St Lucia

A new offshore centre that may be at risk from money laundering in the future, but appears to be keen to establish and maintain an unblemished reputation.

St Vincent and the Grenadines

Named by FATF as 'non-cooperative' in June 2000; remained blacklisted as at February 2003
A cocaine trans-shipment point, a growing offshore sector and International Business Corporations that can be incorporated online without disclosure of beneficial owners are just some reasons why

money laundering is a sizeable risk. If you want more, then the absence of regulations concerning customer identification or suspicious transactions should be enough. The islands are very popular, we are reliably told, with South American drug barons. All of these factors led to their appearance on the FATF's first blacklist, and they remained there as at October 2002. Significant progress has been made, but the FATF still have concerns about customer identification procedures.

Sudan

No significant money laundering problems
Because of its extreme Islamic Government and own internal problems Sudan will not be appearing on anyone's list of places to launder money for the foreseeable future.

Suriname

Suriname is the main entry point for cocaine into the Netherlands, and there is evidence of money laundering taking place.

Switzerland

Because of the size of the country's banking and financial industry it is inconceivable to consider that money laundering is not a problem. Moreover, the clients that the country draws to its private banking and asset management sectors are almost entirely from an international catchment area. Thus it is very commonplace to see banks with subsidiaries in South America (or Miami for South America), Russia and other hot spots. Switzerland however has responded to previous negative publicity and has installed a robust anti-money laundering system. Nevertheless Russian organized criminal groups are active in the banking system, company structures and by physically trying to move to and reside in Switzerland. Interestingly, though, one of the on-going claims made by Switzerland is that many funds that are subsequently shown to have been laundered actually arrive in the country not from Russia or South America, for example, but in a 'clean' state from other reputable Western financial centres. The country has until recently been the favoured location for the funds of corrupt politicians. Member of the FATF.

Taiwan

The country has more than 60,000 heroin addicts and is a trans-shipment point for Chinese heroin, thus creating a substantial money laundering risk. The presence of sophisticated organized crime groups and persistent corruption makes the situation worse. It is estimated that at least half of the funds laundered through Taiwan are then transferred abroad.

Tajikistan

Tajikistan is a drug transit country (from Afghanistan), but an unsophisticated banking apparatus makes the country an unattractive money laundering target.

Tanzania

A major drug transit country, some highly cash intensive businesses, high levels of official corruption and a rise in organized criminal activity are the minus points. Probably the only plus point is that the country is not a major financial centre. Rated 71st out of 102 (where 102 is the worst) of countries where corruption is perceived as a key problem in a survey by Transparency International in 2002 – a substantial improvement on 1999 when the country was rated 93rd out of 99.

Thailand

The country is trying to combat its money laundering problem. But, because of its cash based economy and geographical position, Thailand is particularly prone to money launderers, particularly for funds generated by illegal drugs in South East Asia.

Tunisia

Hard information difficult to obtain
Little information is available, but the presence of an offshore industry including banks, IBCs and casinos suggests that vulnerabilities exist.

Turkey

Turkey is becoming an increasingly relevant financial centre on a regional basis and also is on the transit route for drugs moving from Asia to Europe. However, money laundering problems appear to be domestic rather than international. Member of the FATF.

Turkmenistan

The country is the chief route in Central Asia for exporting opiates and hashish products produced in Afghanistan. Money laundering appears to be part of various 'mysteriously' funded luxury hotel and major building projects that are sprouting up.

Turks and Caicos Islands

This is an offshore financial centre that provides various vehicles to ensure anonymity, including International Business Companies where ultimate beneficial owners are not disclosed. It is vulnerable to money laundering.

Ukraine

Major organized crime problems
Named by FATF as 'non-cooperative' in September 2001; remained blacklisted as at February 2003 – countermeasures imposed December 2002
Large amounts of money are generated by domestic criminal groupings; Ukraine is also used as an entry point to the global banking system by international organized crime groups. In December 2002 the Parliamentary Committee on Combating Organized Crime and Corruption released a report that concluded that:

- The major problem in the country (and the most corrupt entities) is state law enforcement agencies.
- Criminal organizations are able to operate openly in every region of the country because law enforcement agencies do not stop their activities, and in many instances are in league with the criminals.
- Corruption in the country's court system is widespread.

- Organized crime 'has reached such proportions that it constitutes a real danger to the constitutional basis of government in Ukraine'.

Prior to this report a February 2002 opinion poll in the country found that 84 per cent of those questioned said that corruption was a nationwide problem; 67 per cent said that corruption was at its highest level amongst the political elite; and, to add to the depressing picture, 44 per cent said that such corruption can never be stopped. Examples quoted in November 2001 on the Criminal Ukraine Web site are: to bribe a tax inspector costs $87 and to have a telephone line installed incurs a payment of $200. To add to the problems are continuing allegations of government illegal arms dealing with (amongst others) Iraq and the Taliban. In December 2002 the FATF applied countermeasures against Ukraine, as the country had not addressed the deficiencies in its AML regime identified by the FATF in June 2001. The 2002 US Department of State report on human trafficking rates Ukraine at Tier 2 (a country not in compliance with minimum standards for the elimination of trafficking but making significant efforts). The report states that Ukraine is a source country for women and girls trafficked for sexual exploitation to Central and Western Europe together with the Middle East. Whilst the report praises the Government for efforts it has made in this respect, it is stated that 'a number of law enforcement officers may be corrupt thereby facilitating trafficking'. The country was rated 85th out of 102 (where 102 is the worst) of countries where corruption is perceived as a key problem in a survey by Transparency International in 2002. This is a marked decline from 1999 when the country was rated 75th out of 99.

United Kingdom

Because of its key strategic position as a global financial centre, the United Kingdom is a major laundering centre. In 2002 it was claimed that London is the cocaine capital of the world, with financial institutions indirectly fuelling the market through their staff. The continuing and accelerating trend of globalization and the ease of funds transfer make the City even more vulnerable to money laundering. If you are a money launderer then you know you have made it safely and successfully if your funds are accepted without question in London. The United Kingdom has its own domestic problems with home-grown criminal groupings, but also acts as a magnet for the new criminal order. Russian and other Eastern European crime groups favour London properties and banking system. They are also active in the vice trade, London metal market, art world and financial fraud. Hong Kong/Chinese Triads are active in fraud, drugs and prostitution (including human trafficking). Turkish/Kurdish gangs are responsible for 80 per cent of heroin smuggled into the country each year. There is increasing evidence of Colombian groups utilizing London Heathrow Airport as a gateway to mainland Europe. The Nigerian criminal gangs are heavily active in all types of banking and financial fraud. Member of the FATF.

United States

The United States is the country with everything: all major (and some not so major) organized crime groups are active here; specifically, there are large scale problems with drugs from across the border in South America. It is the one country in the world that has taken the threat of organized crime and money laundering seriously from the word go. New developments include Russian organized crime groups (both on their own account and in league with others such as Colombians) active in extortion, protection, drugs, prostitution, money laundering, credit card fraud and counterfeiting. They have a strong presence in Brooklyn, Los Angeles, Philadelphia, Boston, Miami and San Francisco. The Japanese Yakuza have a sizeable influence together with portfolio of property holdings in Hawaii. That is not to forget the traditional criminal elements such as New York crime families. The position of the United States at the cutting edge of new technology poses additional risks particularly to the country's citizens who compose a substantial proportion of the world's Internet users. The aftermath of 9/11 has put the prevention of money laundering very near the top of the US administration's agenda. One side effect of the focus on stopping terrorist funding is that the previous focus on tax evasion as money laundering has taken a back seat. Member of the FATF.

Vanuatu

As at April 2002 Vanuatu was classified as being an 'uncooperative tax haven' by the OECD because of its lack of commitment to the specified concepts of transparency and effective exchange of information.

Venezuela

Corruption, a weak banking system and proximity to Colombia make the country an important destination for drug money generated by the Colombian cartels. Rated 75th out of 99 (where 99 is the worst) of countries where corruption is perceived as a key problem in a survey by Transparency International in 1999 (the country was not included in the 2002 survey).

Vietnam

There exists little evidence to suggest that money laundering is a serious problem in Vietnam, but the country has a substantial grey economy that makes the identification of dirty money difficult. Vietnam, because of its geographical position, is a trans-shipment country for drugs from the Golden Triangle together with being an attractive target for overseas crime groups. Vietnam was rated 85th out of 102 (where 102 is the worst) of countries where corruption is perceived as a key problem in a survey by Transparency International in 2002.

THE FATF 'BLACKLIST'

On 22 June 2000, the Financial Action Task Force published its 'Review to identify non-cooperative countries or territories (NCCTs): increasing the worldwide effectiveness of anti-money laundering measures'. This report was picked up by many of the world's newspapers with many stories referring to the report as providing a 'blacklist' of countries that are negligent in their response and attitude to money laundering. It should also be noted that this was the review of the first set of jurisdictions – not a complete overview of all countries.

The countries named as being 'non-cooperative' in June 2000 with the reasons for this are:

1. Bahamas:
   - Lack of information about beneficial ownership of trusts and IBCs (which issue bearer shares).
   - Certain intermediaries can avoid revealing the identity of their clients.

   - Delays and restricted responses to requests for assistance from other jurisdictions.
2. Cayman Islands:
   - No legal requirements for customer identification and record keeping.
   - No mandatory regime for the reporting of suspicious transactions.
   - Large class of management companies unregulated.
3. Cook Islands:
   - No relevant information on *circa* 1,200 IBCs registered there.
   - Seven offshore banks are registered that do not have to identify customers or keep records.
4. Dominica:
   - Outdated proceeds of crime laws.
   - Company law provisions frustrate identification of beneficial ownership.
5. Israel:
   - No anti-money laundering legislation.
6. Lebanon:
   - The country has a strict banking secrecy regime that frustrates investigations and international cooperation; suspicious customer relationships can be terminated without reporting to relevant authorities.
7. Liechtenstein:
   - System for reporting suspicious transactions is inadequate.
   - No proper laws for exchanging information about money laundering and international cooperation.
   - Resources devoted to tackling money laundering are inadequate.
8. Marshall Islands:
   - Absence of a basic set of anti-money laundering regulations including criminalization of money laundering, customer identification and reporting of suspicious transactions.
   - 3,000 IBCs registered here with strong secrecy concerning beneficial owners.
9. Nauru:
   - Absence of a basic set of anti-money laundering regulations including criminalization of money laundering, customer identification and reporting of suspicious transactions.
   - It has licensed 400 offshore 'banks' that are badly supervised – no disclosure of relevant information on such entities or IBCs.

10. Niue:
    - Lapses in customer identification requirements.
    - Strong concerns about regulation of five offshore banks and *circa* 5,000 IBCs registered here.
11. Panama:
    - Money laundering (apart from drug trafficking) is not criminalized.
    - Strange system of reporting suspicious transactions.
12. Philippines:
    - Absence of a basic set of anti-money laundering regulations including customer identification and reporting of suspicious transactions.
    - Excessive secrecy of bank records; no suspicious transaction reporting procedure.
13. Russia:
    - Lack of comprehensive money laundering law and regulations.
    - No customer identification requirements; no suspicious transaction reporting procedure.
    - No central reporting/intelligence unit.
    - FATF commented: 'Russia faces a unique challenge in combating money laundering as it continues its transition to a market economy. The existence of a continued large scale capital flight, underdeveloped market institutions and lack of fiscal resources all complicate the fight against money laundering.'
14. St Kitts and Nevis:
    - Money laundering is only a criminal offence in relation to narcotics trafficking.
    - No reporting of suspicious transactions.
    - In Nevis: little supervision of the offshore sector; no relevant procedures in place; non-residents can operate an offshore bank account with no ID being taken; strong bank secrecy laws which hide beneficial owners even in criminal cases; company law frustrates customer identification even more.
15. St Vincent and the Grenadines:
    - No anti-money laundering regulations/guidelines exist for offshore financial institutions – thus no customer identification.
    - No system to require reporting of suspicious transactions.

Crucially the FATF report recommended that 'financial institutions should give special attention to business relations and transactions with persons, including companies and financial institutions, from the non-cooperative countries' (ie the list of 15 territories given above).

On 22 June 2001 the FATF issued their revised blacklist; removed from the previous year's list were:

- Bahamas;
- Cayman Islands;
- Liechtenstein;
- Panama.

All were commended for making significant progress over the previous 12 months in tackling the problems of money laundering and introducing significant new legislation/regulation to control it.

However, FATF singled out three countries as having failed to make any progress in fighting money laundering. These were:

- Russia;
- Philippines;
- Nauru.

Each of these jurisdictions was given until 30 September 2001 to make progress on money laundering issues in line with FATF's overall strategy. Punishments against these countries unless they 'enact significant legislation before 30/09/01 to address these problems' were stated as possibly to include: requiring US and other banks to gather detailed information before doing business with any individual or company from any of these countries; and issuing official warnings to international companies against doing business in any of the three countries.

As at 22 June 2001 the FATF 'blacklist' of countries in full was:

- Russia: no progress – remained on list from previous year;
- Philippines: no progress – remained on list from previous year;
- Nauru: no progress – remained on list from previous year;
- Cook Islands: remained on list from previous year;
- Dominica: remained on list from previous year;
- Israel: remained on list from previous year;
- Lebanon: remained on list from previous year;
- Marshall Islands: remained on list from previous year;
- Niue: remained on list from previous year;

- St Kitts and Nevis: remained on list from previous year;
- St Vincent and the Grenadines: remained on list from previous year;
- Egypt: new listing;
- Guatemala: new listing;
- Hungary: new listing;
- Indonesia: new listing;
- Myanmar (Burma): new listing;
- Nigeria: new listing.

On 7 September 2001 the FATF issued an update on the 'Non-cooperative countries and territories (NCCTs) list', together with a recommendation that:

> *Financial institutions should give special attention to business relations and transactions with persons, including companies and financial institutions, from countries which do not or insufficiently apply these recommendations. Whenever these transactions have no apparent economic or visible lawful purpose, their background and purpose should, as far as possible, be examined, the findings established in writing, and be available to help supervisors, auditors and law enforcement agencies.*

In June 2001 FATF singled out three nations as major problems, and gave these countries until 30 September 2001 to enact significant money laundering legislation. These were Russia, Nauru and the Philippines. FATF considered the progress made by each of these countries, and concluded:

- Russia: remained on the main NCCTs list, but because of significant legislation that had been enacted was removed from the 'top three'.
- Nauru: had enacted an Anti-Money Laundering Act but FATF commented that 'this new legislation is found to have several deficiencies and does not address the major money laundering problem in Nauru'. FATF urged the Nauru Government to amend the legislation accordingly, and, if it did not, countermeasures would apply to Nauru from 30 November 2001.
- Philippines: put simply, this country had done nothing and FATF called for its members to implement countermeasures unless the Philippines enacted significant legislation by 30 September 2001.

Additionally FATF added Ukraine and Grenada to the main NCCTs list, for the following reasons:

- Grenada: authorities had inadequate access to customer account information and inadequate authority to cooperate with foreign counterparts; Grenadian financial institutions did not have adequate qualification procedures for owners of financial institutions.
- Ukraine: lacked a complete set of anti-money laundering measures; no efficient mandatory system for reporting suspicious transactions; inadequate resources to tackle the problem.

The 'blacklist' of countries as at 7 September 2001 in full was:

- Cook Islands;
- Dominica;
- Egypt;
- Grenada;
- Guatemala;
- Hungary;
- Indonesia;
- Israel;
- Lebanon;
- Marshall Islands;
- Myanmar (Burma);
- Nauru;
- Nigeria;
- Niue;
- Philippines;
- Russia;
- St Kitts and Nevis;
- St Vincent and the Grenadines;
- Ukraine.

On 21 June 2002 the FATF updated the list by removing four countries: but perhaps somewhat surprisingly in view of events since 11 September 2001 no new countries were added.

The four removals from the list were Hungary, Israel, Lebanon and St Kitts and Nevis. All four will be under observation for some time. Israel was removed from the list because of the laws that had been recently enacted and the country's plans to introduce a proper financial regulator. The Justice Minister of Israel rather pre-empted FATF's announcement by confirming that the country had been removed from the blacklist a few hours before the official announcement. Hungary escaped from the list because it has introduced a law banning anonymous accounts.

Russia edged closer to removal from the list: it had, by this stage, introduced the laws requested by FATF but the organization wants to see how and whether they actually work before taking the country off the list. Grenada and St Vincent and the Grenadines were also identified as making progress.

The full list as at 21 June 2002 comprised 15 states and territories, as follows:

- Cook Islands;
- Dominica;
- Egypt;
- Grenada;
- Guatemala;
- Indonesia;
- Marshall Islands;
- Myanmar (Burma);
- Nauru;
- Nigeria;
- Niue;
- Philippines;
- Russia;
- St Vincent and the Grenadines;
- Ukraine.

The FATF also commented that it would recommend taking sanctions against Nigeria at the end of October 2002 if the Government failed to enact legal reforms. Ukraine is also a subject of concern – FATF officials commented that, 'in plain English, nothing has been done'.

At the time of the issue of this list I observed in an interview on BBC TV that it actually predated 11 September 2001, and thus had no specific focus on money laundering by terrorists. Moreover, none of the countries identified by the US administration as the 'axis of evil' (Iraq, Iran and North Korea; and in an expanded form also Cuba, Libya and Syria) appear on the list. Moreover, based on intelligence concerning the entry point into the global banking system of terrorist funds, it is equally surprising that no Middle Eastern country (or countries) is on the blacklist. I also expressed concern as to whether money laundering has now 'bypassed' the banking system and is being carried out through such methods as:

- the purchase of gold and diamonds;
- informal money transmission services (such as hawala and hundi);
- money transmitted through casinos;
- property transactions;
- the use of professional advisors such as lawyers and accountants.

On 11 October 2002 the FATF changed its list of non-cooperative countries. By this stage, as it had been widely observed that the task of tracing terrorist funds had not been wholly successful and was a long term, uphill struggle, I was somewhat surprised that FATF managed substantially to reduce the number of blacklisted countries. In summary the changes were as follows:

- Countries added: none.
- Countries removed: Russia (implementation of significant reforms to its anti-money laundering system), Marshall Islands, Niue and Dominica (all removed because of progress made in improving their anti-money laundering systems).
- Remaining on the blacklist: Cook Islands, Egypt, Grenada, Guatemala, Indonesia, Myanmar (Burma), Nauru, Nigeria, Philippines, St Vincent and the Grenadines, Ukraine.
- Still subject to countermeasures: Nauru.
- New countermeasures: to be imposed on Nigeria and Ukraine if suitable steps were not taken by each country to improve their anti-money laundering regimes. Date for implementation: 15 December 2002.

I could not help but be cynical about what criteria are used to select countries for inclusion on the blacklist, what political pressures are exerted to have countries taken off the blacklist (or not included in the first place), whether the list bears any relation to the reality of the global money laundering problem (particularly as it relates to the funding of terrorism) and whether the list has any practical effects. Little wonder then that there are growing calls for an international body to be set up that solely deals with the problem of terrorist money laundering.

Following a FATF meeting on 14 February 2003, the FATF blacklist was as follows:

- Cook Islands;
- Egypt;
- Guatemala;
- Indonesia;
- Myanmar (Burma);
- Nauru (subject to countermeasures);
- Nigeria;
- Philippines (may be subject to countermeasures from March 2003);
- St Vincent and the Grenadines;
- Ukraine.

Grenada was taken off the blacklist because of its 'implementation of significant reforms to its anti-money laundering system'. The Philippines may (or may not) be the subject of 'countermeasures' if the country does not improve its AML regime. Ukraine, on the other hand, subject to countermeasures for just under two months since December 2002 had those countermeasures withdrawn because of the country's recent enactment of 'comprehensive' AML legislation, but it remains on the main blacklist.

In the Philippines this latest move has not been well received, one commentator observed of the FATF that it is 'a body whose authority to dictate on countries no one seems able to pin down, whose membership makes the countries under its threat want to throw up, and whose exceptions of the usual suspects enrage everyone else'.

The FATF also confirmed that no further countries would be blacklisted for a year because of the discussions going on between the FATF, the IMF and World Bank. Various commentators have speculated that because of these moves this may be the final FATF blacklist. Based on the somewhat haphazard nature of the FATF blacklist to date (both in terms of countries included and those not even considered for inclusion) it is my hope that these discussions would lead to a more effective world body to robustly tackle the problems of money laundering and terrorist financing.

Further information

Future changes to the FATF blacklist, and analysis of these changes, can be found in the newsletter section of www.proximalconsulting.com.

Details of international initiatives to combat money laundering can be found at http://www1.oecd.org/fatf/Initiatives_en.htm.

Details of AML legislation of individual countries can be found at http://www.imolin.org/map.htm.

APPENDIX II: WEB DIRECTORY

General Web sites

www.proximalconsulting.com
My own firm's Web site, which is updated with new money laundering information and regular newsletters.

www.oecd.org/fatf/index.htm
The Financial Action Task Force on Money Laundering, which is an essential place to visit. You will find the following: a full version of the FATF's 40 recommendations, full copies of all of the FATF's reports and latest news and press releases.

www.occ.treas.gov
The United States Office of the Comptroller of the Currency Web site: good general information and links.

www.fincen.gov
The United States Department of the Treasury Financial Crimes Enforcement Network Web site: comprehensive information including relevant advisory notices issued.

http://www.laundryman.u-net.com
Billy's Money Laundering Information Web site, which is a private Web site solely concerned with money laundering with no commercial angle. Good overview and background information.

Relevant international money laundering legislation

www.imolin.org
The Web site of the International Money Laundering Information Network, which is run by the United Nations Office for Drug Control and Crime Prevention. Contains details of, and links to, current national AML legislation.

www1.oecd.org/fatf/Legislation_en.htm
Pages on the FATF Web site that review its members' compliance with the FATF's recommendations and provide details of relevant national legislation.

Narcotics issues

www.whitehousedrugpolicy.gov
The United States Office of National Drug Control Policy Web site: detailed information on US national drug control initiatives.

www.odccp.org
The United Nations Office for Drug Control and Crime Prevention Web site: information on the international legal framework, crime prevention, drug supply reduction and drug demand production.

www.state.gov/www/global/narcotics_law/index.html
The Web site of the US State Department Bureau of International Narcotics and Law Enforcement Affairs. Detailed information including the annual International Narcotics Control Strategy Report, which contains a separate and ever larger sub-report on money laundering problems on a country by country basis.

www.ogd.org
The Web site of the Observatoire Geopolitique des Drogues, an independent body based in France that receives funding from, amongst others, the European Commission. Very interesting annual reports.

Quantifying the amount of money laundering

www.ozemail.com.au/born1820/mlmethod.htm
A full version (as far as I'm aware) of the thought-provoking paper by John Walker on the global extent of money laundering, calculating a total of $2.85 trillion.

National sites

www.imolin.org
See reference under 'Relevant international money laundering legislation' above – also has links to national money laundering FIUs.

www.austrac.gov.au/
The Web site of AUSTRAC, the Australian Transaction Reports and Analysis Centre, containing a large volume of useful data including relevant legislation, past annual reports, newsletters and forms.

www.cia.gov/cia/publications/factbook/index.html
The CIA world factbook – provides key background information on each individual country.

Organized crime

www.cisc.gc.ca
The Web site of the Criminal Intelligence Service of Canada, which publishes annual reports on the scale, nature and extent of organized criminal activities in Canada.

www.yorku.ca/nathanson/
The Web site of the Nathanson Centre for the study of organized crime and corruption: contains a very good listing of links to other sites of relevance.

www.alternatives.com/crime/menu.html
The Web site of the Committee for a Safe Society, which has a good organized crime set of links.

Corruption issues

www.transparency.com
The Web site of Transparency International, the global group dedicated to fighting corruption, including the Corruption Perceptions Index.

Warning lists

www.ustreas.gov/offices/enforcement/ofac/
The US Office of Foreign Assets Control – contains full details of all individuals and companies against which the United States has sanctions, including terrorists (note: the lists are mainly in PDF form, which on occasions makes loading them a tedious process).

http://www.nasdr.com/1200-ofac.asp
A free search facility for the US OFAC lists, which appears to be very effective and removes the need to view PDF files in their entirety.

http://www.bankofengland.co.uk/sanctions/main.htm
Complete listings of all sanctions in force by UK authorities.

http://www1.oecd.org/fatf/NCCT_en.htm
The current list of the FATF's non-cooperative countries and territories.

http://www.fincen.gov/pub_main.html
The complete list of FinCEN advisory notices, specifically relevant to individual country risks.

Appendix III: Glossary of terms

419 Fraud
The infamous letters from Nigeria and neighbouring states offering you untold riches, named after the section in the Nigerian penal code that deals with fraud.

AML
Anti-money laundering: abbreviation now widely used when referring to relevant legislation and regulation and their enforcement.

Anonymous account
The only 'official' anonymous account available was the Sparbuch; Switzerland, for example, does not offer anonymous accounts. True anonymous accounts are where the financial institution has no idea whatsoever who holds the account and has no records concerning the client's identity. It can be effectively argued (and the accounts certainly are promoted as such) that an IBC that opens a bank account is in effect creating an anonymous account. Numerous 'anonymous' accounts and facilities are still offered via the Internet.

BCBS
Basel Committee on Banking Supervision.

Bearer shares
In very simple terms the documents that show ownership of the company: if you have them you own the company but such ownership is not recorded in any official records. A substantial facilitator of anonymity and confidentiality in company ownership.

BMPE
Black Market Peso Exchange (see 'Peso Exchange' below).

CDD
Customer due diligence.

CFT
Combating the financing of terrorism.

Coca
The shortened version of the name of the South American shrub Erythroxylon coca, the dried leaves of which are the source of cocaine.

Cocaine
Extracted from the leaves of the coca tree and the drug of choice in the United States where there are over 2 million addicts. It has limited use as a medical application, mostly as a local anaesthetic. However, it is highly toxic and addictive. Crack is a derivative of cocaine.

Correspondent bank
A perfectly legitimate banking arrangement where a bank accepts deposits and performs banking services for another bank. However, there is a specific money laundering risk where the bank using the services is a 'shell bank' (see below).

FATF
FATF stands for the Financial Action Task Force on Money Laundering (also known as GAFI: the Group d'Action Financière sur le Blanchiment de Capitaux), which was established by the Group of Seven Nations summit in Paris in July 1989 to examine methods to combat money laundering. Its secretariat is based at the OECD in Paris. At January 2003 the members of FATF were: Argentina, Australia, Austria, Belgium, Brazil, Canada, Denmark, Finland, France, Germany, Greece, Hong Kong China, Iceland, Ireland, Italy, Japan, Luxembourg, Mexico, Netherlands, New Zealand, Norway, Portugal, Singapore, Spain, Sweden, Switzerland, Turkey, United Kingdom,

United States, the European Commission and the Gulf Cooperation Council. In 1990 the FATF issued 40 recommendations to control and prevent money laundering, which were revised in 1996 as a result of changing events and trends. FATF also issues annual reports and typology papers. Both of these give extremely comprehensive information on trends, issues, methods, preventative measures and other useful material. These reports and the 40 recommendations can be downloaded in their entirety from FATF's Web site (see Appendix II: Web directory).

FinCEN
The United States Department of the Treasury Financial Crimes Enforcement Network (also see Appendix II: Web directory).

FIU
Financial Intelligence Unit: the national central unit/authority as recommended by the FATF, which receives, analyses and acts upon suspicious activity reports and deals with AML matters.

Front company
Normally a company that is a front for organized crime or other illegal activities. It is argued that by their very nature all IBCs are front companies.

IBC
International Business Company or Corporation. Can be incorporated in most offshore financial centres and although some attributes may vary typically such a company is not permitted to trade in the country of incorporation; is not taxed or only low tax is applied; and it is possible to own such an entity anonymously through nominee directors and bearer shares. Additionally there are very few corporate reporting requirements.

Integration
The final part of the money laundering process whereby the funds that were originally a direct result of, and directly associated to, criminal activity are fully integrated into the banking system and are thus now clean.

KYC
One of the fundamental precepts of global anti-money laundering regulations: Know Your Customer. The process whereby the identity

of a new customer must be established before a business or financial relationship can begin or proceed.

Layering
The second stage of the money laundering process where funds are split up and given more authenticity and a better provenance by financial tools such as shares, stocks, loans and any other mechanism that pushes the criminal money further into the monetary system and disguises its origins.

ML
Money laundering.

NCCTs
Non-cooperative countries and territories; FATF abbreviation for 'blacklisted' countries and territories.

Nominee director
When a professional (or another person) acts as a director for a client without revealing or recording the identity of the client. In offshore financial centres it is quite common for company formation agents to be nominee directors of thousands of companies.

Numbered account
Fairly common and not to be confused with anonymous accounts. This is where a bank, to hide the identity of the customer, gives the account a number or code name. However, the bank itself should know the identity of the customer and have verified it.

OFC
See 'Offshore financial centre' below.

Offshore bank
These are primarily banks that are domiciled in an offshore financial centre and conduct their business with non-residents of that jurisdiction. At their extreme, in some of the more dubious locations, they have no physical presence in the jurisdiction; very little regulation; zero or low tax rates; little or no capital reserve requirements. Because of these factors they are an ideal money laundering vehicle. However, it should be appreciated that there are many legitimate offshore banks – the real danger group are shell banks (see below).

Offshore company
A company registered in an offshore financial centre; normally but not exclusively an International Business Company.

Offshore financial centre
There is some on-going discussion as to how an offshore financial centre or OFC can be defined. In broad terms it is a jurisdiction where a concerted governmental effort has been made to attract foreign business and investment through tax incentives, confidentiality and investor-friendly regulations. In most cases the provision of financial services in an OFC is to non-residents only.

Patriot Act
The United and Strengthening America by Providing Appropriate Tools Required to Intercept and Obstruct Terrorism ('USA Patriot') Act of 2001. The Money Laundering Abatement and Anti-Terrorist Financing Act of 2001 is Title III of the Patriot Act, signed into law by President Bush on 26 October 2001. Rightly claimed by the US administration as 'the most significant legislation of its kind since 1970'.

PEP
Politically exposed person.

Peso Exchange
Has been described as the 'the single most efficient and extensive money laundering scheme in the Western hemisphere', involving the washing of funds from Colombia – described fully in Chapter 3.

Phantom banks
A bank that simply does not exist, as it is not registered or licensed anywhere; rather it is merely a front for criminal or laundering activity.

Placement
The initial and most difficult stage of the money laundering process where the direct results and proceeds of crime need to be inserted into the business and banking system. There is a vast variety of methods used but the key objective is to make all amounts resemble legitimate business transactions.

SAR
Suspicious activity report or reporting: generic term that may have a different title in individual countries. The report(s) submitted by financial institutions and other bodies subject to AML regulations to the FIU when suspicious money laundering activity is suspected. In the United States (as an example) there are SARs for financial institutions, SARC (suspicious activity report for casinos) and SAR-S (suspicious activity report for securities brokers and dealers).

Shell bank
A specific money laundering risk, particularly via correspondent banking relationships established by shell banks. A shell bank is generally defined as 'a foreign bank without a physical presence in any country'.

Smurfing
A technique used in the placement of funds that are being laundered, where the funds are divided into smaller amounts so that such amounts will fall below the threshold at which the relevant financial institution (or other body) is required to file a suspicious transaction report.

Sparbuch
From the German *Sparen* meaning save, *Buch* meaning book. An anonymous passbook based account that was available in Austria, the Czech Republic and some other locations. Now officially banned or withdrawn. No identification was taken when the account was opened and the account was operated under a password: the bank did not hold details of the account holder. Cash withdrawals were allowed on production of the passbook and code word (thus the account holder did not necessarily have to be present and could send a representative).

Tax haven
A country that has a low or zero rate of taxes across the board (also see 'Offshore financial centre'). The OECD define a tax haven that conducts harmful tax competition as:

- any nation that imposes nominal or no tax on income;
- any nation offering preferential treatment to certain types of income at no or low tax rates;
- any nation that offers or is perceived to offer non-residents the ability to escape taxes in their country of residence.

The OECD notes further activities that identify a tax haven as:

- practices that prevent the effective exchange of relevant information with other governments on taxpayers benefiting from a low or no tax rate;
- general lack of transparency;
- the absence of a requirement that the activity be substantial (investment that is not purely tax driven).

Trust
A legal structure created by a trust agreement through which the instigator or settlor transfers the legal ownership of assets to a trustee who then holds those assets under the terms of the agreement for the benefit of the beneficiaries, which may include the settlor.

REFERENCES AND FURTHER READING

To get a comprehensive overview of the global money laundering problem I would unhesitatingly recommend that you read the annual reports issued by the following organizations. I have made use of all of these documents as background material. Every relevant report can be downloaded from the Internet, and the relevant site addresses are listed in the Web Directory section of this book:

- The Financial Action Task Force (FATF). In particular: *Review to Identify Non-cooperative Countries or Territories: Increasing the Worldwide Effectiveness of Anti-money Laundering Measures*, Paris, June 2000.
- The Observatoire Geopolitique des Drogues (OGD).
- The US Department of State Bureau for International Narcotics and Law Enforcement Affairs (Compilers of the US Government International Narcotics Control Strategy Report).

Additionally I suggest you read John Walker's *Modelling global money laundering flows*, published on his Web site (see Web Directory section for details).

I would also recommend the following books for further reading on various aspects of money laundering, organized crime and related issues:

Aubert, M (1995) *Swiss Banking Secrecy*, Geneve Place Financiere – Stampfli and Co, Bern

Ehrenfeld, R (1992) *Evil Money*: *Encounters along the money trail*, Harper Business, New York

Freemantle, B (1995) *The Octopus: Europe on the grip of organized crime*, Orion Books Ltd, London

Hal, J (1995) *Behind Closed Doors, The complete text to investing in tax-free havens*, Treasury International, Ontario

Handelman, S (1995) *Comrade Criminal – Russia's New Mafiya*, Yale University Press, New Haven

Robinson, J (1999) *The Merger: How organized crime is taking over the world*, Simon and Schuster, London

Roth, J (1998) *Die Roten Bosse*, Piper Verlag GmbH, Munich

Sterling, C (1994) *Crime without Frontiers*, Little, Brown, London

Trepp, G (1996) *Swiss Connection*, Unionsverlag, Zurich

In researching this book I have made use of the following print and online sources:

Associated Press
The Washington Press
The Observer (UK)
Montreal Gazette
The Wall Street Journal
The Guardian (UK)
Le Temps (Geneva)
Tribune de Geneve
USA Today
The British Swiss Chamber of Commerce Weekly News Digest
The Times (UK)
The Financial Times
The Sunday Times
Russia Today
The Independent (UK)
The Daily Telegraph
The New York Times
The Sunday Telegraph

Sunday Business
Publications of the US Office of National Drug Policy
News Releases of the OECD
Publications of the Office of the Comptroller of Currency (US)
Publications of the United States Department of the Treasury Financial Crimes Enforcement Network
Publications and press releases of the United Nations
Annual reports on Organized Crime by the Criminal Intelligence Service Canada
Press Releases and the first Annual Report of the Money Laundering Reporting Office, Switzerland
Various US Congress and Senate documents
The Observer (UK)
FBI press releases and publications
The annual reports, press releases and other documents published by the Financial Action Task Force on Money Laundering
Reuters
The Bergen Record (US)
The Economist
The Evening Standard (UK)
Press releases and publications of Transparency International
Fortune Magazine
The Los Angeles Times
International Herald Tribune
www.excite.com news service

Index